BASIC GRAPHIC DESIGN

FROM **PRENTICE-HALL, INC.** ENGLEWOOD CLIFFS, NEW JERSEY 07632

SC	TITLE CODE	QTY.	TITLE	ED.	AUTHOR
1	062190	P 1	BASIC GRAPHIC DESIGN D19811 SMITH	1	

Thank you for considering our texts

```
PERFORMING AND CREATIVE ART          4HU6   ST52 109
LANSING COMMUNITY COLLEGE      LNF   84353-10258 1843
419 N CAPITOL AVE              1 *LR 9999 073    092685
LANSING MI  48914

ATTN. PROF S BRAINARD                 039-4715-0169 COL
```

SENT WITH THE COMPLIMENTS OF YOUR P-H REPRESENTATIVE

SUSAN RENWICK, 514 NO GRANT STREET, WESTMONT, IL 60557

BASIC GRAPHIC DESIGN

Robert Charles Smith

Washington University

Prentice-Hall, Inc., Englewood Cliffs, New Jersey 07632

Library of Congress Cataloging in Publication Data

SMITH, ROBERT CHARLES, (date)
    Basic graphic design.

    Bibliography; p.
    1. Printing, Practical—Style manuals.
2. Printing, Practical—Layout. 3. Graphic
arts. I. Title.
Z253.S643 1986   686.2'252   85-496
ISBN 0-13-062191-9

Editorial/production supervision: Barbara Alexander
Interior, color insert, and cover design: Sue Behnke
Page layout: Meryl Poweski
Art paste up: Gail Collis
Manufacturing buyer: Harry P. Baisley

Printed in the United States of America

10 9 8 7 6 5 4 3 2 1

ISBN 0-13-062191-9 01

PRENTICE-HALL INTERNATIONAL (UK) LIMITED, *London*
PRENTICE-HALL OF AUSTRALIA PTY. LIMITED, *Sydney*
PRENTICE-HALL CANADA INC., *Toronto*
PRENTICE-HALL HISPANOAMERICANA, S.A., *Mexico*
PRENTICE-HALL OF INDIA PRIVATE LIMITED, *New Delhi*
PRENTICE-HALL OF JAPAN, INC., *Tokyo*
PRENTICE-HALL OF SOUTHEAST ASIA PTE. LTD., *Singapore*
EDITORA PRENTICE-HALL DO BRASIL, LTDA., *Rio de Janeiro*
WHITEHALL BOOKS LIMITED, *Wellington, New Zealand*

CONTENTS

6 DESIGN RESOURCES 152

BIBLIOGRAPHY 162

PREFACE

Graphic design is a broad new field reaching into every educational, industrial, and communications activity. Those of us who have participated in its development since World War II have found it to be an exciting and stimulating profession.

I discuss many subjects in this text, and I include information concerning fundamental design form, concepts, and skills that the reader can immediately put to practical use. There can be no consensus on priority in a text such as this: All the issues and techniques are valuable and interdependent tools whose common goal is to encourage the development of visual conceptualization and an understanding of the roles of form and technique in creative communication.

I hope this book will stimulate beginners to investigate graphic design further and perhaps continue with professional study to prepare for design careers. Firm knowledge of the basics is vital to pursuing such an option.

ROBERT CHARLES SMITH
St. Louis, Missouri

DESIGN HERITAGE

1

Background Influences

Graphic design has generally been understood to be the design of printed matter, but such a definition is too limited for what is now becoming an increasingly complex activity with broadening applications. Graphic design involves the transmission of information and ideas by visual means. Because technology is opening new directions for this to take place, signage, environmental graphics, television audio-visual presentations, filmmaking, word processing, and computer-generated design and images must now be included in any discussion of graphic design.

New technical developments in publication and production techniques are also expanding opportunities for new design, especially by combining processes such as computer typography and layout, scan-plate-making, long-distance transmission of images, microfiche storage, and so on. Few fields remain unaffected by graphic design.

In spite of the rapidity with which we are acquiring new technological tools, the most basic processes of organizing information remain the same: A problem to be solved needs research and definition; answers need to be considered and selected, refined, produced, and reviewed. The graphic basics of the visual designer also remain the same: shape, form, texture, color, scale, movement, images, symbols, and time, cost, and production.

The present flux of design activity is stimulating and exciting. As we become caught up in this excitement, however, we should also pay some attention to our design heritage, not only to understand the roots to which we are indebted but also to use them as a valuable source of reference when considering present problems.

Historical Development

The earliest graphics seem to have developed along with the earliest language. Prehistoric paintings were personal expressions as well as attempts at communicating or signifying important events either to a deity or to a social audience. Early artists responded creatively to the basic beauty and power of nature. This is especially obvious in their depictions of animals. As primitive as we may consider these artists and their works to be, any contemporary designer trying to stylize an animal, perhaps for a symbol or illustration, must still experience some respect for their ability to simplify or reduce a form to its essence. Today we still use simple basic symbols; restroom signs, for instance, suggest a relationship to these early figures.

As civilization developed, so did the application of graphic information and the desire to refine it into something visually enjoyable as well as understandable. Architectural applications of graphic work, constructed of more lasting materials than other manifestations, remain today. The victories and conquests of the ancient kings, for example, were recorded in an exquisite balance of shape, space, letter, and line.

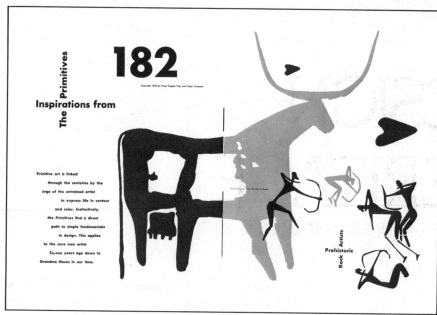

Figure 1.1
Primitive artists reduced subject matter to minimal details and contours yet retained the identity and vitality of the object. This work is an excellent reference for logo and symbol design. *From Westvaco Inspirations for Printers, No.182. Bradbury Thompson designer. Reprinted with permission of Westvaco Corporation.*

Figure 1.2b
This example of a primitive design relationship is used as a humorous illustration by designer Malcolm Grear. By working in a cut-paper technique, Grear forces himself to reduce detail and allows contours to flow from the knife blade, which in turn symbolizes the flow of the music. *Malcolm Grear Designers, Inc.*

Figure 1.2a
The simplicity of this symbol for the Toronto Zoo reminds us of primitive design. The geometric forms and the well-balanced use of light and dark make it an elegant, yet practical, modern symbol. *Peter Ulmer, Stewart & Morrison, Ltd.*

(a)

(b)

Figure 1.3
The "stick" figure (a) is universally used as a symbol for information, especially in architecture and travel. With subtle variations of weight and contour, designers can still develop uniqueness even from such a fundamental form. In addition, the stick figure is appropriate for an illustration that needs to be brief and to the point, as in these pamphlet cover examples (b) from the American Cancer Society.

Figure 1.4
Throughout the history of art, lettering has often been integrated with images. Besides their documentary content, the words also become a pattern related by texture to the whole design, as in this relief from the Palace of Ashurbanipal II. This is an example of art literally communicating to a public. *All rights reserved, The Metropolitan Museum of Art.*

Because only a few highly respected specialists acquired writing skills, the forms of letters took on their special styles and configurations. This area is a complex study in itself, but one does not need to be a specialist to appreciate the basic structural quality of letter forms as an inexhaustible source of design information. Consider the Japanese, Chinese, Islamic, and Hebrew, characters, for example. These are possibly even richer in variety, expression, and construction than our Western—roman and gothic—alphabets.

Although the history of graphic design reaches far back and parallels or overlaps that of art and literacy, the obvious impetus to and rapid development of this area started with the invention of printing and publishing in the fifteenth century. By today's standards the original printing process was quite tedious. Although the products were printed mechanically in multiples, the designs reflected the beauty of proportion and quality of details that characterized the hand-made books of the preceding periods.

3

Figure 1.5a
As widely as they have been interpreted, these Hebrew letters, designed by Stan Brod, retain the thick-thin humanistic quality of the pen. Writing traditions have had to adapt to the technical problems of typesetting and signage design. Simplification need not mean a loss of tradition and grace. *Design/calligraphy Stan Brod.*

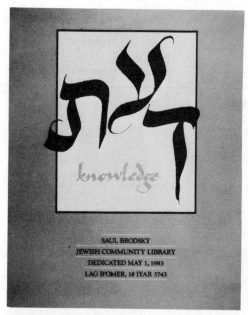

Designer: Susan Minturn.

Designer: Cynthia Hewitt.

Figure 1.5b
The three posters here illustrate well the use of letter forms as a major element in design.

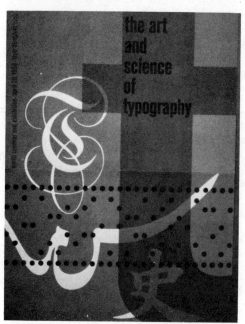

Designer: Will Burtin.

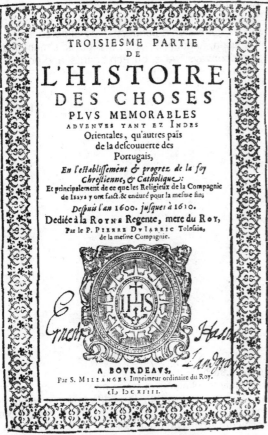

Figure 1.6
Early examples of printed books show a loving care for the balance of letter sizes, styles, spacing, and decorative matter. Although this example may seem filled in, much relief is introduced by the textural use of the type and borders.

Social and Political Application

The history of social-political action art and publicity is a fascinating subject with which all designers of information and advertising should be familiar.

Historically, as mass production became more widespread, considerably more printed information reached a wider public at lower cost. Because trade, science, and transportation were also expanding at that time, society wanted to be aware of what was occurring. News of current events could spread faster while it was still news. With this thus increasing quantity of available information and graphic products, competition for the audience increased dramatically; today's remnants of this development are our advertising or publicity media.

We also cannot ignore the importance of graphic matter as a pervasive historical political tool. The pamphlets of the American Revolution and later of political issues were effective graphic communications. Any community bulletin board or telephone pole attests that today posters and flyers are still a viable source of public interchange.

During World War I the publications industry was the major vehicle for communication. Posters were abundant. Magazines, journals, and books were devoured by a generation taught to read by an equally developing public education system in most Western countries. Almost every urban community had access to printing sources. Graphic design was generally in the hands of trained artists or printers; many practiced their craft well and were highly respected. The extensive

Figure 1.7
Flyers or broadsides with political-social content played an important part in the history of Western culture. The editorial cartoon is now a regular part of most newspapers. Many notable artists produced cartoons or other graphic art to support their interests in important issues. This Civil War cartoon from a series by Currier and Ives mimics Jefferson Davis as a coward, in a woman's clothes, fleeing in protest with his gold.
Cartoon from the collection of the Missouri Historical Society.

THE LAST DITCH OF THE CHIVALRY, OR A PRESIDENT IN PETTICOATS.

Figure 1.8
The ease of reproduction made available by rapid printing services generates a constant flood of personal information, announcements, and public statements that adorn doorways, walls, bulletin boards, and poles.

Figure 1.9a.b.
Frequently, sentiments such as pride, heroics, patriotism, and fear are employed to persuade the community; symbols also play a large persuasive role in emotional public concerns. Wars and political campaigns seem to generate the most graphic material of this nature.

Poster from the collection
of the Missouri Historical Society.

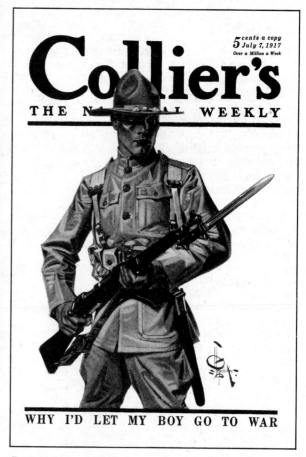

Frank X. Leyendecker.

Figure 1.10a.b.c.
The swastika is probably history's most negatively regarded symbol. After centuries of acceptance, it now only represents the Nazi era. Previous to the Nazis, however, the swastika appeared in countless forms, from printed matter to jewelry.

THE CUSHMAN-BARNEGAT PRESS

graphic propaganda campaigns of World War I and the later social-political conflicts were widely distributed.

The full potential of politically oriented information and propaganda was unfortunately discovered and exploited by Adolph Hitler. Today the swastika symbol means "Nazi" and represents all that is reprehensible about it, although the symbol itself is an ancient motif in Greek decoration and in American Indian Art. Hitler successfully used a wide range of visual graphic media, such as colorful and emotionally charged spectacles of massed rallies, films, posters, banners, uniforms, and insignia, to capture his "audience." He also knew the value of repetition in mass publicity. Nothing visual was left out of his plans—from architectural forms to the style of type for publications.

Influence of Technical Progress and Artistic Styles

Before and during the technological developments of the nineteenth century, the designers of publications, signs, posters, and so on, were either trained in particular crafts or in the fine arts. Illustrators were expected to produce whatever lettering and design was required. Often typesetters and printers organized the layouts and assisted the clients in composing their copy.

Over time, a wide choice of machine-produced type became available and photos became economically reproducible. The development of lithography offered expanded color-printing opportunities, and paper manufacturing produced a broader selection of paper. These and parallel developments—such as the popularity of magazines, advertising posters and novelties, calendars, mail-order catalogs, and outdoor advertising—demanded specialized artists who with expertise could ensure successful delivery of the required graphic in-

formation. Much of this early material is readily available in libraries, old book stores, and antique shops and is well worth your seeking out. Although most of the work is decorative and elaborate and reflects the style of the fine arts of the period, some work showed remarkable insight into the future. Today we see frequent revivals from other periods adapting type and layout styles to contemporary tastes. We need to be responsive to the problems of the present, but having an awareness of the solutions of the past can add depth to our experiences and can frequently even be a source for new ideas.

The most direct stylistic influences on present graphic design originated in the radical fine-arts movements before and after World War I. Revolutionary movements, such as the Constructivist, Dadist, Surrealist, and Cubist, reached for new visual directions and frequently included typographical forms, words, and photos in their art or even as their art. They designed and produced extensive writings, publications, and posters to publicize their new concepts. Photography, film, printing, exhibits, and other new technologies were incorporated as welcome new means of expression and information.

The German design center, the *Bauhaus* (1919–1933) organized the first instructional program that especially trained artists to design within the new technology, materials, and media, and broke away from the academic teaching traditions of art and decorative design. Their foundation design courses emphasized artists' understanding the new materials through experimentation and adapting these experiences to new applications for their products. These goals are still a fundamental part of the basic design educational process; today much design continues to reflect the Bauhaus influence. Their acceptance of and interest in the creative use of new technology should inspire us now, as we confront a new revolution in graphics with electronically generated graphic materials and new uses for graphic problem solving.

(a)

(b)

(c)

Figure 1.11a.b.c.
In none of these three examples, incredibly, is the copy typeset; it is all hand lettered. Note the decorative embellishment and ornamental letters characteristic of the pre-World War I period. Notice, too, that the layout is essentially symmetrical in all these examples.

(a)

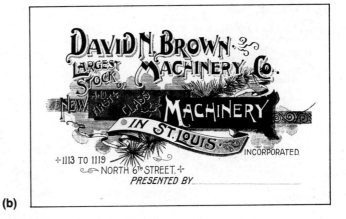

(b)

(c)

Figure 1.12a.b.c.
Many examples of early advertising and printing displayed original and whimsical letter styles, decoration, and symbols, as is evident on the "cabinet" card photograph back and the engravers' ad here. Catalogs were particularly interesting; their bold engravings and artistic layouts enabled them to attractively accommodate all the required information.

(a)

Figure 1.13
The diagonal layout and the use of bars and rules (a) give a feeling of movement or action to this Jones Company ad from the 1930s. This same technique also appears, in spirit, in the recent Amway ad (b) shown here. Until the influence of the Constructivist and Dada artists, design was dominated by symmetrical layouts.

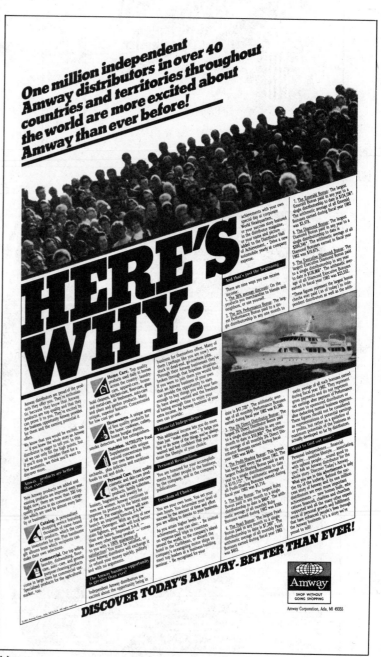

(b)

(a)

Designer: Paula Scher.

(b)

Figure 1.14
The radical artists of the early twentieth century introduced new attitudes toward composition which were readily adapted to typography and layout. Their departure opened the way to break from traditional forms such as centering and serif type. The Paula Scher poster (a) is contemporary, but it shows a relationship to Constructivist design and art of 60 years earlier by Joost Schmidt (b).

Figure 1.15
The clean, right-angular arrangement, and the use of white space balanced with type, bold rules, and heavy black accents, typify the Bauhaus look as shown in (a) the ad for Kleinwohnungsbau, Staatliches Bauhaus, and (b) the layouts for a German architectural book from the late 1920s. (c) The Bendix ad comes from the same period and shows the influence in layout but not yet in typography. (d) The black-and-white magazine layout by PGAV Design shows the Bauhaus influence adapted to today's typographic problems.

(a)

Figure 1.15 (continued)

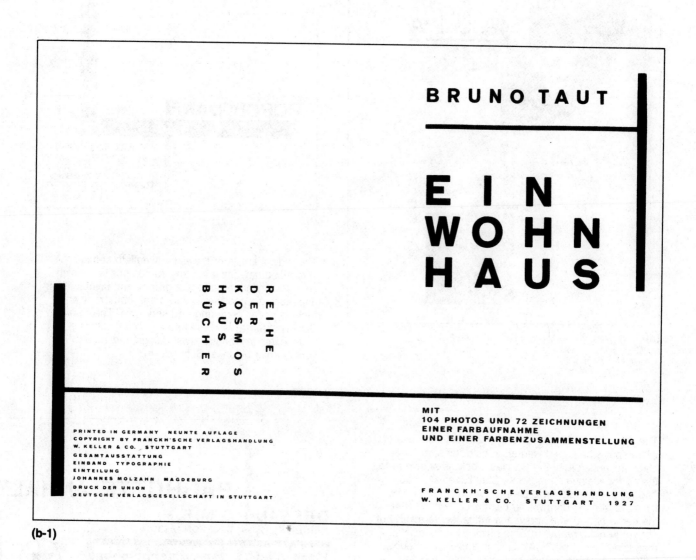

(b-1)

Figure 1.15 (continued)

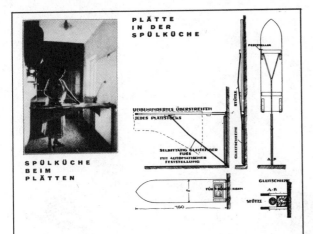

meladen des täglichen Gebrauchs. wieder ein anderes Fach für Kaffee-, Teekannen und so fort. also alles Geschirr, das in der Kochküche gebraucht wird. Unten Schiebetürfächer, darüber zwei Ausziehplatten. Ein Drehstuhl ist zur Regelung der Sitzhöhe nach den Empfehlungen von Dr. Erna Meyer vorhanden. Die Beleuchtung geschieht bei diesem kleinen Raum durch eine gleichmäßig streuende Mattglaslampe mit Reflektor.

Prinzipiell ist in dieser Küche kein Gegenstand offen aufbewahrt; deshalb ist es nicht schwer, sie bei Nichtbenutzung stets völlig aufgeräumt zu halten. Ihre Anlage beruht auf reiner Zweckmäßigkeit; trotzdem oder vielleicht gerade deshalb macht sie einen fast „gemütlichen" Eindruck (ohne Vorhänge!) und wird nicht ungern von Kindern selbst zum Essen benutzt. An dieser Stelle dürfte das Urteil eines amerikanischen Professors nicht unbeachtlich sein, der die Küche für den gelungensten Teil dieses Hauses erklärte.

In unmittelbarer Nähe, dicht neben dem Herd, ist die Tür zur Spülküche. welche das geschilderte Büfett. den Spültisch, den Junkers-Warmwasserbereiter für das ganze Haus und das herunterklappbare Plättbrett nebst Ablageklapptischchen enthält. Leider müssen wir in Deutschland die Vorrichtungen für ein solches Plättbrett erst neu entwerfen und anfertigen lassen, anstatt es fertig kaufen zu können. Neben ihm eine kleine Kammer zur Aufbewahrung des Bügeleisens (mit Birkaregler. für das Schlüsselbrett und in seinem Hauptraum für Eingewecktes auf Fächern, die sich nach unten verbreitern. Dieser Raum hat mit 1,75 m Breite die kleinstmögliche Abmessungen. Von ihm führt eine Tür mit drei Stufen unmittelbar zur Waschküche und weiter zu den Wirtschaftsräumen, zum Seiteneingang nebst Hof und zur Garage.

(b-2)

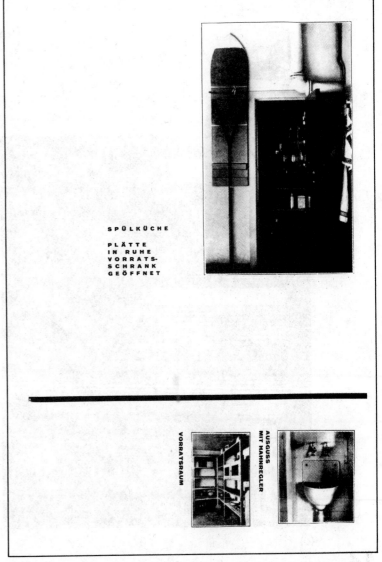

(b-3)

Figure 1.15 (continued)

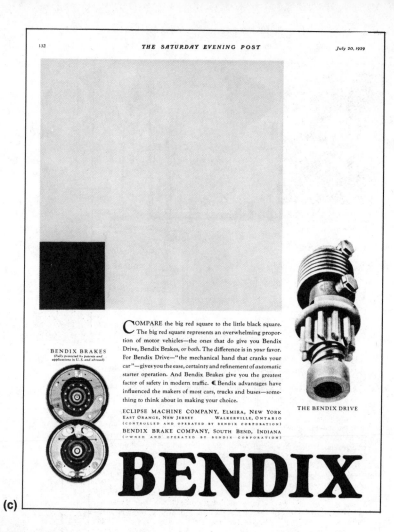

COMPARE the big red square to the little black square. The big red square represents an overwhelming proportion of motor vehicles—the ones that do give you Bendix Drive, Bendix Brakes, or both. The difference is in your favor. For Bendix Drive—"the mechanical hand that cranks your car"—gives you the ease, certainty and refinement of automatic starter operation. And Bendix Brakes give you the greatest factor of safety in modern traffic. ¶ Bendix advantages have influenced the makers of most cars, trucks and buses—something to think about in making your choice.

ECLIPSE MACHINE COMPANY, ELMIRA, NEW YORK
EAST ORANGE, NEW JERSEY   WALKERVILLE, ONTARIO
(CONTROLLED AND OPERATED BY BENDIX CORPORATION)
BENDIX BRAKE COMPANY, SOUTH BEND, INDIANA
(OWNED AND OPERATED BY BENDIX CORPORATION)

BENDIX BRAKES
(Fully protected by patents and
applications in U. S. and abroad)

THE BENDIX DRIVE

BENDIX

(c)

Checker Day 1982

William P. Stiritz

Try to find better ways to do things as if you were the owner of your job.

September 30 is Checker Day, the end of the Company's fiscal year. Across the country, Ralston Purina employees celebrate this day in different ways: quietly at some locations, with fanfare and hoopla at others. Checker Day festivities at St. Louis headquarters were observed in a new way this year.

One employee described the event as "dignified and businesslike...in keeping with the economy." Another viewed it as a "...timely return to what Checker Day is really all about —a report on the state of the Company."

With music by the Ralston Purina Show cast to brighten the mood, the core of the celebration was Company business—a review of the past year's successes and a look at the expectations for Fiscal 83.

Short speeches by four group presidents informed employees about the activities of our different businesses. Although Jack Goodall, President of Foodmaker in San Diego wasn't present, CEO Bill Stiritz reviewed our restaurant operations. Attitude was the thrust of Mr. Stiritz's message, which is excerpted along with other speeches on the following pages.

I would like to give you a brief update on the state of the Company—and secondly, talk about the type of working environment we are attempting to create here at Ralston Purina.

This has been a good year, but not a great one. It has been a year when the Company moved to get a clear definition of who we are and where we are going. We've recognized our core businesses as *a major strength* of the Ralston Purina Company. We intend to grow in our core businesses.

In a tough year, all of our core businesses have done well. To recap:
—Dog food share is trending up for the first time in several years and we are now taking share from our competitors in the premium segment.
—Chow, in a very tough farm economy, has cut costs and is outperforming others in the industry.
—Restaurants, not heard from today, has been very innovative in its approach to the business. If you've eaten in a Jack in the Box restaurant lately, you've not only seen but you've tasted the improvements. Jack in the Box unit volume is up substantially.

—Finally, Protein Technologies has had a terrific year. This is a year when both volume and margins have come together to put this group on the map.
The point is: Our core businesses have never been healthier. They are very well managed—I believe the best managed in their respective industries.
The second point I want to make is that we do have problems. But we are moving to solve those problems and soon. And when they're solved, Ralston Purina will be the premier food company. Which leads me to my third and final point.
In order to be successful, we must seek out and find innovative/creative solutions to our problems.

The point is: It's you, the individual (not the corporation), that makes the difference. The corporation is no more than the sum of your individual actions. If the individual isn't pulling his load then the corporation is diminished. To be fair, the individual can perform at his very best—and that should be our goal—only when challenged in an environment that fosters creativity and innovation. I am committed to creating such an environment at Ralston Purina. We're close, but we're not there yet.
What we seek on the part of every individual is an ownership attitude toward his or her job. Do your job, make decisions, and try to find better ways to do things as if you were the owner of your function.
Easy for me to say, but how can you do that?
Here are some thoughts—
First, be alert to what's going on around your job.
Second, spot the bottlenecks, the inefficiencies, the duplications, the items that "cost too much", the systems or ways of doing things that are outmoded and need to be changed.

Third, seek out better ways to solve these problems. In your day-to-day work, don't be consistent for consistency's sake. If it doesn't make sense anymore, work to change it.
Finally, focus on those few things that are critical to the success of your job—there are probably only three or four. Focus on the things that matter the most and you're certain to do a better job.
I want to particularly thank you—the employees—for all your efforts. You're the most important element. If all our factories and buildings burned, we could build them back and shortly be back in business. But without you—the employees—our most important asset—the Company would be nothing.
We very much appreciate your dedication.

(d)

14   *RP magazine layout by PGAV Design.*

DESIGN ACTIVITIES

2

Responsibilities and Skills of Designers

Graphic design is one of the few professions that periodically sheds its name. Graphic artists have been identified as commercial artists, advertising designers, graphic designers, and visual communicators in the ongoing attempt to define their role. The concerns of graphic design have now extended far beyond those of the early days: lettering and illustration for publications, posters, advertising novelties, and so on.

Today, most design activities require an ability to *conceptualize* visually. Considerable value is placed on the skills of defining and sensing the basics of a communication problem and of creating specific attitudes toward the solution process. In addition, the designer needs to reveal solutions through the graphic skills of layout, drawing, lettering, typography, photography, film, and diagramming. Visual communication includes a major involvement with words, and graphic work usually begins with a manuscript or other written copy. Familiarity with or skill in writing are, therefore, invaluable tools for the graphic designer. The designer must also be familiar with the technical processes involved in the design procedure and in the assembly of a final product.

Most graphic-design products are the results of group or team efforts by designers to communicate instructions and record information clearly in verbal and written form using, for instance, the telephone and audio-visual equipment. Individual designers must be able to cooperate with others in large or small group assignments. Many beginning designers, in their early design education, are motivated from highly independent positions and prefer to process their materials independently. They must learn early, however, to participate responsibly as team members and to effectively function as creative leaders. Even free-lance designers or illustrators work jointly with several clients and their staffs, plus a large number of special suppliers.

Typically, beginners enter the business of design in a production-oriented capacity or as junior members of a design group. Even though the development of original, inventive conceptualizations is ultimately of primary importance, the beginning designer first needs to rely on and perfect such hand skills as paste-up, rendering layouts, proposal assembly, matting, and mounting. These are invaluable experiences, especially for understanding the processes, time, and economics involved.

Functions of Design Firms

The demands of any design position often force the designer to work quickly and under pressure. Newspaper work almost constantly requires it.

Graphic design functions within conditions that vary considerably. The work opportunities extend into all commercial services: manufacturing, advertising, education, government, entertainment, transportation, architecture, and so on. The largest employers of graphic-design skills are advertising agencies, graphic-design studios, and publishers.

The advertising industry uses the largest number of graphic specialists for print advertising, television commercials, direct-mail materials, packaging, and special promotions. Advertising agencies need art directors or creative managers who develop the visual concepts, designers and illustrators who create and execute the visual materials for the concepts, and production or mechanical artists who produce and assemble the parts for reproduction. Design services are also purchased from outside studios or individual specialists. (See box.)

The graphic-design studio sometimes parallels the advertising agency and may produce advertising-marketing programs for clients. Usually such studios can service a wide range of client needs, from a one-time brochure directly for a manufacturer to all the graphic-design services for advertising agencies or corporations. Graphic studios frequently concentrate on illustration, photography, medical advertising, packaging, or annual reports. Their personnel requirements can be similar to those of advertising agencies.

Publications, including magazines, newspapers, books, and journals, need art directors, designers, and production artists responsible for their layouts and their visual "personality(ies)." The composition and size of the staff depends on the scale of the particular publication. Most publications use some outside services from studios or free-lance specialists such as illustrators, cartoonists, photographers, lettering artists, and so on.

Other areas with significant needs for design-art services include the greeting-card industry, department stores, architectural firms, television production studios, and film producers.

Regardless of the specific environment in which a graphic designer works, other individuals are inevitably involved in the creative process: writers, editors, and business executives, for instance. Working together and successfully producing a product or an ad program has personal as well as economical benefits for all involved. Seeing their designs and conceptual efforts function in publications or on television is the pleasure in this process that motivates artists to work in the design area.

Following is a general outline that illustrates the career opportunities available for graphic designers to acquire experience. Many of the services and staff titles overlap or may be combined; use this list as a basis on which to expand as you investigate your specific areas of interest.

As you can probably surmise, the physical working environment for designers can be as diverse as individual lifestyles. The facilities can range anywhere from being a panoramic corner office with a view from the

---

Art Director: Originates the visual concept. Selects other specialists—illustrators, photographers, stylists. Establishes the look or style of the product. Supervises the overall concept through all the development stages. Assimilates the research and goals relative to the problem. Works more as a coordinator than as a hands-on artist.

Designer: Produces the detailed visual concept. Converts the problem into a form to be proposed to the client. Actually draws or lays out a prototype. Works with the specifics of type style, paper, colors, and so on. Often overlaps the activities of the art director, and vice versa.

Production Artist: Produces the mechanical material necessary to reproduce the product. Follows the creative activity with the technical material needed by the printer or manufacturer.

Illustrator: Creates the images that need to be delineated or painted. Also, may produce the preliminary "comps" or sketches needed by the art director or designer. May be specialized by product—machines, charts, clothing, story boards—or technique—air brush, pen and ink, collage.

Typographer: Converts the original manuscript into typesetting instructions. Translates the layout into practical and legible type size and spacing. Designers must be knowledgeable of this field.

Free Lancer: Artist, designer, photographer, or production artist who works independently. Many are very specialized in areas such as greeting cards, fashion, annual reports, scientific subjects, signage, and so on. Often they receive work through a representative who shows their work to agencies, studios, and publishers.

A. COMMUNICATIONS INDUSTRY

EMPLOYERS	SERVICES	STAFF
1. Advertising agencies, marketing firms	Ad campaigns and marketing programs for print, TV, other media	Art director, designer, production artist, illustrator, TV producer
2. Design studios	Corporate identity programs, publications design, product and package design, exhibit design, illustration, photography, miscellaneous art services	Designer, production artist, illustrator, photographer, lettering specialist, air-brush or retouch artist
3. Publishers	Book or magazine layout, promotions for same, cartoon and feature syndicates	Art director, designer, production artist, illustrator, photographer
4. Newspapers	Daily, weekly news, specialized tabloids, advertising for same	Art director, designer, production artist, illustrator, cartoonist, photographer
5. Public relations, marketing	Specialized promotional and publicity campaigns for products, services, events	Art director, production artist, free-lance designer
6. Printers, typesetters	Printing, production services, often specialized such as color printing or packaging	Designer, production artist, typographer
7. Exhibits and displays	Trade-show booths, product displays and presentations, store displays, educational exhibits	Art director, production artist, illustrator, 3-D designer, model maker
8. Signage firms	Outdoor advertising, directional and informational systems for architectural sites, store identification	Designer (2- and 3-D) production artist, lettering specialist
9. Television	Advertising for products, graphics for programs, station identity, news, entertainment and special features, and their own services	Art director, designer, production artist for video and print, set designer
10. Film or videotape stations, audio-visual media	TV commercials, instructional and promotional films, entertainment and documentary presentations	Art director, photographer, animator, set designer
11. Governmental agencies	Publications, exhibits, displays, public information	Art director, designer, production artist, illustrator
12. Free lance	Any of preceding independently managed and produced	Any of preceding

B. MANUFACTURING, MARKETING

EMPLOYERS	SERVICES	STAFF
1. Packaging	Product image and container, manufacturing and graphic services for boxes, bags, plastic wrapping, etc.	Art director, designer, production artist
2. Specialized novelty and decorative products	Producing cards and gifts, wrappings, displays, novelties, product promotions, calendars, decals, t-shirts, party supplies, matchbooks, novelty displays	Art director, designer, production artist, illustrator, free-lance artist, lettering specialist
3. Manufacturers	Corporate graphics, sales information, in-house publications and public relations, sometimes product design and advertising	Art director, designer, production artist, product designer, free-lance artist
4. Department or retail chain stores (grocery, hardware, etc.)	Advertising, in-store promotions, displays, signage, interior graphics	Art director, product illustrator, fashion illustrator, production artist
5. Graphic products	Fabrics, floor and wall covering, furniture, toys, games, stationery supplies	Designer, production artist, product designer

C. PROFESSIONAL SERVICES

EMPLOYERS	SERVICES	STAFF
1. Architectural and planning firms	Building design, municipal and community planning; theme sites, entertainment centers, play areas, corporate identity, presentation graphics	Art director, designer, production artist, illustrator, model maker
2. Interior design and products firms	Similar to architecture with focus on interiors and contents, plus advertising for products, may be specialized such as homes, hospitals, or banks	Similar to architecture
3. Public institutions: museums, zoos, galleries	Exhibit design, catalogs, publicity, signage, educational material, fund raising	Designer, production artist, 3-D designer, free-lance artist
4. Hospitals	Publications, instructional materials, scientific presentations, public information, signage, audio-visual media	Designer, production artist, illustrator, visual-aids designer
5. Schools, colleges, libraries	Promotions for programs, instructional materials, catalogs, signage, exhibits, audio-visual media, journals, sometimes publishing	Art director, designer, production artist, visual-aids designer
6. Instructional	Teaching in college, technical, or other school programs	All design specializations, many on a part-time basis

D. OTHER

EMPLOYERS	SERVICES	STAFF
1. Artist's representative	Selling art, design, illustration and photography services	General art and design skills valuable, business experience necessary
2. Supplier sales	Selling printing, paper, and type services	Same as artist's rep
3. Working with ad agency art directors to select photographers or artists for specific jobs	Good knowledge of business and sensitivity to good suppliers of art and photography	
4. Art-supply sales	Selling and demonstrating materials for stores and manufacturers	Same as artist's rep
5. Contract art	Decorative art for hotels, restaurants, and decorator market	Illustrator, artist

thirtieth floor of a large agency occupying three floors to a crowded cubicle in the center of one of the floors. Some firms occupy charming Victorian buildings in older residential communities; others may work in converted bedrooms or basements.

Steps of Design Development

It is impossible to cover design requirements inherent in every problem, but some general guidelines should help you in planning.

When you first receive a project do not assume anything; ask questions about what is to be accomplished and for whom. Do not neglect including time, cost, and final application or media requirements. Frequently, the original problem described by the project originator or client is not the *real* problem. For example, maybe a project needs redesign or a better name rather than a new package or logo.

Write out everything. Keep visual notes and records of all of your references and especially of your early ideas. Solving problems is a process that may take months of development, such as in a corporate identity program (see page 101). The process includes intuitive experience as well as highly developed research. Many projects follow a similar progression. The following diagram and discussion outline some key stages.

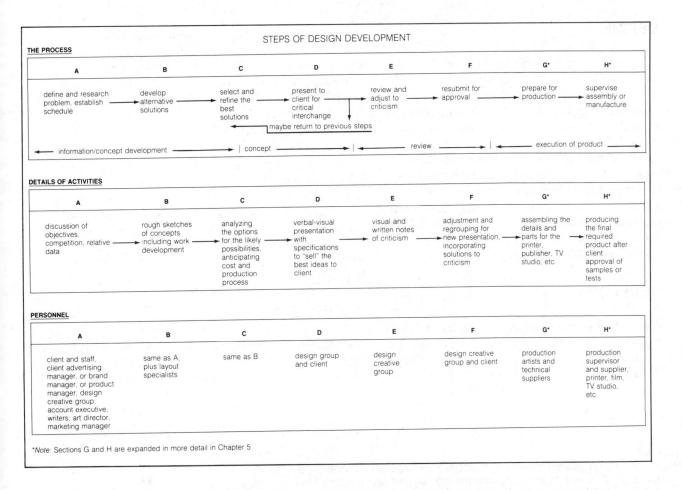

STEPS OF DESIGN DEVELOPMENT

THE PROCESS

A	B	C	D	E	F	G*	H*
define and research problem, establish schedule	develop alternative solutions	select and refine the best solutions	present to client for critical interchange	review and adjust to criticism	resubmit for approval	prepare for production	supervise assembly or manufacture

maybe return to previous steps

← information/concept development → | concept ——————→ | ← review ——— | ← execution of product →

DETAILS OF ACTIVITIES

A	B	C	D	E	F	G*	H*
discussion of objectives, competition, relative data	rough sketches of concepts including work development	analyzing the options for the likely possibilities, anticipating cost and production process	verbal-visual presentation with specifications to "sell" the best ideas to client	visual and written notes of criticism	adjustment and regrouping for new presentation, incorporating solutions to criticism	assembling the details and parts for the printer, publisher, TV studio, etc.	producing the final required product after client approval of samples or tests

PERSONNEL

A	B	C	D	E	F	G*	H*
client and staff, client advertising manager, or brand manager, or product manager; design creative group; account executive; writers; art director, marketing manager	same as A, plus layout specialists	same as B	design group and client	design creative group	design creative group and client	production artists and technical suppliers	production supervisor and supplier; printer, film, TV studio, etc.

*Note: Sections G and H are expanded in more detail in Chapter 5.

Figure 2.1
The oversized portfolio is the symbol of the graphic designer on the run.

DEFINE

Clients vary greatly: Some have considerable experience in developing graphic concepts; others simply consider graphic design as a way to cosmetically improve something's appearance. When first starting a project, define the objectives. Collect all possible data available about the project: What has preceded it? How do the clients see their product or service in relation to competition or in its functional context? Have they previously explored this specific area? What were their conclusions? What are time and cost constraints? Who in their organization will make the final decisions? Collect names and responsibilities of all members of the client group. Develop a schedule for the entire process.

DEVELOP

Assemble the data from the clients and related sources and form a profile of who the firm is, what the clients will need, and what design attitudes can be explored: traditional, humorous, expedient? Work with the copy available and relate visual ideas to the words. Pro-

duce as many small sketches, called *thumbnails,* as possible. Do not dismiss anything at this stage. Be open-minded and able to record an idea at any moment. Some of the best solutions come to the surface when you are not concentrating directly on the problem.

SELECT AND REFINE

Arrange the obviously applicable material from step B. Compare and begin to eliminate. Keep in mind that even at this stage a combination or new alternative may appear. At this time the dialogue of others involved is important. Through discussion, the "right" words may generate the very "connection" that makes something work. When the selection is narrowed, initiate estimates of production costs relative to budget.

PRESENT

Now further refine the selected graphic ideas by approximating the final product in as much detail as is required by the project. The project may dictate simply a "rough" layout form to give a general impression, or

Figure 2.2
Make the first rough visual concepts or *thumbnail* sketches about scratch-pad size. Although small, they should indicate color and they should account for all the components that will appear in the final layout. Most designers use markers for these. Because they can be produced fast, they are made in large quantities to allow for thorough investigation before the design direction is established.

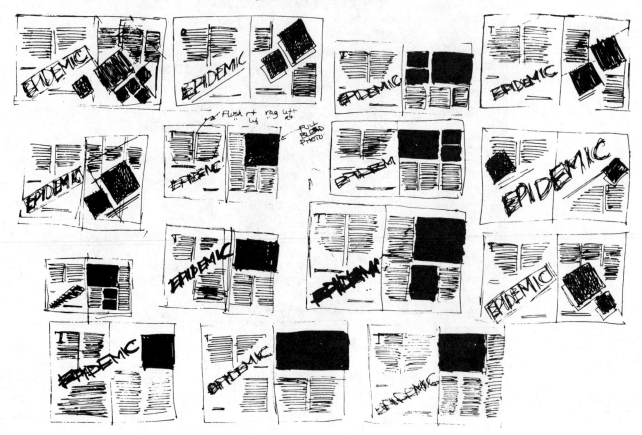

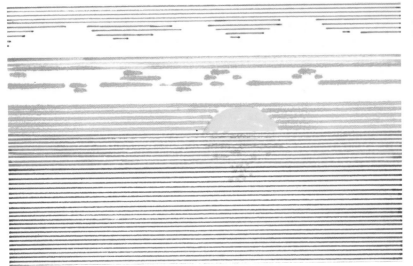

Plate 5
At sunset, the warm colors recede because of context.

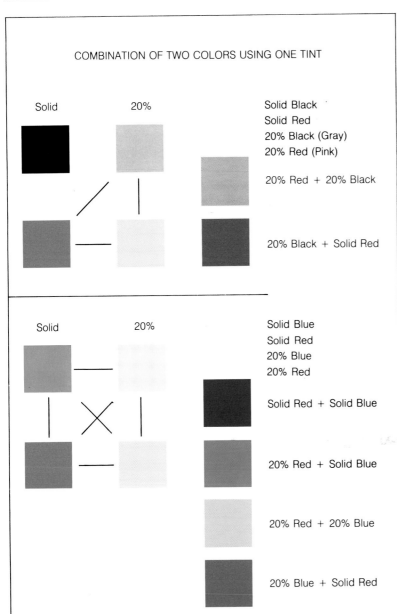

COMBINATION OF TWO COLORS USING ONE TINT

Solid   20%

Solid Black
Solid Red
20% Black (Gray)
20% Red (Pink)

20% Red + 20% Black

20% Black + Solid Red

Solid   20%

Solid Blue
Solid Red
20% Blue
20% Red

Solid Red + Solid Blue

20% Red + Solid Blue

20% Red + 20% Blue

20% Blue + Solid Red

Note: Tints are available 10% through 90%. This technique probably is most effective at 50% or less. Remember that the paper is an additional color.

Plate 6
Tints provide the effect of much more color at less cost.

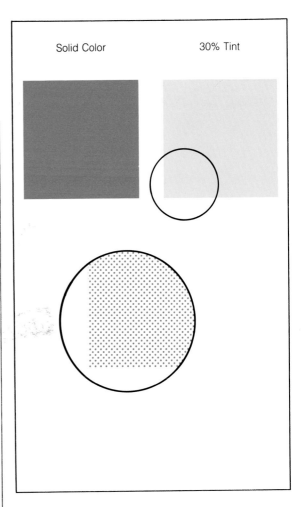

Solid Color   30% Tint

Plate 7
The ink is still solid but, when broken into tiny dots, the open spaces (usually white) mix optically with the color of the ink to create the effect of pink.

Halftone

Line conversion screened 30% combined with negative

Posterization

Horizontal straight line halftone combined with 30% screen

Line conversion combined with halftone

Duotone

Plate 8

The original photograph should have sufficient contrast to avoid a severe loss of identification of detail. With the advantage of two colors, halftones may utilize techniques that create striking interpretations of the image. Very dark or very light photos will be ineffective originals for these techniques.

Plate 9

A mechanical or camera ready art *must* be accurate. All instructions should be on, or attached to, the mechanical. Careless work or instructions waste time and add to the costs.

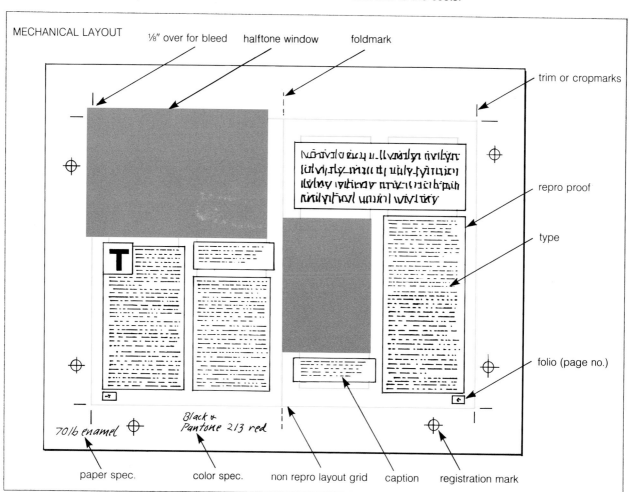

MECHANICAL LAYOUT

⅛" over for bleed halftone window foldmark

trim or cropmarks

repro proof

type

folio (page no.)

70lb enamel

Black & Pantone 213 red

paper spec.   color spec.   non repro layout grid   caption   registration mark

Plate 10
The values are very close between the brown and black, which makes the drama in the VD poster tense and blunt. *Design: Barbara Hueting.*

Plate 11
The Ferrario poster uses only pure colors; notice that there is no black. A brown appears where the purple overlaps the green, because of the mixing of complements. The colors here are red, blue, and yellow and were all separated on overlays for the overlap effect. *Design: William Kohn.*

Plate 12
The Berlyn catalogs use color as a form of individual identification for each catalog, yet retain the stripes as the corporate identity.

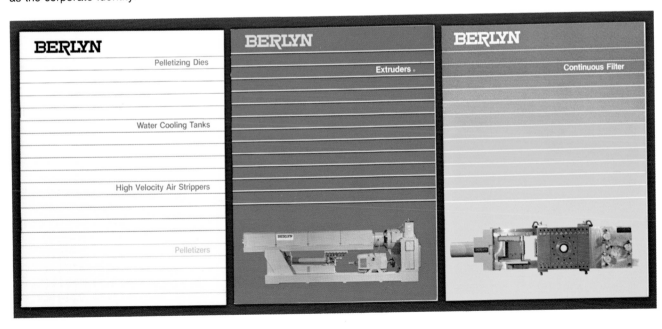

(a)

(b)

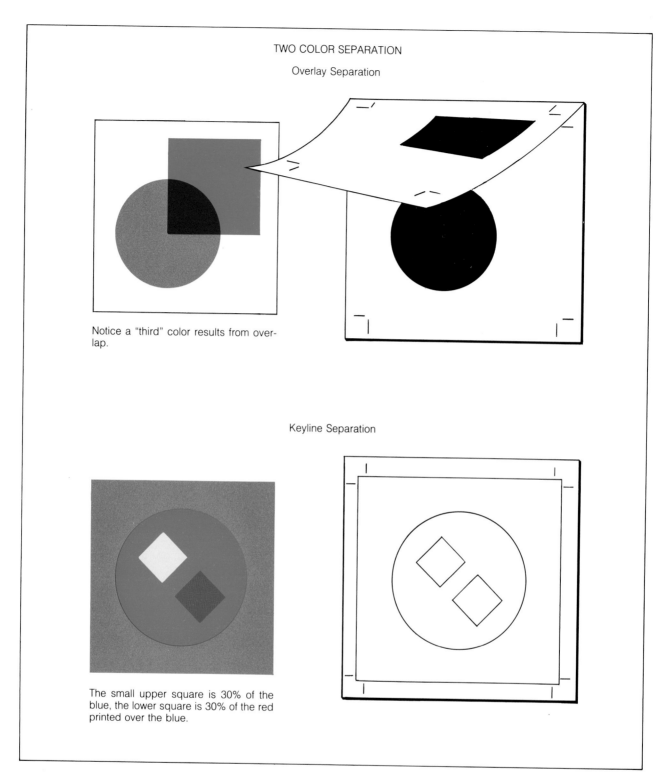

TWO COLOR SEPARATION

Overlay Separation

Notice a "third" color results from overlap.

Keyline Separation

The small upper square is 30% of the blue, the lower square is 30% of the red printed over the blue.

Plate 18
Two colors may require more than two separations if the use of tints becomes complex. Even a one color layout might require separations indicating tints. If colors do not touch they may be drawn on one sheet.

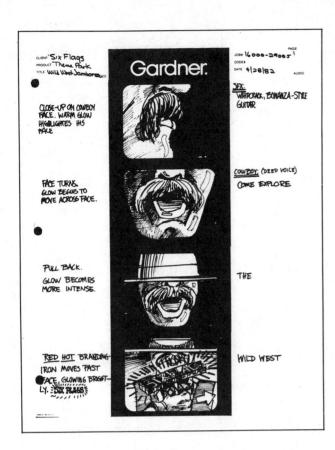

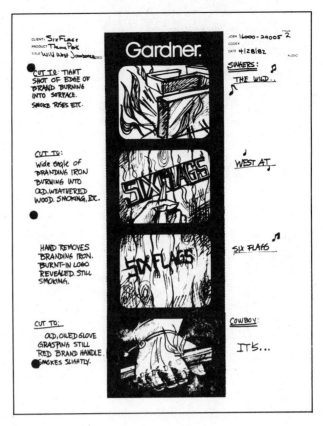

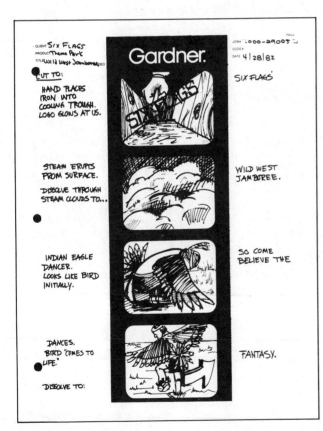

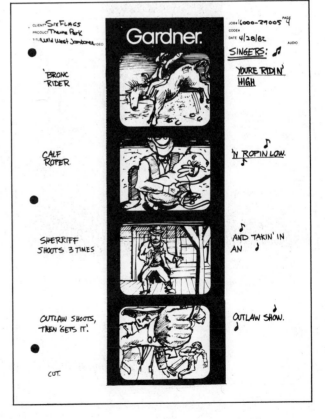

Figure 2.5

The story-board concept emphasizes the changes in the commercial sequence. The drawings are rough but give the feel of the action. Notice that the copy and the camera movements are written along with the images. *Art Director: Art Webb, Gardner Advertising. Writer: Sallie Ervin, Gardner Advertising.*

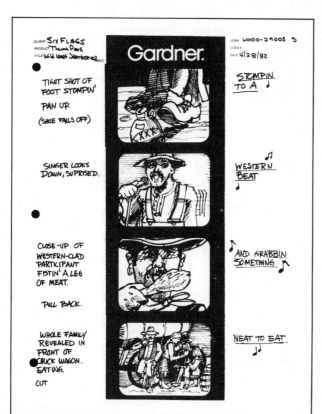

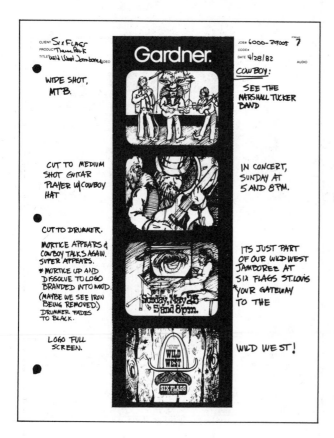

Figure 2.5 (continued)

ELEMENTS OF FORM FOR LAYOUT

3

Concept and Layout

The objective of graphic design is to interest the readers or users to the extent that they will first take notice, then be motivated to digest more of the information and remember the contents, and finally either purchase, think favorably about, or apply the information. In an advertisement, for example, the motive is to persuade observers to eventually purchase the subject, whereas in a technical textbook layout, the motive is to present information clearly so it can be learned and applied.

The components of a good layout must be presented in a systematic manner with clear major and minor emphases, and without design distraction, ambiguous images, or difficult-to-read copy.

Basically there are two components in a graphic design: concept and layout. The *concept* is the driving force behind all elements, including the meaning of the words (or copy), the subject matter in the images, and the symbols.

These elements of meaning, in turn, are emphasized or clarified further by the *layout* of the formal elements of visual design: the use of space/field, placement, pattern, contrast, color, movement, shape, arrangement of type, surfaces, materials, and so on.

What is called composition in painting and drawing is called layout in design. In each case—whether it is called composition, layout, or visual organization—the design fundamentals apply universally; only the motivation and context are not the same. The fine artist and the designer have parallel and overlapping, but not identical, roles. But both must understand the relationships of basic design principles in order to direct their instruments of communication.

CONCEPT

Concept is the reason for the design to exist in the first place. Work without concept is aimless or purely decorative. To a designer, concept means variety of pur-

25

pose for the words and the images and the symbols. Color, type style, paper texture, and layout all mesh and relate to the visual-literal idea. The words usually come first, generally from someone who thinks creatively but lacks art skills. The graphic designer then makes the verbal visible. Many designers also have developed writing skills, which makes them doubly valuable. The best results emerge when visually creative artists and innovative writers get together at the early stages of planning a concept.

LAYOUT

The design layout or plan of the visual material is organized to reinforce, emphasize, or complement the concept. If the layout supports the content successfully, the concept should be communicated.

As simple as this seems, design solutions are often ineffective, either because a design layout overwhelms or competes with the content or because it is inappropriately conceived through superficial design tricks.

Space/Field. Most graphic design exists on a flat surface that can be as small as a matchbook cover or as large as an outdoor board (billboard). The proportion of the surface is the first apparent design element. The empty surface is called the *space* or *field* or *ground.*

This space and its shape are frequently not the designer's choice but may be predetermined by manufacturing or business economics and standards common to magazines, TV screens, ad space, letterhead, and so on.

The systematic sectioning of a design field, or *grid,* offers a framework in which designers can arrange a coherent sequence of pages. A grid divides a page vertically and horizontally into sections of squares or rectangles. Columns of type and photographs, captions, and headings are aligned within the guidlines of the grid. This system can produce a coordinated layout from page to page, but also allows for variations in size and placement locations to avoid tedious repetition. Grids are particularly valuable when the information to be communicated is complex and lengthy, and needs to be clearly available for reference.

Figure 3.1a
This national food ad, from a newspaper insert, tests the layout skills of the designer to the limit. Although the products totally fill this ad, they are clearly and attractively displayed. *Courtesy National Supermarkets.*

The Executive Committee: clockwise from upper left, Arthur Ochs Sulzberger, chairman and chief executive officer; Walter E. Mattson, president and chief operating officer; Sydney Gruson, vice chairman.

Stock Price, Year-End

77 78 79 80 81

To Our Shareholders: The New York Times Company Annual Report for 1981

It was a good year for our Company. Despite the recessionary economy, net income in 1981 rose 23 percent to a record $50.0 million, or $4.03 per share, from $40.6 million, or $3.37 per share, in 1980. This growth was achieved on a 15 percent gain in consolidated revenues to $845.2 million, from $733.2 million in 1980.

It was a year of excellence and accomplishment in the newspaper group. A year in which we completed our first cable TV acquisition–a large, growing system that will have two-way electronic information capabilities. A year of high contribution from our forest products group, during which the new Maine paper mill in which we hold an important equity position began production well ahead of schedule of a versatile magazine-grade paper.

For the fifth time in a little more than four years, the Company's dividend was raised. Effective with the September 1981 payment, the annual rate on the Class A and Class B common stock was increased from $1.00 to $1.10 per share.

John M. Crewdson, national correspondent, and Dave Anderson, sports columnist, congratulate each other after winning in 1981 the 47th and 48th Pulitzer Prizes awarded to The Times or to members of its staff.

Newspaper Group

New York
The New York Times

Florida
The Ledger, Lakeland
Gainesville Sun
Ocala Star-Banner
Palatka Daily News
Leesburg/Commercial
Lake City Reporter
Sebring News
Fernandina Beach News-Leader
Avon Park Sun
Marco Island Eagle
Anna Maria Islander
Golden Gate Eagle
Zephyrhills News

North Carolina
Wilmington Star-News
Lexington Dispatch
Hendersonville Times-News

Louisiana
Houma Daily Courier
Daily Comet, Thibodaux

Newspapers: Advertising and circulation growth produce 26% gain in operating profit

The operating profit of this group, comprising The New York Times and 18 regional newspapers in the South, rose by 26 percent to $54.1 million from $42.9 million in 1980.
Record advertising linage and significant circulation gains accounted for the strong advance.

The New York Times

Readers and advertisers alike find The Times indispensable–readers for the thoroughness, interest and readability they find in this unique newspaper, and for the interesting and useful advertising that runs in its pages; advertisers for the high-income, well-educated readers The Times attracts in increasing numbers.

In the evolutionary process of making The Times an ever better newspaper, several improvements were made during 1981. The Sunday Travel section took on an entirely new design and was expanded to include new features. "Washington Talk," a page of behind-the-scenes items, profiles and analyses, began in late summer and appears every weekday.

The excellence of The Times is not only affirmed by such awards as the Pulitzer Prizes–more of which have been awarded to it and its staff than to any other newspaper–but also by increases in its circulation in the city, suburbs, region and nation.

Circulation: Average weekday circulation for the year was 912,500 copies, a gain of 11,400 copies over 1980. Average Sunday circulation was 1,485,000 copies, up 27,500 copies. The suggested newsstand price of the weekday editions was scheduled to be increased from 25 cents to 30 cents a copy within 50 miles of New York City on March 1, 1982.

A second printing site for the national edition was established at The Ledger in Lakeland, Fla., one of the Company's regional newspapers. Production at this site enables readers in the Southeast to get early-morning delivery, just as readers in the Midwest have been reading the paper at breakfast-time since the national edition began printing in Chicago in August 1980. The two plants make conventional offset page plates with masks produced by a laser device, having received the image information by satellite

---

The New York Times Company	Annual Report 1981

Earnings: a record year, up 23 percent

Revenues: $845 million, a new high

The Times: 98 million ad lines, a record

The Times: 47th and 48th Pulitzer Prizes

Cable TV: year-end subscriptions top 84,000

Forest Products: Maine mill in production

Figure 3.1b

The New York Times 1981 Annual Report shows a grid in use with great vitality. Notice that the design has a vertical emphasis and images that occasionally break across the grid to bring them spatially forward. The white space is also beautifully balanced with the type and photos.
Copyright © 1981 by The New York Times Company. Reprinted by permission. Copyright Art Director: Louis Silverstein, V.P., the New York Times and Corporate Art Director, The New York Times Company. Designer: Philip Gips, Gips & Balkind, Inc., NYC.

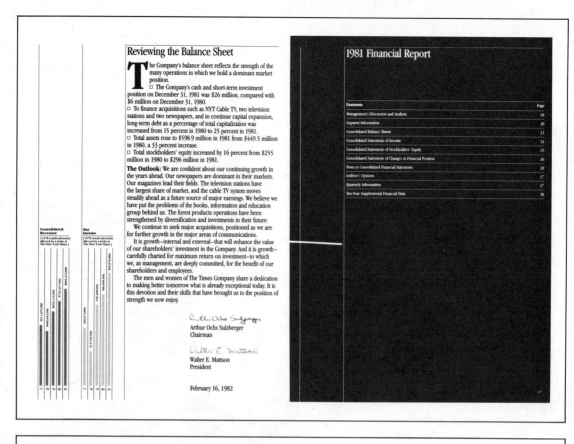

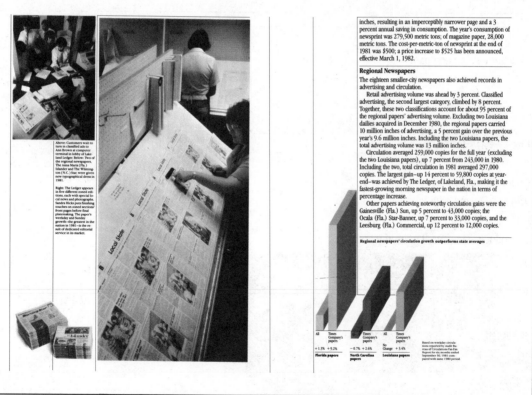

Figure 3.1c
In brochures, catalogs, and books the most common grids are based on two, three, or four columns. Notice that within these dimensions it is also possible to double or triple the column widths—that is, to use wide and short widths together, such as in *The New York Times Annual Report. Copyright © 1981 by The New York Times Company. Reprinted by permission. Copyright Art Director: Louis Silverstein, V.P., the New York Times and Corporate Art Director, The New York Times Company. Designer: Philip Gips, Gips & Balkind, Inc., NYC.*

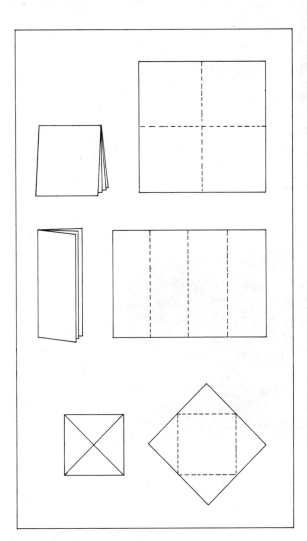

Most space or field areas, obviously, are rectangles. The designer must, therefore, find endless means to create visual interest within vertical or horizontal rectangular space. Probably the most common proportion is the letter size of $8\frac{1}{2}'' \times 11''$, or proportionately related sizes. Standard measurements, however, are not necessarily limiting. An unfolded rectangular sheet may become a square when folded. Or it may have a vertical axis when folded, but a horizontal axis when unfolded. The process of unfolding can itself be related to the flow of the copy; proper timing can reveal the shape as the sheet is gradually opened. Greeting cards, particularly, use this technique.

A single empty surface also has an axis (vertical or horizontal), a texture (glossy, rough), a color (bright white, off-white, blue, brown), thickness, and form (flat, curved, flexible). A designer must consider all these elements before placing anything on the surface; each element must have a relationship to the other design elements and the function of the piece.

A designer must see the surface as *space,* not merely as paper or board. As soon as objects are placed in this space, it becomes the field for the objects, and the objects are related spatially by depth and interval. *Depth* results when the objects overlap or are placed in perspective. Space is also *interval,* which is referred to as "negative space." This is easily defined as the area and shape between the contours of objects and between objects and edges. Some of the best examples of negative space are found in logos.

Figure 3.2a
The top shows a right angle fold. In the middle is an example of parallel folding. The bottom is a unique special purpose fold which can contain extra sheets.

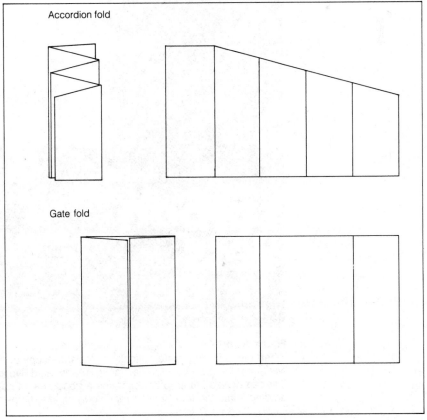

Figure 3.2b
A simple cut at the top adds a secondary dimension to the format. The gate fold is often used to dramatically reveal a product as it opens and expands.

29

Figure 3.2c
When the unfolding systematically reveals the copy or other visual elements, the graphic effect is kinetic or animated. Notice that the 3-M carbonless paper folder contains a good deal of copy, but dividing it into the folds invites reading in smaller steps. *Courtesy 3M Printing Products Division.*

A new carbonless paper with all the benefits of "Action" 100 but many ways better

3M is proud to present a bright new star among carbonless papers, "Action" 100 PLUS. An extraordinary uncoated self-contained carbonless paper with significant improvements over our famous "Action" 100.

"Action" 100 PLUS is substance 11# —combining the best features of the old substance 10# and 12#.

"Action" 100 PLUS satisfies all forms market requirements with no need to stock two weights.

While "Action" 100 PLUS retains all the desirable benefits of "Action" 100, it gives you additional "plus" features:

"Action" 100 PLUS has more opacity, more brightness, more contrast, denser image, more body, more strength, and excellent press performance.

"Action" 100 PLUS puts together the most-wanted carbonless paper characteristics for the benefit of forms designers, manufacturers and users.

must be back-printed with information or instructions • Business machine and teleprinter rolls, used with or without a ribbon.

100 PLUS is now available for immediate shipment, roll and sheet stock, in substance 11#, white and five colors.

"Action" 100 PLUS. The new one, the better one for forms manufacturer's in today's economy.

For further information and samples, please write 3M Company, Box 33050, Dept. BRF-76, St. Paul, MN 55101.

A new carbonless paper with all the benefits of "Action" 100 but many ways better

3M is proud to present a bright new star among carbonless papers, "Action" 100 PLUS. An extraordinary uncoated self-contained carbonless paper with significant improvements over our famous "Action" 100.

"Action" 100 PLUS is substance 11# —combining the best features of the old substance 10# and 12#.

"Action" 100 PLUS satisfies all forms market requirements with no need to stock two weights.

While "Action" 100 PLUS retains all the desirable benefits of "Action" 100, it gives you additional "plus" features:

"Action" 100 PLUS has more opacity, more brightness, more contrast, denser image, more body, more strength, and excellent press performance.

"Action" 100 PLUS puts together the most-wanted carbonless paper characteristics for the benefit of forms designers, manufacturers and users.

For the manufacturer, 100 PLUS, with its superior press and collator performance, offers improved productivity and faster turn-around. Less inventory, too, with no mated coatings to match up, because 100 PLUS is totally self-contained. 100 PLUS is the least expensive self-contained carbonless to buy and to ship. You can save as much as 60% in shipping weight with "Action" 100 PLUS.

Because 100 PLUS is uncoated and self-contained, it has versatility and usefulness for a far greater variety of forms than any other carbonless paper. It is the choice paper for forms used in machine entry systems, and is recommended for ribbonless entry applications, especially where clean performance is essential.

Here are just a few recommended applications for your new "Action" 100 PLUS: Automated teller forms • Automated medical diagnostic equipment forms • Credit card imprinter forms • Carbon and carbonless combinations forms • Standard multiple part business forms, invoices, repair forms, purchase orders, etc. • Fuel meter and other automatic measuring equipment forms • Label forms for register, unit set or continuous applications • Forms that

must be back-printed with information or instructions • Business machine and teleprinter rolls, used with or without a ribbon.

100 PLUS is now available for immediate shipment, roll and sheet stock, in substance 11#, white and five colors.

"Action" 100 PLUS. The new one, the better one for forms manufacturer's in today's economy.

For further information and samples, please write 3M Company, Box 33050, Dept. BRF-76, St. Paul, MN 55101.

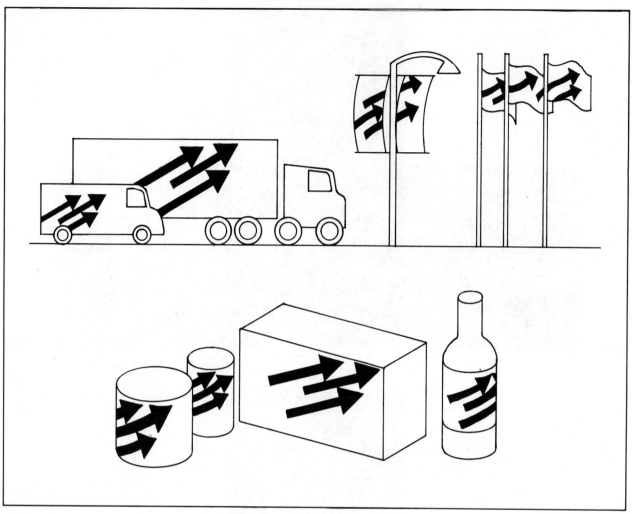

Figure 3.3
Design techniques that work well for printed matter do not necessarily apply to other forms. Scale, movement, and surfaces plus environmental limitations must be considered. A good example is the diverse and unpredictable potential applications to which a corporate symbol might have to adapt.

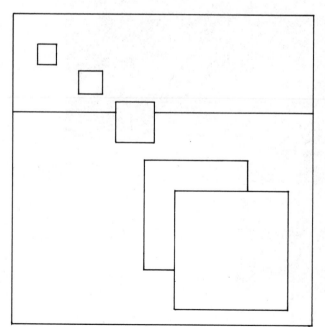

Figure 3.4
Depth can be implied simply through diminishing shape size, establishing a horizon, and overlapping. Shapes near the top of an area usually appear further away. However, this illusion can easily be contradicted by the use of color contrasts.

Figure 3.5a
The 7 UP logo uses the spatial overlap of the 7, the dot, and UP, as well as a diagonal movement to reinforce the upward thrust. *Courtesy The Seven Up Company.*

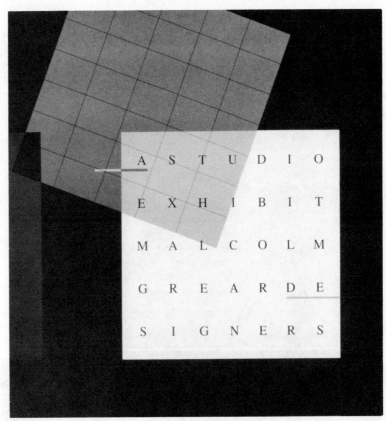

Figure 3.5b
This studio exhibit announcement shows transparency, a more subtle form of overlap.

Figure 3.5c
The Mackey newsletter scatters the pages to suggest informality and immediacy. *Design: Obata-Kuehner, Inc.*

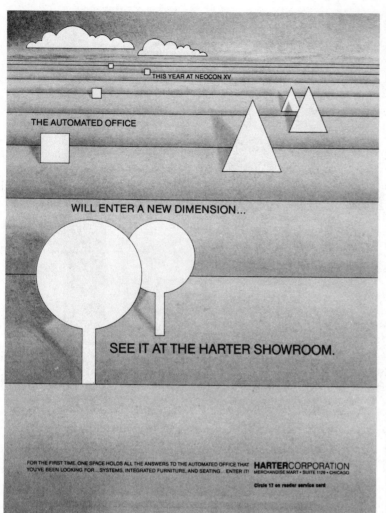

Figure 3.6
The Harter ad shown here combines diminishing shapes and type, receding ground lines, a horizon, and shadows to invite you into Harter's "new dimension." *Designer: Mr. Bob Bender, Creative Art Director @ Lord, Sullivan & Yoder, Marion, Ohio.*

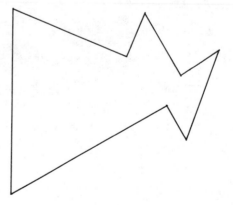

Figure 3.7
Interval or negative space. Notice that the shape of the space may include the edge of the layout.

(a)

Malcolm Grear Designers, Inc.

(b)

Jon Tomas for Hair and Skin,
St. Louis, Missouri.

(c)

Courtesy KMOX.

Figure 3.8
A positive-negative interchange of shapes results in a reverse of attention, which in turn develops visual activity. One logo here (a) is simple and typographically based, the other logo (b) is complex and objectively based, yet both are significant and memorable. (c) The KMOX ad uses positive-negative type and a strong diagonal emphasis to pull your attention to it in the context of a newspaper.

Placement. Among the variables of space, object, and color (or value contrast) are endless methods of arrangement to organize elements into significant visual statements.

A single shape as simple as a square can be large and suggest impact or small and imply space or emptiness. In a diagonal position it can seem to be in motion as if falling or disappearing. A change in color can reverse brightness to darkness. If you add more shapes, the design possibilities are compounded: One object will be compared to the other, which in turn will invite multitudes of other relationships to emerge.

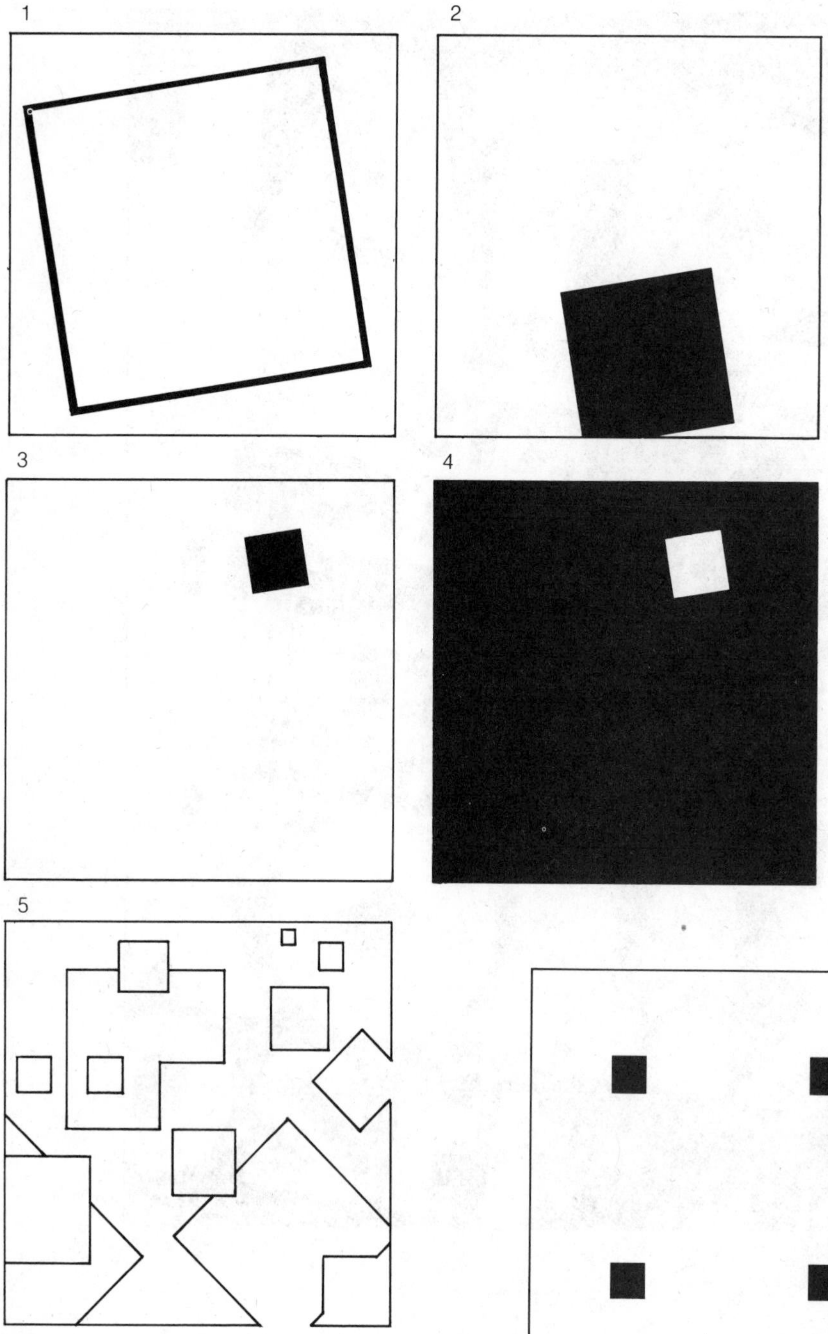

Figure 3.9
When the mark appears on the paper, the
surface changes from paper to space.

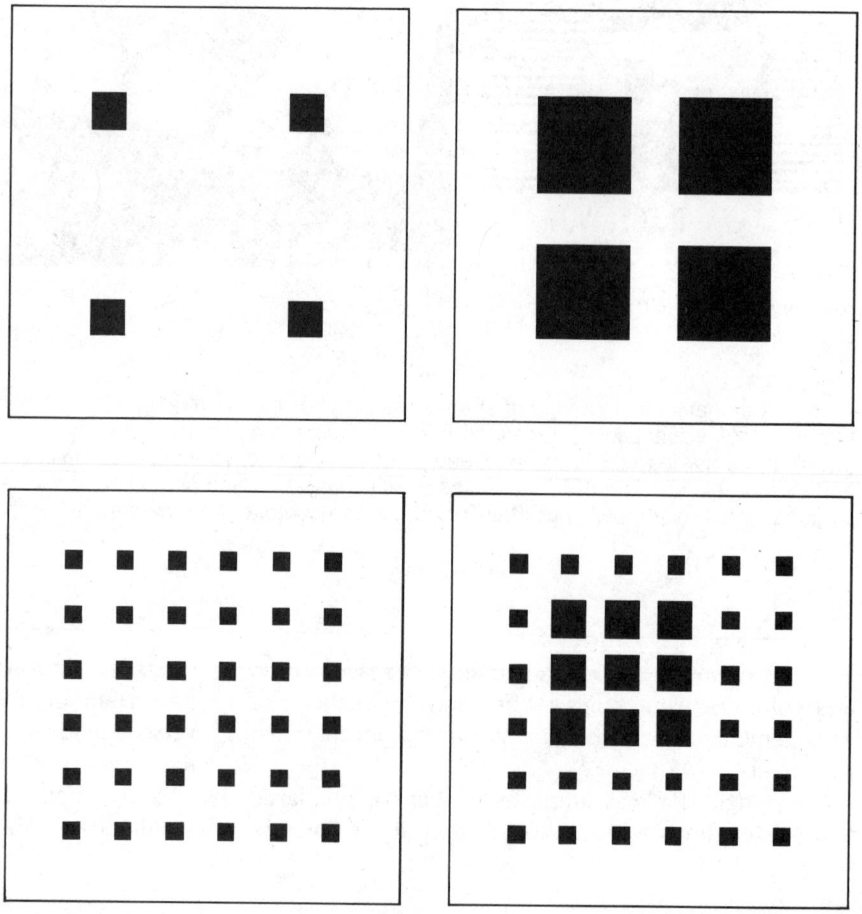

Figure 3.10
With the addition of color these
groupings could incorporate
secondary patterns or a change in
emphasis from the black-and-white
examples.

Pattern. Visual relationships are composed of more than one activity at a time. Are there only four squares in Figure 3.10, or are these the four corners of an implied outline of a larger square? If we change the size, another idea occurs: A shape appears between the shapes (negative space). If we multiply the number of shapes, the individual shapes are now subordinate to the whole or what has become a repeat pattern. But even within strong patterns, secondary variations can make the visual experience more interesting and can introduce systems within systems, a principle used often in advertising and typography.

Isolating the design components from one another may result in one's destroying the others. If a designer concentrates on shape relationships and ignores color, the byproduct might be loss of information. For example, a common "mistake" is to place bright green letters on a bright red background: This initiates a diffusion of definition at the edges. The error is one of concentrating on brilliance but ignoring value contrast. The colors seem to vibrate even though the shapes are really sharp and separate. The result is a distortion of legibility.

Contrast. In order for the design elements to operate together, they must also take places in a sequence of relative importance or they will merge into a pattern with no emphasis.

Figure 3.11
Patterns can be more than simply decorative display. (a) In the Sudden Infant Death Syndrome booklet cover, the logo (a single square) made up of *i*'s with one missing conveys the issue sensitively. It then repeats further to comprise a simple, attractive brochure cover. (b) The Envision 9 poster, complex in detail but simple in concept, is a fine example of a pattern within a pattern. (c) Type alone can also be a lively decoration, as is evident on the Boston Museum of Fine Arts gift-shop bag. (d and e) Patterns can also be used successfully in logos, as the Lindenwood and Camelot designs here show.

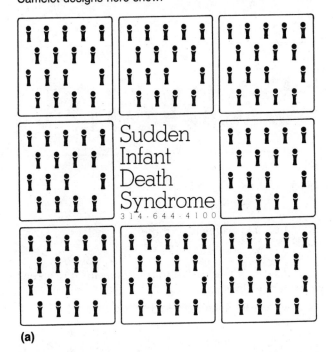

(a)

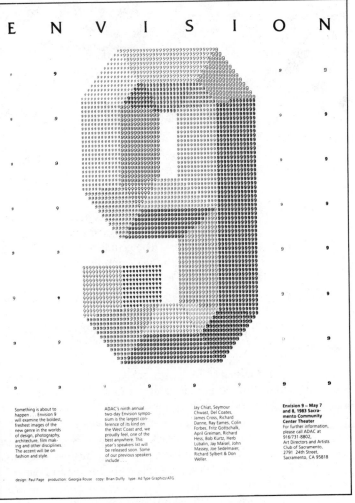

(b)

Designer: Paul Page, Page Design.

Figure 3.11 (continued)

(c)

Shopping bag designed by Barbara Hawley and Carl Zahn for the Museum of Fine Arts, Boston.

LINDENWOOD

(d)

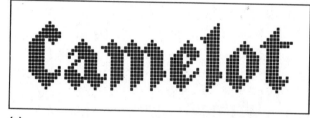

(e)

Design: Obata-Kuehner, Inc.

To develop some priority, designers can use *contrast* or opposing forces: large against small, one against many, light against dark. The actual content of the copy could also contrast with the design forms to develop an interchange of interest between the parts. An example would be lettering constructed from objects to create a visual metaphor or pun. Often the designs are made up of combinations of contrasting parts that are not so obvious.

Color. Color is probably the most complex yet fascinating design element; it can also be the most misunderstood. As a designer, you must be familiar with its structural properties. (See color plates.)

First, consider black and white as color. If you look at the black ink of newsprint against the white newspaper and compare this with the ink and paper of a popular magazine, you will see that they have different characteristics. This should make you aware that how and where an ink or paint is placed has a serious effect on the color.

Inks and paints have three "dimensions" to consider:

Hue (or chrome): Which color something is: green, red, yellow, and so on.
Value: Its lightness or darkness. (Note that black and white only have value.)
Intensity (or saturation): How bright or "pure" the color is. (See color plates 1 and 2.)

Other functional color factors are whether a color is opaque, transparent, dull or glossy, including surface. In addition, certain symbolic meanings are traditionally attached to certain colors.

The simple name of a color is its hue. The term *pure color* visually refers to the color, unmixed, when the hue is obvious. The color "pink" is really a red hue with white mixed into it. So pink is a red with a higher value (lighter) and also a loss of intensity (brightness).

Notice the changes that occur when one ink is printed over another or when a color is printed on a

38

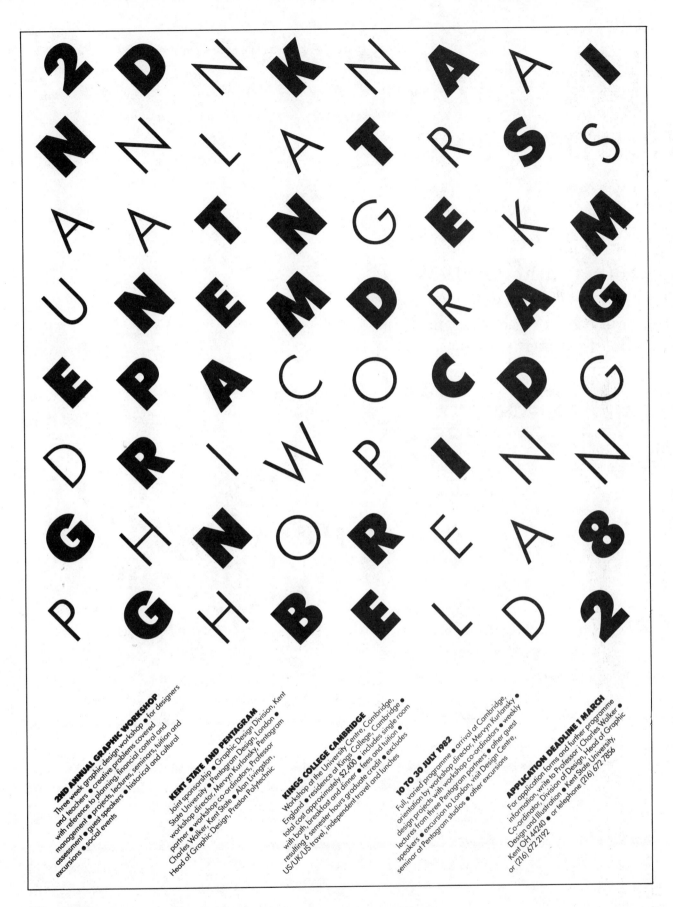

Figure 3.12a
The Kent State poster here, by Pentagram, uses light and heavy type to separate
the two parts of the heading. The result is not easy to read, but it is visually worth
the effort. *Design: Pentagram, Mervyn Kuriansky A.D.*

Figure 3.12b
These IBM ads illustrate contrast in size and placement.

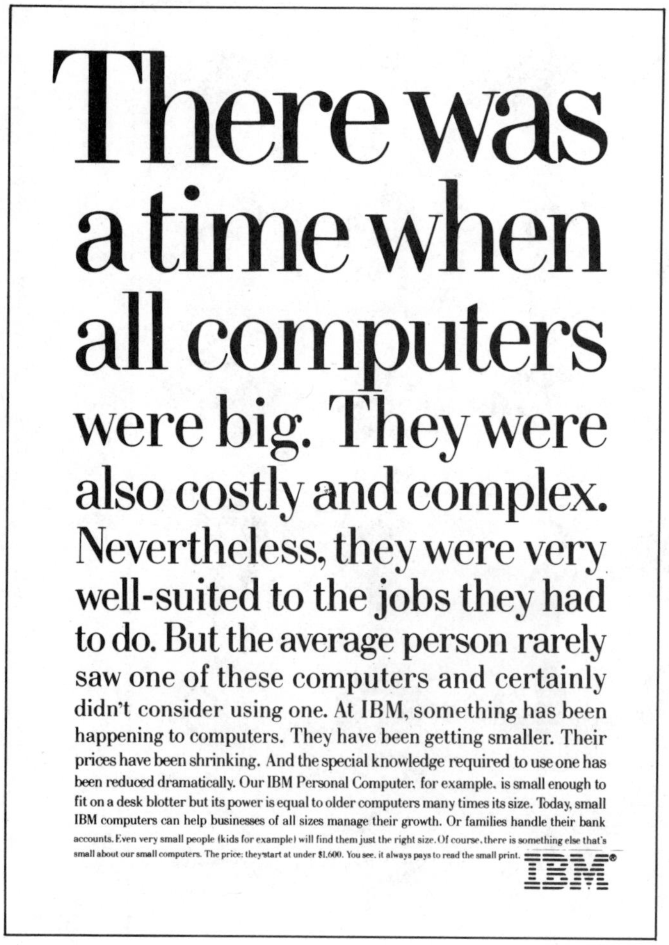

There was a time when all computers were big. They were also costly and complex.

Nevertheless, they were very well-suited to the jobs they had to do. But the average person rarely saw one of these computers and certainly didn't consider using one. At IBM, something has been happening to computers. They have been getting smaller. Their prices have been shrinking. And the special knowledge required to use one has been reduced dramatically. Our IBM Personal Computer. for example. is small enough to fit on a desk blotter but its power is equal to older computers many times its size. Today, small IBM computers can help businesses of all sizes manage their growth. Or families handle their bank accounts. Even very small people (kids for example) will find them just the right size. Of course, there is something else that's small about our small computers. The price: they start at under $1,600. You see, it always pays to read the small print. **IBM®**

Art Director: John Marcellino, Lord, Geller, Federico, Einstein.

The three most important letters in typing.

IBM.

Call *IBM Direct* 800-631-5582 Ext. 4. In New Jersey 800-352-4960 Ext. 4. In Hawaii/Alaska 800-526-2484 Ext. 4.

Art Directors: Andy DeSantis and Hal Kaufman, Doyle, Dane, Bernbach.

THE WINNING TEAM IN HEALTH CLAIMS ADMINISTRATION

1 QicCLAIM—HEALTH CLAIMS MANAGEMENT SYSTEM

In just two short years, QicClaim has set the standard for excellence in automated health claims administration systems. With more than 60 installations nationwide, QicClaim provides in-depth management information reporting for cost containment analysis, loss reporting and benefit utilization to more than 5000 companies every day. More than just a system...QicClaim is the affordable solution to your organization's needs... including analysis, design, installation, training, maintenance and ongoing support.

2 QANTEL BUSINESS COMPUTERS

A proven record of performance and reliability with more than 20,000 business systems installed. Qantel combines this experience with the support of more than 2500 sales and service personnel worldwide and a major commitment to the employee benefits administration industry. From NFL playing fields to insurance companies...Qantel is the computer of champions.

3 EMPLOYEE BENEFITS ADMINISTRATION PROFESSIONALS

With the systems and support of QicClaim and Qantel, employee benefit plans are currently being administered covering more than 2 million people. Third Party Administrators, insurance companies and self-administered organizations are joining the Q Team for systems, solutions and support that only a champion can provide.

For Q Team membership information, contact:

RiMS RESOURCE INFORMATION MANAGEMENT SYSTEMS, INC.

2015 Spring Road, Suite 220
Oak Brook, IL 60521 • 312/789-0230

Figure 3.12c
This Q team ad uses exaggerated type to make its point. *Courtesy Resource Information Management Systems, Inc.*

Figure 3.13
The outstanding use of three dimensionality makes the concept on this page from
a booklet for the Champion Paper Company extend from the page. The contrast
here between the flat sheet and the distribution of the letters contributes to the
visual pun. *Design: Robert Cipriani, Cipriani Advertising, Inc.*

colored paper. Obviously, when you apply a blue to a yellow surface, some sort of "greenness" will occur. This is a change in hue. If you mix certain colors that are "complements" they will appear darker and get brown or "muddy," which can be desirable or not. When this happens there is a maximum loss of brightness (intensity) and minimum hue is apparent. Brown and black inks and paints reveal some touch of hue. If you thin them with water or add white the hues become more apparent.

You must also be aware of the relative *value* contrast of black, white, and gray to determine how the elements of a design will be perceived. This is more difficult with colors. (See color plates 2 and 3.) When the color (hue) is by nature a high (light) value, the contrast scale will be limited and design details will be less defined on a white ground.

The value scale of light to dark is maximum when printing with black ink. Colors will reduce the value range resulting in less detail and less contrast. This is especially important when reproducing photographs with significant details. When type is printed in color on a field of gray paper that has a similar darkness (value) as the type, it will seem to merge or diffuse. This effect,

however, could be used effectively as an exciting color activity when it is an approrpriate device for the intent of the design. (See color plate 10.)

Intensity is the degree of purity. A hue with no white, black, or gray mixed into it is maximum in intensity. If you mix white into a pure color, the color gets lighter in value and reduced in intensity. It does *not* get brighter. Notice that yellow at its purist (or maximum intensity) is lighter in value than the brightest blue or red. It is almost impossible to understand bright yellow or orange small type or thin lines printed on white paper. The problem is one of values' not having enough contrast. On the other hand, what might not work where legibility is important might be dramatic as a design color effect for the right problem.

A color is affected by the other colors surrounding or adjacent to it. For example, a bright red on an orange area will appear darker than the same red on a bright blue. A simple exercise to show this is to place swatches of a scale of grays on various colors and to notice how the gray values change.

Colors are also called *warm* or *cool*. If you examine a blue, it will probably seem on the greenish side or the reddish side. If it is red directed (ultramarine blue) then it probably will make a good purple; if it is more of a green-blue (cobalt blue) then it will readily mix with yellow to produce green. The warmer colors are said to *advance,* the cool ones to *recede.* However, this has to be considered in context because an effect can be contradicted by what shape the color has, how much of it there is, and where it is placed. (See color plate 5.)

Furthermore, we all have some attitudes and prejudices toward color that are part of our cultural-social backgrounds. For example, blue is for boys, pink for girls, apples are red, and so on. Other colors have environmental significance: black and yellow for warning signs, blue for police officers. Indeed, when something with a traditionally accepted strong color association is printed in black and white, we still perceive the color subconsciously.

We use many color terms in our everyday language: "white as a sheet," "blue-collar workers," "getting the pink slip," a "green" beginner, a "yellow" coward, "feeling blue," and so on. Such associations can, at times, be tapped for design purposes but they can also become

Figure 3.14a
We know that some apples are green or yellow and that hearts can be made of brown chocolate, but the pattern of color association with common objects is well established in our culture. Even when such strongly associated objects are reproduced in black and white, we understand them to be in their usual colors.

Figure 3.14b
The American flag is perceived in color even when it is shown in black and white. *Art Director: Herb Lubalin.*

Figure 3.14c
Do we really see the bouquet of roses as gray, as they are here, or do we think of them as red with tints to indicate variations of pink? This is a simple, informal, sensitive, small poster for the American Red Cross. *Designer: Robin Rader for St. Louis Bi State Chapter, American Red Cross.*

burdensome when their assumed meanings interfere with unrelated design concepts.

Basic design principles are not actually "rules." Many of the best graphic designs break some basic rules or traditions. This, however, requires that a designer have control over the elements as well as a thorough knowledge of the accepted principles. By becoming familiar with the characteristics of color mixing you can predict the changes that will occur, and can use them to great advantage in printed matter. Especially notice that when you are using two colors you actually acquire three by overlapping. (See color plates 11 and 18.) The paper (ground) is also another "color." Testing combinations of transparent and translucent color films and tissues by overlapping them can give you a good idea of what happens. Also, save examples of color printing and examine them through a magnifying glass.

In printed matter a pattern of dots (screen) can extend the use of a color. Bright red printed in a dot pattern, for instance, will look pink even though it really is composed of the same red.

Movement. The implication of direction or of objects moving through the space of a page is a useful element of visual dynamics. It can suggest speed, instability, or a passing event recorded.

There are many means of implying movement: A path of lines trailing from an object like a comet or a sequence of objects diminishing into a deep perspective space are only two of them. Movement seems more dynamic when depth is implied.

Shape. The specific area or outline quality of each design element can also add character to a graphic design: It can be sharp and clean in contour or rough and diffused; colors can be textured, smooth, reflective.

Concept and Layout Summarized. Although we are systematically examining the working parts of the design process, we should recognize that successful designing requires a relative order of all of the parts: shapes, colors, format, copy, images, and so on. All these parts, in turn, must be related to the concept at hand

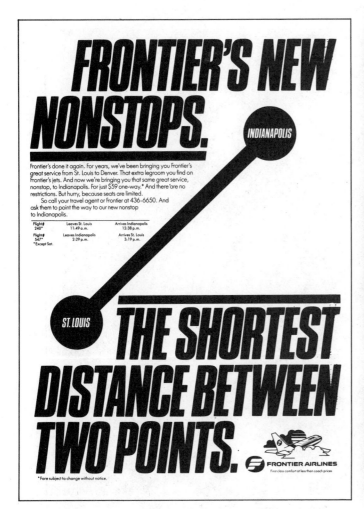

Figure 3.15a
The slanted type and the diagonal air route give this Frontier Airlines ad a strong direction to drive home the message.
Courtesy Frontier Airlines.

Figure 3.15b
The Pirelli circles move like wheels across the page.
Courtesy Pirelli Tire Corporation.

Figure 3.15c
Symbolic graphic waves make the design flow across the page for a booklet cover for the Missouri Botanical Gardens.

Figure 3.15d
The beer can breaks through the sheet with a sense of Surrealism. © *Anheuser-Busch, Inc., 1983. Art Director/Designer Credit: D'Arcy MacManus & Masius, Inc.*

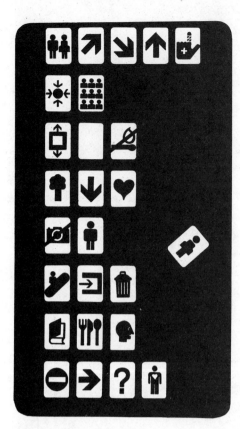

Figure 3.15e
In the "graphic poem" by Jean McCarthy, the movement is out and down for one subject; arrows imply directions in other places. *Designer: Jean McCarthy.*

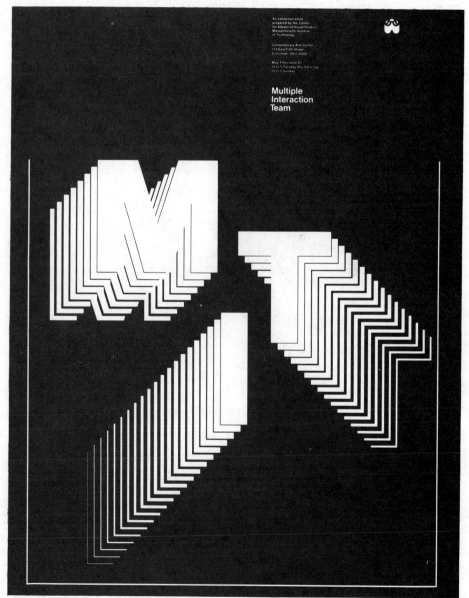

Figure 3.16
As the letters in the *Multiple Interaction Team* move from the background in steps, they appear to extend out from the sheet. *Designer: Joe Bottoni.*

Figure 3.17
The casual, shaky character of the line drawings contrasts with the serious business subject of and the elegant, traditional headline type in this series of magazine ads for *Barron's*.
Reprinted by courtesy of Barron's National Business and Financial Weekly.

Barron's readers have the highest median household income—and the highest median individual employment income—of any audience measured by Simmons.

Source: SMRB, 1982. Copyright, Dow Jones & Company, Inc., 1983.

Barron's has the highest concentration of top management executives of any publication measured by Simmons, including Business Week, Fortune and Forbes.

Source: SMRB, 1982. Copyright, Dow Jones & Company, Inc., 1983.

Figure 3.18
This spread layout from an Apple Computers ad is about as complex as it could be; yet the copy and the images are well placed. The lengthy copy looks less formidable because of the emphasis of the numbers and the variety of images.
© 1982 Apple Computer, Inc.

and must allow for the successful reproduction or distribution of the information. Designing is more than cosmetic afterthought or simply moving things about until they "look nice."

The circumstances under which a particular design object will be experienced is another primary consideration in its construction. Who will see it? Where? How will it be used? How long will it be used? With what competition? Is this for information? Attention? Is it expedient or of high value?

Design can be a rational and planned process through schematic steps or it can be intuitive and spontaneous. Both approaches involve a balance natural to each individual designer, which depends in part on the dictates of each particular problem. Either attitude can be obvious in visual form. If a subject itself is of a highly specific schematic nature—instructional, historic, or scientific, for instance—then order and restraint are probably the qualities indicated. For a more kinetic or emotional work, such as a dance poster or political-social announcement, a spontaneous graphic element might better convey the emotional content.

The total design should be perceived in a manner directed by the design parts, not in spite of them. You must, in other words, consider the purpose of a design as you create it. This requires an open-minded approach, and a willingness to adjust the parts of a graphic project to enhance its effective communication. Once the concept is established, all the relationships of the parts need to support the intent of the solution. The basics of design are best understood by extensive practice: The more you pursue alternatives, the more experience you are accumulating to apply to future problems.

Copy

The most direct designs are those made up simply of words (typographic). These can be the most difficult to produce. A layout may consist of only a headline, especially when there would not be time for the audience to pause and examine, but merely to identify quickly or grasp a message. In newspaper or magazine advertising, this simple technique can make a design stand out from others of more complexity simply by contrast. Other contrasts—of type size, location, scale, and value, for example—can also result in simple yet exciting variations.

Even when a large amount of copy is required for an informative ad or within the layout of a magazine or catalog, careful design accents can clarify the main points and make the data less formidable.

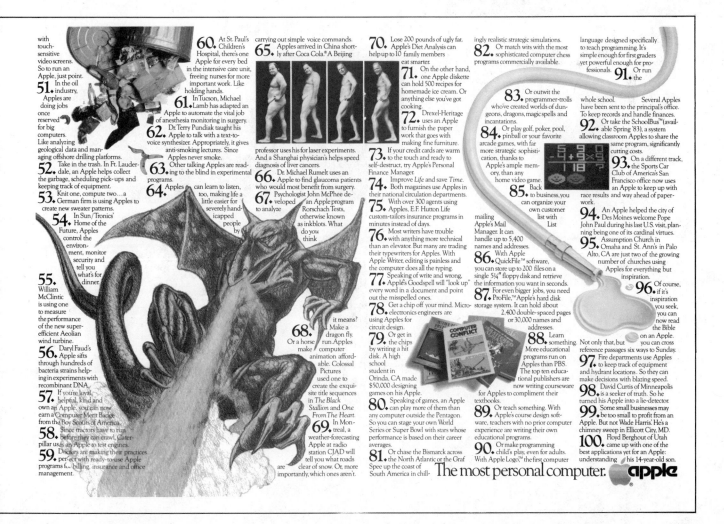

Figure 3.19
The need to emphasize four lectures equally
indicated a regularity of design for this poster.

Figure 3.20a
The Eat Art is a visually shocking combination of images with the
activity clearly symbolized. *Designer: Barron Krody.*

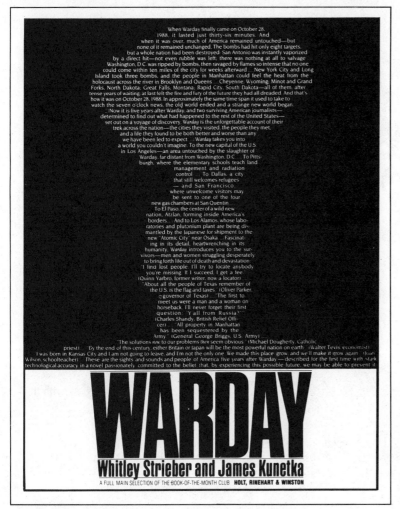

Figure 3.20b
This Warday ad makes the nuclear cloud of type move up and out of the title. *Art Director: Dan Silverstone, Jameson Advertising, Inc.*

Figure 3.21a
This now-classic Rabbit ad is the essence of simplicity, a typographic pun. *Art Director: Gary Goldsmith. Copywriter: Shawn Cooper. Courtesy Volkswagen of America.*

GUTS. *GREAT-WEST LIFE WOULD BE GOOD FOR YOUR BROKER- AGE BUSINESS. WE DON'T HAVE A PROBLEM SAYING THAT. WHY SHOULD WE? WE KNOW WE CAN GIVE YOU THE FLEXIBILITY AND COMPETITIVE PRICING YOU NEED. AND SERVICE? YOU'LL FIND IT'S A PLEASURE WORKING WITH US. YOU SAY, "THOSE PEOPLE AT GREAT-WEST LIFE. THEY HAVE GUTS MAKING HOT-SHOT PROMISES LIKE THAT." CALL IT CONFIDENCE. CALL IT MOXIE. BUT FIRST, CALL YOUR GREAT-WEST LIFE MANAGER. OR MAKE A COLLECT CALL TO YOUR BROKER BUYLINE.* **303-892-3000**

Great-West Life
UNITED STATES HEADQUARTERS DENVER COLORADO

GREED. *SO WE SAY WE WANT YOUR BROKERAGE BUSINESS. YOU SAY, "SO WHAT. A LOT OF PEOPLE WANT MY BUSINESS. WHAT DO I GET OUT OF GIVING IT TO YOU?" YOU'LL GET GREAT-WEST LIFE – A COMPANY THAT WILL BEND OVER BACKWARDS FOR YOUR BROKERAGE BUSINESS BY GIVING YOU FLEXIBILITY, COMPETITIVE PRICING, TER- RIFIC SERVICE AND COMPENSATION. WHAT DO WE GET OUT OF IT? BIGGER AND STRONGER. CALL IT GREED. BUT IS THAT SO BAD? SOME PEOPLE THINK GREED IS A VICE. WE THINK OUR VICE IS YOUR VIRTUE. GIVE YOUR LOCAL GREAT-WEST LIFE MANAGER A CALL. OR CALL COLLECT TO YOUR BROKER BUYLINE.* **303-892-3000**

Great-West Life
UNITED STATES HEADQUARTERS DENVER COLORADO

Figure 3.21b
The shock of words like "guts" and "greed" amplified by their light-bold contrast has to make the reader take notice of Great-West Life. *Art Director: Bill Hook, Broyles, Allenbaugh & Davis.*

Figure 3.21c
In one of a clever series of ads, Haute Stuff amplifies the copy with outlined and faded type. *Art Director: Bob Barrie. Copywriter: Jim Newcombe.*

Figure 3.22a

These spreads from an Illinois tourism brochure are packed with information. The type is relieved through the random placement of photos, drawings, and a box, which suggest the variety of activities the spreads are promoting. *Courtesy Illinois Department of Commerce & Community Affairs, Office of Tourism.*

Figure 3.22b
The Ferrario Tabloid spread makes maximum use of type weights and sizes to identify its featured products. *Design: Frank/James Productions.*

Figure 3.22c
Vogue crams every space with information, but keeps it separate by rule-breaking changes in type style and weights, and the contrast of light and dark in an updated Dadaist style. *Courtesy Vogue. Copyright © 1983 by The Conde Nast Publications, Inc. Art Director: Roger Schoening. Designer: Ron Kajiwara.*

Most copy in publishing and advertising falls into the following categories:

Headlines: Briefly worded summations of content in a layout; the leading messages in advertments.

Headings: Titles of sections of copy, such as chapters.

Titles: Names of books or plays or reports.

Text: Longer running copy detailing information or persuading the reader in adversiting.

Captions: Information related to photographs, illustrations, or diagrams.

Others: Credits, call-outs, bylines, addresses, contents, footnotes, lists, schedule, dates, and so on.

Organizing and designing the copy is the process of *typography*.

Although the headings seem to be the most interesting copy material and probably stimulate more creative design responses, other copy must not be ignored by the designer because it participates in the *total* design. The designer should organize the copy in a manner that allows the reader to visually grasp the order in which the content or value is to be understood.

The effect of only a few words of the right style, size, and weight and in proper relationship can be very powerful. When specific layout standards exist—magazine formats, grid systems, business formats, or corporate graphic systems, for instance—inventive options at first may seem limited, but designers can still discover interesting design directions by assessing what design basics are available. For example, business cards usually follow a common $2'' \times 3\frac{1}{2}''$ format. They generally consist of a logo, the individual with title, company name, address, and phone number. But within this seemingly narrow layout constraint the design solutions and variations are endless.

Typographic design is easier to comprehend if you think of it as an extension of language. By using design effects you can suggest quiet, loud, informality, formality, systematic order, spontaneity, and countless other situational variables. (See Figures 3.25 and 3.12b.) In addition, the use of quotes, word balloons, exclamation marks, question marks, underlines, dots, and dashes parallels speech effects which people clearly understand. Messages can acquire additional emphasis if their designs contrast size, weights, and spacing. Combining letters with objects or symbols, or cutting and rearranging, are also design techniques for turning a work into a

Figure 3.23
This section from the *Globe-Democrat* newspaper shows most of the common parts of typographic layout. *The St. Louis Globe-Democrat.*

Department heading

Line art illustration

Headline

Subhead

Byline

Initial cap

Body copy (text) flush left ragged right

Bold lead in

Credit line

(a)

Design: Jan Rosamond.

(b)

Design: Nadine B. Sokol.

(c)

Design: Wayne Webb.

(d)

Design: Jeffrey Pike and Charles Harmon.

(e)

Design: Bill Vann.

Figure 3.24
Even though the business-card format is fairly standard, creative variations of style abound. (a) Nightblooming graphics gracefully refers to a late-in-the-day free-lance business. (b) Sokol converts her name into surgical sutures and leaves ample hospital white space. (c) Ball uses a rather large name but refeines it nicely with warm-toned colored type and textured paper. (d) Pike makes good use of a natural pun: The fish floats in the sea of white space. (e) This Bill Vann card expresses an informality and directness with simple shadowed lettering.

DON'T TURN THIS PAGE. STILL DON'T TURN IT. NOT YET DON'T TURN IT. HOLD ON A LITTLE LONGER. PATIENCE, PATIENCE. JUST A COUPLE MORE MINUTES. YOU'RE GETTING WARMER. O.K., NOW YOU CAN TURN IT.

Now you know how a typical reader reads U.S.News.

Slowly. Carefully. That's how our readers read.

Because they know that when they read U.S.News, anything that's worth missing is already missing.

And what's left is the cream. For our readers. And for our advertisers.

WE GIVE YOU THE CREAM. NOT THE SKIM.™

Figure 3.25
The *U.S. News & World Report* ad suggests a voice getting softer as the type size diminishes. *Ted Littleford, Creative Director Forte, Cole & Belding, New York.*

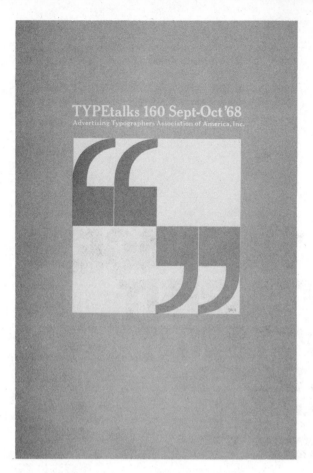

Figure 3.26a
The *Type Talks* cover appropriately uses quotes purely as the design focus and symbol for this issue. *Designer: Erwin Raith. Artist: B. Weil.*

Figure 3.26b
The Whalen chair is paired with the huge exclamation for maximum attention. *Concept: Vincent J. Danesi, Vice President Marketing.*

Figure 3.26c
In No More War the exclamation mark ends the headline with a graphic punch. *Art Director: Herb Lubalin.*

Figure 3.26d
The word balloon in *Changing Times* personalizes the message isolated in the office. *Courtesy* Changing Times.

Figure 3.26e
The earlier *Herald Tribune* ad animates the headline in a clever collage piece. *Courtesy the* Herald Tribune.

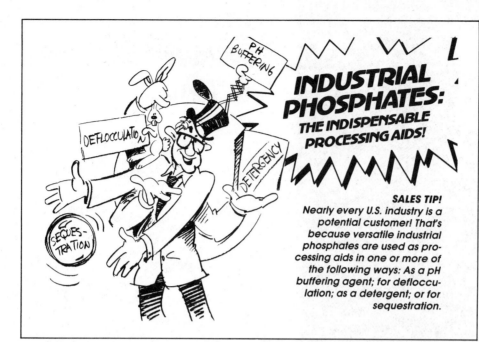

60

Figure 3.27a
The rebus, as shown in the old Sunday school book page, is a technique that, though not always used in the purest sense, works attractively as an image for relief in layouts with long headlines.

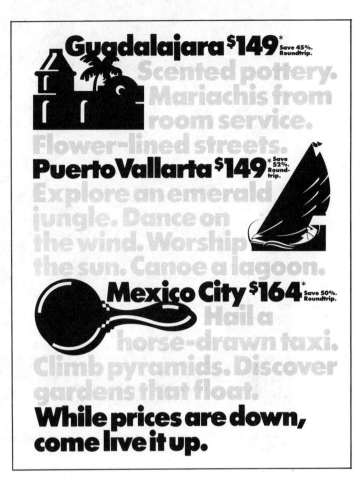

Figure 3.27b
The Mexicana ad also uses value contrast to emphasize the lead points in this somewhat rebus-oriented layout. *Courtesy Dailey & Associates.*

visual pun. Designing visual puns is often one of the more entertaining processes. Perhaps we should call it visual pfun. The style or character of a particular type of lettering also has much to convey about the ideas and information in the layout. The choices here should also be related to the other type in the design. Avoid design clichés, however: A delicate, light type is not necessarily feminine, nor is there any guaranteed ecclesiastical benefit in "Old English." Style choices depend on the words, the context, the color, the size, and, of course, the other parts of the layout.

Images

Images—in the form of photos or illustrations—are necessary in designs for descriptive purposes, as in magazines, catalogs or product advertising, or purely to convey a mood or symbolic concept.

The most common image, a descriptive photo or drawing with a caption, is frequently found in annual reports, catalogs and newsletters. Frequently, such images are not very interesting in themselves so the designer needs to organize them into various sizes and positions to induce the reader, who in turn will then pay some attention to them. Exciting creative images are found in posters, billboards, magazine title pages for articles, album covers, and book jackets.

The relationship of an image to the type is always vital. Designers have to keep both in mind and design for a balance between content and format related to the message. One aspect may dominate the other, or both can be combined into one: Attention can then vacillate between image and copy. Probably the only rule to which to adhere is that the concept of the design should not be confused or sacrificed by the flashy or weak execution of any of its individual parts.

The more typical design solutions, especially in advertising, include copy with photos or illustrations. The problem is to relate the literate parts with the visual

To celebrate their triumphs, quench their thirsts and drown their sorrows, the people who buy LIFE will down almost six million beers next week.
Don't you belong in LIFE? **LIFE**

Source: LIFE Marketing Services Department using 1981 SMRB and household purchasing data from 1981 LIFE Subscriber/Newsstand Study

Figure 3.28a
The 6 million *Life* spread here emphasizes a numerical point with a sense of humor. *Art Director: Lisa Scott. Illustrator: Dick Sakahara. Writer: Peter Swerdloff.*

Figure 3.28b
The GTE Flip Phone layout shows that even a difficult-to-read technique can work for the right concept.
Courtesy GTE.

Figure 3.29
The Broadway Deco style of type expresses Marilyn as well as her kiss in this poster. *Designer: Janet Nebel, Gellman Design.*

THE TELEPHONE YOU'LL FLIP OVER.

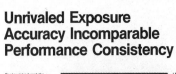

Unrivaled Exposure Accuracy Incomparable Performance Consistency

Figure 3.30a
The Contax booklet photos emphasize technical interest but the images vary in size and outline so as not to intimidate or bore the reader.
Courtesy Yashica, Inc.

Figure 3.30b
Photos or drawings in sequential steps suggest animation of movement similar to film or video images in the Walker ad.
Courtesy Somerset Importers Ltd.

WOULDN'T IT BE WONDERFUL
IF EVERY BIRTHDAY
THIS MONTH
ENDED WITH RED.

GIVE JOHNNIE WALKER® RED
SO SMOOTH, IT'S THE WORLD'S BEST SELLING SCOTCH.

Figure 3.30c
The TIAA-CREF brochure uses the collage technique to incorporate a variety of subjects. *Courtesy TIAA-CREF.*

Figure 3.30d
The NEA brochure cover centers around a photographic pun combining
apple = teacher + world and the map = travel.
National Education Association Special Services—Travel Programs. Design and Production: The Publishing Group, Rockville, Maryland.

KDTV channel 14, the only Spanish language TV station in the Bay area is also the best way to reach the 671,000 Hispanics in San Francisco.
KDTV has won the loyalty of San Francisco Hispanic audiences not only by broadcasting seven days a week in their own language, but also by being involved in the community.
In fact, the KDTV audience is so large and so loyal that, during prime time TV hours, more Hispanic adults 18-49 watch KDTV than the NBC, ABC or CBS affiliates.
For more information about the SIN affiliate station in San Francisco, contact: Lou Sweeney (415) 641-1400.

14 kdtv
ANOTHER SIN TELEVISION NETWORK AFFILIATE

For the 2.2 million people in New York who speak Spanish, WXTV channel 41 is number one.
Not just sometimes. But, Monday through Friday, from morning to early evening, WXTV is their #1 choice.
In addition to being the only Spanish language TV station in New York broadcasting 7 days a week, WXTV also reaches Hispanics in New Jersey, Connecticut and Philadelphia. So it's no surprise that WXTV has more local accounts on the air than any other New York Spanish language television station.
For more information about the SIN affiliate station in New York, contact: Wayne Casa, General Sales Manager, (201) 348-4141.

WXTV 41
ANOTHER SIN TELEVISION NETWORK AFFILIATE

Among women ages 25-54, WLTV channel 23 is simply the number one independent television station in the United States.
That stands to reason, because for Miami's 773,000 Spanish speaking Americans, WLTV is the only full-time, all-Spanish language TV station.
Which accounts for the fact that the November Arbitron proves that WLTV often draws a larger audience than CBS and ABC affiliates.
For more information about the SIN affiliate in Miami, contact: Damaso Santana (305) 856-2323.

WLTV 23 MIAMI
ANOTHER SIN TELEVISION NETWORK AFFILIATE

Figure 3.31a
In this striking series of small ads for the S.I.N. TV network, each city is important and is emphasized by large type plus highly stylized images. The headlines and illustrations have about equal graphic emphasis. Notice that the layout accommodates the individual station logos. *Courtesy S.I.N. Television Network.*

65

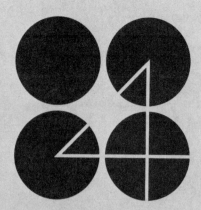

A Community for Learning

LINDENWOOD 4 is a new kind of College attracting a new kind of student. Who is this student?

A woman who after ten years of raising children wants to complete her college education.

A counselor at a community mental health center who wants to broaden his skills in working with adolescents.

A feminist who wants to understand the psychology of pregnancy and childbirth.

An environmental chemist who wants to gain proficiency in the field of air pollution.

A community leader who wants to explore the origins of the Black community in the tribal structure of African life.

4

Typically, Lindenwood 4 students will be working and over 25 years old. They will be mature, purposeful people who seek in higher education an opportunity to focus and enhance their lives and work. Some may be unable to attend regular classes or may find no school which gives them instruction in their chosen field. Or they no longer find the conventional lecture an acceptable means of instruction.

Lindenwood 4 recognizes the value of their past experience. Undergraduates have the option of receiving as much as three years' advanced standing, computed from previous college work, nationally recognized tests, and critical life experiences. At Lindenwood 4, there is no distinction between learning in the classroom and learning in the life situation.

At the graduate level, exceptional applicants may be admitted without having completed all undergraduate requirements when they can demonstrate advanced competence and expertise in their proposed fields.

Community Organization

The first citizens of the learning community are the students themselves. Their competence and imagination are the most vital resources of Lindenwood 4.

Other citizens of the community are Faculty Administrators, Faculty Sponsors and Resource Persons.

Faculty Administrators serve a nucleus of 30 students as advisors, mentors, and academic and career counselors. They act as general administrators of the Lindenwood 4 program in the regional center and serve as the students' main avenue of communications with the Colleges.

Faculty Sponsors work with no more than ten students, and are chosen for each trimester by the student and Faculty Administrator. Interacting with students on a one-to-one basis, the Faculty Sponsors assist students in developing their program of studies and work substantively with individuals through a regular schedule of meetings. Faculty Sponsors may be independent psychologists, physicians, artists, scientists, writers, community organizers, or professors employed at The Lindenwood Colleges or other institutions.

At the graduate level, a student may nominate his or her own Faculty Sponsor in the student's area of concentration, subject to approval by the Faculty Administrator. In the M.A. program, Faculty Sponsors must be able to work at a level of considerable specialization.

Resource Persons provide the student with a broad range of expertise and help integrate Lindenwood 4 into the

5

larger community. Regional centers maintain long-term relations with individuals and groups at various institutions such as mental health facilities, hospitals, video centers, business and government agencies, and other colleges and universities. These provide a permanent resource for Lindenwood 4 in career counseling, internships, job placement, and setting academic perspectives. Reciprocally, the regional centers contribute services and provide programs for their communities.

Students, faculty and resource persons work for mutual reinforcement, critique and development. All are teachers, all are learners contributing to the community, opening up new avenues of awareness and developing new skills.

Interaction

THE UNDERGRADUATE PROGRAM
While each regional center establishes its own style of interaction, the following is a typical format.

After acceptance, the student attends a weekend workshop. Here a decision is made concerning the student's Faculty Sponsor and the nature of the internship. Next, with the assistance of his *study committee* (the Faculty Administrator, a Faculty Sponsor, other students, and perhaps resource people), the new student reviews his study goals and refines the preliminary *program overview*, submitted at the time of application. The program overview is the plan for a student's entire participation in Lindenwood 4. As a contract between the student and The Lindenwood Colleges, it says generally what the student has agreed to do each trimester and states his overall objectives.

Then, in consultation with his committee, the student designs and submits for approval a detailed *trimester study plan* (as discussed on page 11).

Students meet an average of two hours a week throughout the trimester with their Faculty Sponsor, other students, and perhaps the internship supervisors. Typically, such a meeting would involve two or three students presenting work-in-progress for commentary and critique.

Once a month, the entire regional group meets for an all-day colloquium in a particular field of inquiry. Presentations are given by students, faculty, and resource people. In discussions and workshops, there is exchange of information and points of view, providing a lively interaction among the participants and the community at large.

To supplement the regular meetings, a student may arrange additional meetings of his committee. Throughout the year, faculty, students and resource people offer seminars and

6

workshops in which they share their research and experience with the learning community.

At least once a year all participants and graduates of each regional program come together for a week-long conference of seminars, lectures, workshops and special events. Such yearly gatherings provide a unique opportunity for prolonged interaction among students, faculty and community resource people.

At the end of the trimester there is a weekend workshop at which the student meets again with his study committee to evaluate the trimester's work and to begin discussion of the study plan for the next trimester.

After the three-week break, a new trimester begins, and the cycle is repeated.

THE GRADUATE PROGRAM
Students in the M.A. program meet a minimum of one hour weekly with their Faculty Sponsors about their studies. In addition, they meet frequently with their internship supervisors, community people, and study committees to critique and enrich their work. Graduate students have the option of serving on undergraduate committees and/or tutoring individual undergraduates. Furthermore, they participate in all functions of the program, particularly the monthly colloquia (discussed above) in which they give presentations and lead discussions.

Governance

Shared responsibility is implicit in the notion of a learning community. Education at Lindenwood 4 means being independent but still participating in the mutual concerns of the whole group. The more participation by all concerned, the more learning takes place. Procedures for admission, evaluation, topics and organization of colloquia, community service and involvement are matters always open to community discussion and assessment. While the Faculty Administrator has responsibility to Lindenwood 4 and The Lindenwood Colleges for maintaining quality within established guidelines, all faculty and students work together to create the unique character of each regional program.

7

Figure 3.31b
To introduce some relief to an otherwise type-only layout, the pages include generalized illustrations to symbolize the heading.

Figure 3.32a
Symbols convey information through a form of visual abbreviation. These four examples are well known. They are an alternative to words under the appropriate circumstances.

Figure 3.32b
Because of their simplicity, symbols can be part of other concepts in advertising, as shown in the drunk-driving ad. The "do not" traffic symbol used in this ad is now often adapted to other symbols. *Design: Drohlich Associates. Concept: Jerry G. Clinton.*

Figure 3.32c
The arrow is very likely the most commonly applied symbol: It is universal and nothing else works as effectively for directional emphasis. © *Newspaper Advertising Bureau, 1984.*

parts whether the design is a presentation of a product or an image conveying an attitude or message.

The graphic requirements of a publication may not need many images. The design is frequently intended simply to clarify and organize, with a concern for continued reader interest. Headings and subheadings often include decorative images in this case. Because mere systematic arrangements without some graphic relief might be boring and result in lack of attention and comprehension, typographic details should not be considered second to the illustrations nor as separate or decorative afterthoughts.

Symbols

When an image is simplified to signify, rather than describe, we call it a graphic symbol. Symbols may represent complex concepts such as the environmental conflicts of the earth or sports events or decoratively interpreted objects. Symbols can also be used as typographic matter: The arrow, star, the pointing hand, and the heart are examples. In a letterhead or other corporate identification, the symbol may be crucial because

Figure 3.33a
The eagle is probably the most extensively used American symbol even though many other nations and societies have used it.

it represents the attitudes and concerns of the people and products that comprise the company.

Of course, a symbol is not always a typographic device. Uncle Sam, the bald eagle, and Ronald McDonald, are also symbols. A symbol really is a type of *sign,* and all signs represent some form of information. The octagonal shape and red color of a stop sign signifies a traffic rule as an abstract design. STOP is a sign (alphabet) that combines and represents a word and sound that mean halt, don't go on. A white dove usually means peace; the dove sign is truly a symbolic design at work, as this particular bird represents an idea.

The new international travel communication signs are excellent examples of how important symbols can become to society. Today, we depend on many complex systems of signs: scientific symbols, sports rules, flags, and so on. Designers produce many signs or marks called *trademarks* or *logos* for the business and industrial community. Correctly a logo is a design using the lettering of a name or title in a unique style and arrangement.

Currently, the graphics industry rarely refers to each form of a sign properly; most are called either symbols or logos. Figure 3.35 illustrates some of the different types. Specialized references on the subject are valuable and interesting to study (see the Bibliography).

A good sign or symbol or logo should be simple to identify under adverse conditions of size reproduction and lighting. It should not be difficult to print, photograph, or reproduce on office copiers. It should be complete and legible in black and white. Above all, it must be memorable or identifiable within the context of its distribution.

There are thousands of symbols (logos, trademarks); it is difficult to create a unique one. Very likely a true logo (a mark using a name) works well for a small user who applies it in a limited area or market. But when a large firm can display a mark/symbol throughout thousands of products and advertising, an abstract symbol can be very successful. Trademarks have now become so well accepted that they are used in a decorative sense on shoes, t-shirts, hats, and even as patterns for fabric. (See Figure 3.26g.)

Figure 3.33c
Like Uncle Sam, the McDonald clown humanizes the corporate organization for favorable personal acceptance. *Courtesy McDonald Corporation.*

Figure 3.33b
Uncle Sam is used mostly in cartoons and the symbol has probably lost some of the impact it had, as in the World War I cartoon shown here.

69

Figure 3.33d
Over time, symbols can lose their meaning, go out of favor, and return; such is the case of the Mobil horse, which has now returned to favor. Although "flying horsepower" has less contemporary value, the uniqueness of the red horse does create a valuable identity. *Reprinted with permission of Mobil Oil Corporation: The Flying Horse symbol is a registered trademark of Mobil Oil Corporation.*

Figure 3.33e
The symbol of the dove of peace dates back to the Old Testament as the messenger received by Noah declaring the end of the flood.

Figure 3.33f
The recent peace symbol, originated as an anti-nuclear symbol in England, has now become accepted worldwide.

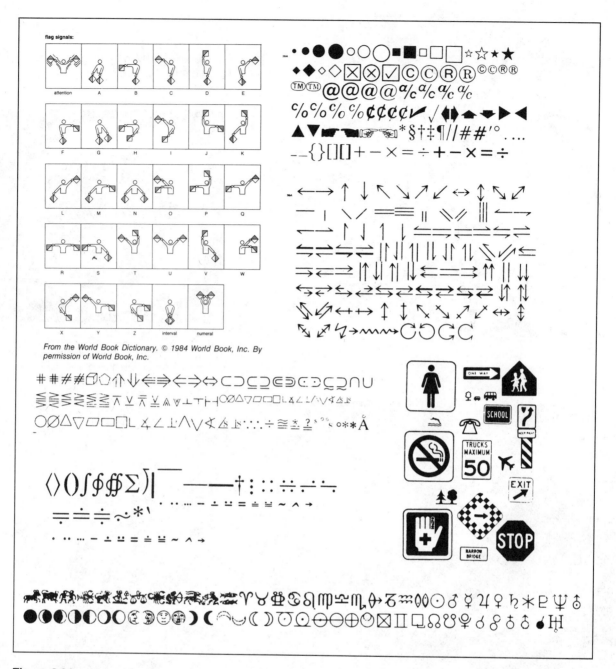

From the World Book Dictionary. © 1984 World Book, Inc. By permission of World Book, Inc.

Figure 3.34
The variety and use of symbols is surprisingly wide. Symbols make specialized information universal among all languages.

Figure 3.35a
A mark using connected type, a ligature. *Design: Stan Gellman Graphic Design, Inc.*

Figure 3.35b
An abstract mark. *Design: Frank James Productions.*

Figure 3.35d
An animated logo. The letters configurate into the name of a collector of tropical fish.

Figure 3.35c
A compound symbol. The heart and the animals together show love and care for them. *Designer/Art Director: Al Klenk, Faller, Klenk & Quinlan, Inc., Buffalo, N.Y.*

Figure 3.35e
A true logo type using the firm's name in a unique manner.

Figure 3.36
Even the most obvious symbols can never be exhausted. The stars here show that the important consideration is the design interpretation, not the specific form of the design. We will probably never see the last rainbow, hand shake, sun, or heart, either.

Design: Anspach Grossman Portugal Inc. Kenneth Love Design Director. Don Kline Designer.

Designer: Roger Cook/Don Shanosky Cook and Shanosky Associates, Inc., Princeton, N.J.

Design: John Waters Associates.

Designer: C.M. Seminario, The Berni Corporation.

73

Figure 3.36 (continued)

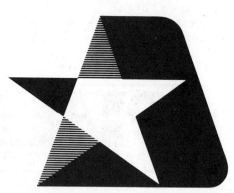

55 K·USA
THE BEST COUNTRY

Design: DeOlivera Creative, Inc.

REVOLUTION
EVOLUTION
1776-1983

Courtesy American Society of Interior Designers.

Design: Walter Landor Associates.

Malcolm Grear Designers, Inc.

MGDA Newsletter

Fall 1980
Minnesota Graphic Designers Association
P.O. Box 24272, Minneapolis 55424

Report on the Proposed National Graphic Design Organization

By Tim Larsen

The following report is the result of a letter from Robert Vogele, one of the Lutsen Conference speakers. In that letter of September 15, 1980 he complimented the MGDA as a "group sincerely interested and dedicated to graphic design as a professional activity."

Mr. Vogele, who is presently president of the S.T.A., a Chicago-based graphic design organization, went on to state "please make a priority out of the question of how we might form a larger alliance of graphic design associations."

Mr. Vogele and I have discussed this further in letters. The MGDA Board of Directors has discussed it at the October 7th meeting, and I was involved in discussions at the S.T.A. Fall Conference at the invitation of Robert Vogele. The following report is a summary of those discussions.

The STA and MGDA along with other organizations and individuals have begun a dialogue about the creation of a National Graphic Design Organization. The national organization would not affect the MGDA structure but would be a national organization of individual members who would have the option to belong to one or both of the organizations.

The MGDA Board of Directors has endorsed the national organization concept, *if* the national organization is for professional graphic designers with some sort of screening mechanism. The screening is necessary because it is not fair to graphic designers making their livelihood from graphic design to be responsible for or associated with amateur designers, vendors, or conflicting professions.

The MGDA Board also believes the name *Graphic Design* should be in the title of the national organization. There is a body of thinking that believes *Visual Communication Designer* is a better term for our profession, or at least the term *Designer* because of its flexibility. The MGDA Board believes the re-education of the public after 20 years of building an understanding of graphic design may be counterproductive. continued on Page 4

Minnesota Graphic Designers Association. Designer: Robert Fleming.

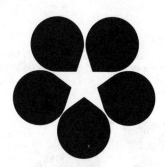

Design: Vanderbyl Design.

Design: Vanderbyl Design.

Design: Vanderbyl Design.

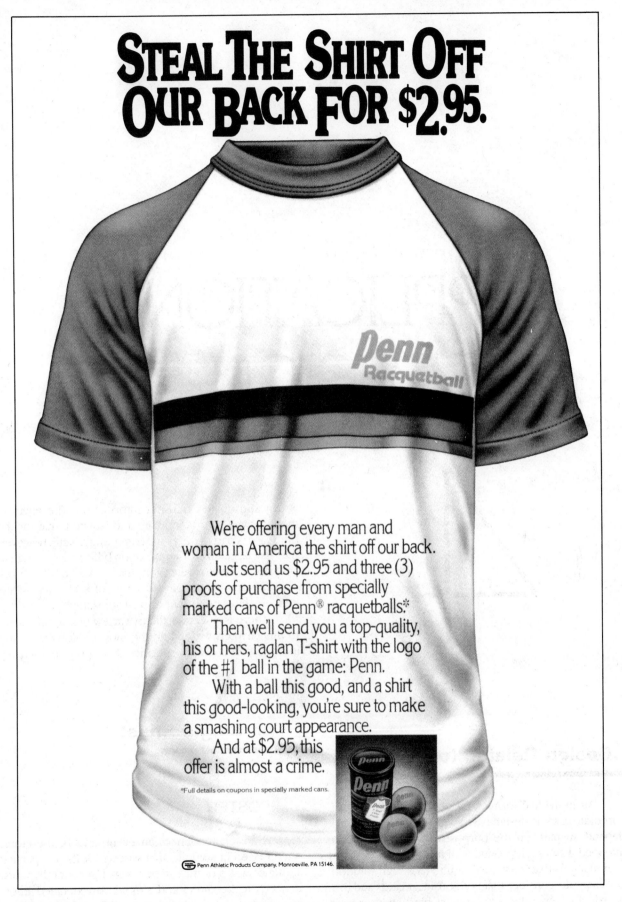

Figure 3.37
No one wears and displays a manufacturer's mark unless he or she feels favorably about the manufacturer. In many cases wearing a particular logo adds social status and publicly declares the purchases one values. *Art Director: Joe Kravek, Ketchum Advertising, Pittsburgh.*

APPLICATION OF DESIGN

4

attract and quickly transmit information. The environment for the card is intimate and isolated; that for the billboard is part of the visual community. Note, however, that the large size of an outdoor billboard is no guarantee of impact or retention; many excellent business-card designs could stand the test of scale. The same, incidentally, can be said of postage stamps.

There is an extraordinary variety of graphic forms. In this chapter, we outline the most obvious ones and indicate some design specifics that apply to each example.

The Single Sheet

Design Related to Purpose

All individual forms, products, or media that incorporate graphic design have special requirements that depend, in part, on the purposes for which they are intended. Each such product will itself have advantages or limitations that must be built into its design solution. For example, consider that both business cards and billboards are generally one-surface objects with simple configurations. However, a business card is a personal form that is convenient to handle and to hand out. A billboard is a mass public promotion meant to widely

POSTER

A poster announces an event, and is, therefore, often placed in a public area past which its prospective audience walks or travels, or at which it generally waits. It needs to be direct and simple. Any detailed information should be as brief as possible and very legible. Highly refined posters comprise a respected art form. (See color plates 13, 14, 15, and 17.) If designed properly posters can gain emphasis by being grouped in patterns.

Design: Frank Roth.

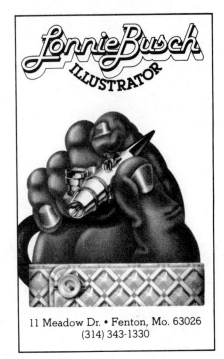

Designer/Illustrator: Lonnie Busch.

Figure 4.1
In these business cards, which center around large visual images, the copy is simple and clear.

OUTDOOR BOARDS (BILLBOARDS)

A billboard, the largest graphic form, is really a poster. Because of their outdoor placement, billboards are subject to extreme variables of lighting as well as environmental distractions. In order to effectively advertise and publicize to a mobile public, then simplicity of design is paramount. The copy must be brief, large, and legible. Standard billboards are based on a proportion of the length being $2\frac{1}{4}$ times the height. Often the design and content of a billboard are related to a broader publicity campaign which includes magazine, newspaper, and TV advertising.

STATIONERY

For the most part letterheads, envelopes, and business cards are designed for one-side use, and usually for occupational or corporate purposes. Stationery should be personal and unique; it should reflect the character of the company, yet not be distracting to the letters to be typed on it. In addition to stationery, various forms, certificates, memos, press releases, and so on, are included within a corporate identity system. Sensitive typography and good use of space are also essential in their design. Much stationery is constrained in concept, but some organizations do sponsor unique activities that can be characterized through unusual die cutting, embossing, colors, and format.

Figure 4.2
In the city it is difficult not to find a billboard in view where public traffic is heavy. Billboards compete in a complexity of other graphic information.

BOOK JACKETS AND RECORD-ALBUM COVERS

Although book jackets and record-album covers are three-dimensional products, they tend to have much in common with posters; indeed, well-done jacket and cover designs can have the same impact as posters, in

77

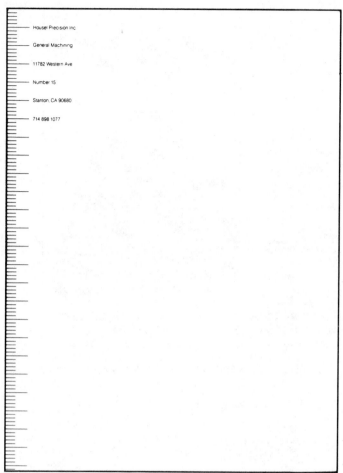

Housel Precision Inc

General Machining

11782 Western Ave

Number 15

Stanton, CA 90680

714 898 1077

Designer: Harold Burch. **(a)**

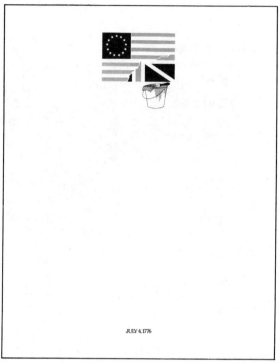

JULY 4, 1776

Courtesy Hammermill Paper Company. **(b)**

The Southside Plaza Stationery Shop

467 Hill Avenue, Milgrove, Ohio 27413

Telephone (683) 745-3824

Hammermill Bond, Gray, Substance 20 Tippletsheerines

Courtesy Hammermill Paper Company. **(c)**

Figure 4.3
Frequently, the solution to a letterhead design lies within the client's occupation or industry. Sometimes, the design does not actually show its complete effect until a typed letter is added to the pages. (a) The Housel letterhead design brilliantly symbolizes the precise activity of the company with minimal, clean typography. (b) In a past series of promotions, the Hammermill Paper Company displayed some delightful spoofs. One example, for the Fourth of July, is shown here. (c) The stationery shop letterhead is an excellent example of a design relating directly to the business of the client. (d) The clean and legible business form for the Yale Summer Program shows that even collateral material can be well designed.

Legal name   last   first   middle   Jr , etc   Current phone no.

Permanent   Zip
home address

Current   Zip
mailing address

Date and place   Social Security no.
of birth

Country of   Passport no.
citizenship

Name of parent,
guardian or spouse

Address

Art schools and colleges attended   Dates of   Field of major   Degree and date
most recent first   attendance   received or expected

Business and professional experience
and present employment

Name and address of references who will be submitting written statements in support of your application

1

2

Name, address and relationship of one individual
who can supply your address at any time in the future

Signature   Date

Designer: Philip Burton.   **(d)**

spite of their smaller size. Albums and books are marketed with strong emphasis on their covers because they need to call attention to their contents or reflect them in some compelling way to induce the observers to examine the products further. Album covers especially typify current design creativity.

FOLDERS

We identify a folder initially in the same manner as we do a book jacket or a small poster. If we find the cover interesting enough, we unfold and examine it until, finally, we are looking at a single sheet. A folder is, thus, complex to create because the design must be considered a sequence; yet after unfolding, all sections must also be related to the one surface, front and back. Deciding on the sequence of the contents from section to section is of particular concern to the designer. Also, guaranteeing the correct unfolding sequence is difficult. The information, therefore, should be understandable during various unfoldings, whether the folder is opened casually or carefully. Folding, itself, can also be a useful design element. Many direct mail promotions and greeting cards inventively incorporate the process of folding into their messages through "pop-up" techniques.

Figure 4.4
Book and record album covers reflect the entire range of design styles: from Surrealism, as in the *Jazz Piano Quartet* cover (a), collage and pattern, as in the *Rubber Stamp Album* (b), pure typography, as in the *Improvising and Arranging* design (c), to Dadaist technique, in *Dexter Gordon* (d).

(a)   **(b)**

Cover: Courtesy of RCA Records. Illustrator: Barbara Bergman. Art Director: Joseph Stelmach.

Louise Fili and Mark Huie. Workman Publishing, New York. Reprinted with permission of the publisher.

Figure 4.4   (continued)

(c)

Courtesy Prentice-Hall, Inc.

(d)

Design: Paula Scher.

Bound or Multiple Pages

BOOKLETS

A booklet is constructed of individual sheets permanently bound (stapled, stitched, glued) together. Booklets, like magazines and books, are essentially handled left to right, or scanned randomly when browsing, so design variety and impact are important. Designers of booklets, such as catalogs and annual reports, as well as magazines and books, which are discussed later, use the grid plan to organize the contents in a systematic, logical manner. They also plan, however, for interesting changes and emphases within the layouts to "pull" the reader to the important areas and maintain attention.

Annual reports are probably among the best examples of booklet design. In some cases, the contents consist of technical information about industries, processes, or services, but in the hands of sensitive designers, photographers, and illustrators, such straightforward material can become visually attractive. Even product catalogs or service manuals containing highly technical or schematic data and charts can be interesting, informative, and very legible to follow, through careful use of typography and layout. Often the subject of the piece can itself yield the best design material.

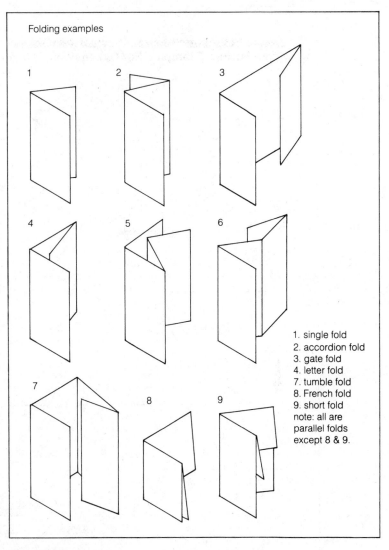

Folding examples

1. single fold
2. accordion fold
3. gate fold
4. letter fold
7. tumble fold
8. French fold
9. short fold
note: all are parallel folds except 8 & 9.

Figure 4.5a
Folding examples.

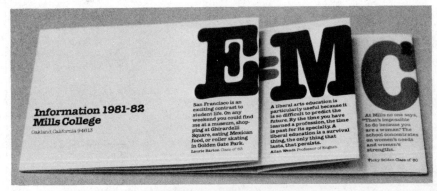

Information 1981-82
Mills College
Oakland, California 94613

Figure 4.5b
This Mills College folder is an outstanding example of using the fold itself as part of the design concept. *Designers: Robin and Heidi Rickabaugh.*

Some Format Examples For Dimensional Inserts (Pop-Ups)

A

B

C

D

E

F

G

H

I

J

K

L

U.S. PATENTS
3 995 388   4 313 270
4 146 983   4 337 589
4 212 231   4 349 973
FOREIGN PATENTS

PAPERMASTERS
545 Thornwood Lane, P.O. Box 8469, Northfield, IL 60093   (312) 441-8420

Figure 4.5c
"Pop-up" designs, which require skillful and creative engineering to work properly,
are becoming popular. Some firms specialize in this work; one such is
Papermasters, whose work is illustrated here.

Figure 4·6
Above all, an annual report must express the activities and character of a company, through legible, interesting design. The Olin-American, Inc. (a) and Southwestern Bell (b) examples rely on precise typography and a well-balanced use of white space.

(a)

Designed by Corporate Annual Reports, Inc.

Figure 4.6 (continued)

(a)

The 1978 Year Compared with 1977

Net income in 1978 was $62.8-million, a decrease of 19.6% from 1977. Improved operating income from the Brass and Specialty Services Groups and Olin-American was more than offset by lower operating profit from the Chemicals, Ecusta Paper and Film, and Winchester Groups. The results for 1978 were adversely impacted by the effects of the three-month strike at the company's plants in East Alton, Ill., operational problems at certain plants and severe winter weather conditions.

Net sales increased by $87.6-million (or 6%) to $1.56-billion. Approximately 57% (or $50-million) of the increase resulted from higher prices, and the remainder from improved volume and mix. All Groups, except for Brass, experienced higher net sales in 1978 when compared with 1977. Product lines which showed the greatest sales improvement were designed and consumer chemicals, construction fastening systems of the Specialty Services Group, and Winchester's international and defense-related businesses. Interest and other income in 1978 remained unchanged from the 1977 level, with both years including nonrecurring gains of $2.3-million and $4.3-million, respectively. The 1978 gain resulted from the sale of lignite deposit leases, while the 1977 gain arose from a Government eminent domain proceeding.

Cost of sales and other operating charges amounted to $1.27-billion, up $97-million from 1977. The increase in costs reflected the higher volume of sales in 1978, as well as continuing escalation in raw materials and energy costs, and increases in wage and salary rates. Also contributing to the increased costs were higher depreciation, principally related to the company's new chlorine/caustic facility at McIntosh, Ala., and the costs associated with the strike at East Alton in the first quarter of 1978.

Selling, general, administrative and research costs increased by approximately $15.4-million (or 8%) when compared with 1977, caused principally by higher selling expenses and administrative costs. Increased interest costs in 1978 reflect higher borrowings and interest rates.

The 1978 reduction in income taxes of approximately $17-million was the result of lower pretax income. Investment tax credits of $14.7-million in 1978 were about the same as in 1977.

Olin-American had pretax earnings of $15.3-million in 1978, up 12½% from 1977, reflecting the continued strong demand for housing throughout the year.

Capital Spending ($ millions)

Long-Term Debt/Total Capital (per cent)

Consolidated Sales and Income Per Share by Quarter

Quarter	Net Sales (in millions) 1979	1978	Net Income Per Share 1979	1978
First	$ 437.2	$ 346.4	$ .73	$ .16
Second	471.8	416.1	1.14	1.08
Third	428.1	389.1	.46	.76
Fourth	441.0	408.5	.64	.62
Year	$1,778.1	$1,560.1	$2.97	$2.62

Industry Segments (in millions)

	1979	1978	1977	1976	1975
Net Sales(1)					
Brass—Copper alloys	$ 314.3	$ 242.1	$ 242.4	$ 229.4	$ 156.7
Chemicals	823.1	714.6	682.2	633.8	604.7
Ecusta—Specialized papers & cellophane	231.1	195.3	178.5	172.7	144.5
Winchester—Sporting arms & ammunition	282.4	299.7	283.2	259.1	283.0
Other	127.2	108.4	86.2	81.5	71.7
Total	$1,778.1	$1,560.1	$1,472.5	$1,376.5	$1,260.6
Operating Income					
Operating Profit (Loss)(2)					
Brass—Copper alloys	$ 42.8	$ 32.8	$ 30.8	$ 24.3	$ 13.3
Chemicals	36.9	35.6	60.1	94.9	101.8
Ecusta—Specialized papers & cellophane	28.2	15.6	18.8	11.7	1.6
Winchester—Sporting arms & ammunition	12.4	19.9	25.0	20.7	20.4
Other	8.6	6.7	2.3	1.1	(3.4)
Total Operating Profit	128.9	110.6	137.0	152.7	133.7
Pretax Income (Loss) of Olin-American, Inc.	17.7	15.3	13.6	4.7	(4.5)
Total	$ 146.6	$ 125.9	$ 150.6	$ 157.4	$ 129.2
Assets					
Brass—Copper alloys	$ 153.1	$ 147.0	$ 132.4	$ 123.5	$ 100.2
Chemicals	776.8	738.3	653.8	481.3	414.3
Ecusta—Specialized papers & cellophane	103.9	105.2	110.3	98.1	90.4
Winchester—Sporting arms & ammunition	230.2	221.6	221.3	209.6	201.7
Other	113.5	102.1	87.6	84.9	75.1
Total	$1,377.5	$1,314.2	$1,205.4	$ 997.4	$ 881.7
Capital Expenditures					
Brass—Copper alloys	$ 11.4	$ 13.0	$ 20.1	$ 21.2	$ 6.8
Chemicals	130.2	126.5	166.9	115.8	62.9
Ecusta—Specialized papers & cellophane	4.7	4.9	4.8	10.3	10.2
Winchester—Sporting arms & ammunition	9.4	11.3	10.4	11.2	10.3
Other	4.4	6.7	3.0	6.6	8.0
Depreciation					
Brass—Copper alloys	$ 9.2	$ 7.9	$ 7.9	$ 7.9	$ 8.0
Chemicals	67.7	54.5	40.3	35.1	32.8
Ecusta—Specialized papers & cellophane	5.8	5.9	5.6	8.2	7.5
Winchester—Sporting arms & ammunition	7.0	8.7	6.3	5.7	7.5
Other	3.8	3.1	2.6	2.6	2.0

(1) Intersegment sales excluded from Net Sales, above, are as follows:

	1979	1978	1977	1976	1975
Brass	$22.2	$17.7	$17.9	$21.3	$19.7
Chemicals	9.8	9.3	9.7	9.9	8.7
Winchester	1.7	1.4	.6	1.3	.8
Other	17.0	13.3	13.8	13.1	12.7
	$50.7	$41.7	$42.0	$45.6	$41.9

(2) The operating profit of each industry segment represents income (excluding equity in income of affiliates) less cost of sales and other operating expenses. Operating profit excludes income taxes, interest expense and general corporate expenses.

(3) See Notes to Financial Statements for information relative to non-U.S. operations for 1979 and 1978.

(4) Segment information has been restated to reflect the transfer of a Chemicals Group operation to "Other." The latter's operating profit for 1979 includes a nonrecurring gain of $1.9-million from the sale of a facility.

(b)

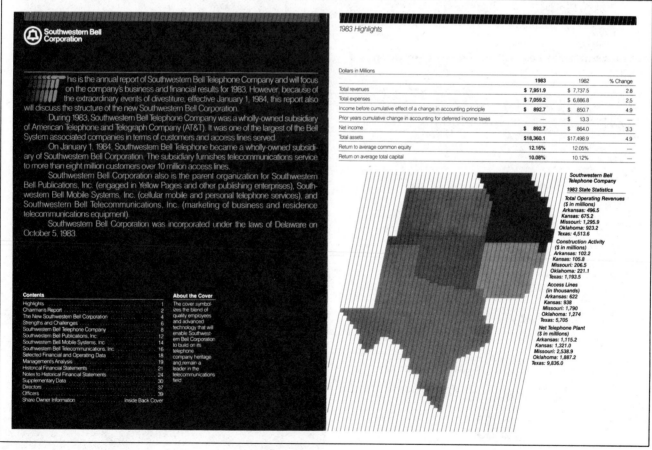

Southwestern Bell Corporation

1983 Highlights

This is the annual report of Southwestern Bell Telephone Company and will focus on the company's business and financial results for 1983. However, because of the extraordinary events of divestiture, effective January 1, 1984, this report also will discuss the structure of the new Southwestern Bell Corporation.

During 1983, Southwestern Bell Telephone Company was a wholly-owned subsidiary of American Telephone and Telegraph Company (AT&T). It was one of the largest of the Bell System associated companies in terms of customers and access lines served.

On January 1, 1984, Southwestern Bell Telephone became a wholly-owned subsidiary of Southwestern Bell Corporation. The subsidiary furnishes telecommunications service to more than eight million customers over 10 million access lines.

Southwestern Bell Corporation also is the parent organization for Southwestern Bell Publications, Inc. (engaged in Yellow Pages and other publishing enterprises), Southwestern Bell Mobile Systems, Inc. (cellular mobile and personal telephone services), and Southwestern Bell Telecommunications, Inc. (marketing of business and residence telecommunications equipment).

Southwestern Bell Corporation was incorporated under the laws of Delaware on October 5, 1983.

Dollars in Millions

	1983	1982	% Change
Total revenues	$ 7,951.9	$ 7,737.5	2.8
Total expenses	$ 7,059.2	$ 6,886.8	2.5
Income before cumulative effect of a change in accounting principle	$ 892.7	$ 850.7	4.9
Prior years cumulative change in accounting for deferred income taxes	—	$ 13.3	—
Net income	$ 892.7	$ 864.0	3.3
Total assets	$18,360.1	$17,498.9	4.9
Return to average common equity	12.16%	12.05%	—
Return on average total capital	10.08%	10.12%	—

Southwestern Bell Telephone Company

1983 State Statistics

Total Operating Revenues ($ in millions)
Arkansas: 496.5
Kansas: 675.2
Missouri: 1,295.9
Oklahoma: 923.2
Texas: 4,513.6

Construction Activity ($ in millions)
Arkansas: 102.2
Kansas: 105.8
Missouri: 206.5
Oklahoma: 221.1
Texas: 1,193.5

Access Lines (in thousands)
Arkansas: 622
Kansas: 938
Missouri: 1,790
Oklahoma: 1,274
Texas: 5,705

Net Telephone Plant ($ in millions)
Arkansas: 1,115.2
Kansas: 1,321.0
Missouri: 2,538.9
Oklahoma: 1,887.2
Texas: 9,836.0

About the Cover

The cover symbolizes the blend of quality employees and advanced technology that will enable Southwestern Bell Corporation to build on its telephone company heritage and remain a leader in the telecommunications field.

Figure 4.6 (continued)

No other period in our 101-year history can compare to 1983. Few if any businesses have ever been confronted with the formidable task we faced. As a result of the court-ordered breakup of the Bell System, we had to reorganize our entire business — a major undertaking for a corporation so large.

Yet that massive job was only part of our challenge. There were eight million telephone customers to be served — one at a time. One industry observer likened it to taking apart a jumbo jet in midair while making sure it keeps flying.

I am proud to report we succeeded on both counts, even if the ride was bumpy at times. That is a tribute to the rare dedication and entrepreneurial spirit of our employees.

Today, divestiture's clouds no longer hang over the company. All steps were completed for the official transfer of assets to AT&T on January 1, 1984. A new course has been mapped for the Corporation and the horizon holds more opportunities than we can count.

I have elected for that reason not to dwell on the past. Even our 1983 financial results speak for a company that no longer exists as it once did. But those numbers document our commitment to continued earnings improvement.

Financial Results

Total operating revenues for Southwestern Bell Telephone Company climbed 2.5 percent over last year. Net income rose 3.3 percent — a modest gain limited by one-time expenses incurred in the fourth quarter.

Total operating expenses were up only 1.4 percent during 1983. Force control was a major factor in keeping the lid on costs.

Improvements also were made in other areas. For example, our return on equity reached 12.16 percent. In addition, we internally generated 98.8 percent of our capital requirements compared to about 60 percent in 1982.

Despite these gains, additional improvements are needed. Our return on equity level remains far below what investors require from a corporation involved in a highly competitive, rapidly evolving industry.

More detailed information about our 1983 financial performance can be found elsewhere in this report.

Seeds for Success

Our success in 1984 and beyond rests not on past performance. This is a "new" Southwestern Bell Corporation with four growing subsidiaries. That means we must invest today to harvest tomorrow's success.

Our first job is to improve the profitability of our primary business — the telephone company. No one realizes its importance more than we do. That business represents the largest revenue stream for the Corporation. It made us the success we are today. It will be the foundation we build upon for the future.

That subsidiary's future looks particularly bright because it serves the dynamic, growing Southwest region. This region continues to outpace the national average in population growth, construction activity, residential housing starts and employment. It is also home base for 47 companies on the *Fortune 500* list.

Serving a high-growth region requires modern facilities. Heavy capital spending in recent years has enabled us to make our plant the most sophisticated anywhere.

Our local network includes some of the most advanced electronic, digital and fiber-optic technology. We are ready to handle complex data systems and innovations still on the drawing boards.

The Corporation's three other subsidiaries have been launched with great expectations, too. All are financially sound, well-managed with clearly defined marketing plans. These companies will provide innovative, quality products and services for the tele-communications marketplace.

The Future

Now let me share with you our vision for tomorrow. It is a future marked by a dramatic shift in this country from an industrial to an information society. Nothing

like it has been seen since the change from an agricultural to an industrial society in the 19th century.

In this new era, the flow of information will dominate society, the economy and business. It will reshape the way we work and live. Many of these changes touch us today, but the full impact of the Information Age has yet to explode on the scene.

Already, vast opportunities are springing up literally overnight. To capitalize, we are positioning ourselves as a *total* communications company to meet these burgeoning information needs as well as others not yet imagined.

Four tenets will drive our Corporation's entry into the new frontiers created by the Information Age. They are:

☐ To aggressively seek removal of any external barriers keeping us from competing on equal footing in markets of our choosing;

☐ To expand into high-growth markets — both inside and outside our five-state region — to achieve long-term financial objectives;

☐ To pursue a policy of diversification that, over time, enables us to reduce financial risk; and,

☐ To insure all subsidiaries build upon our traditional strengths — quality and service — in serving their customers and markets.

These sound principles will guide us as we organize under one umbrella a family of companies designed to fulfill the promise of the Information Age.

In this exciting new environment, the company will not be wedded to the old ways of doing business. At every level of management, we are developing an atmosphere that fosters creativity, entrepreneurship and sensible experimentation. Above all, we are building a bias for both independent and concerted action.

This year we begin writing the history for a new corporation with a successful record spanning more than a century. Not many companies ever get this kind of an opportunity. We intend to do all we can to make the most of it.

Zane E. Barnes

Zane E. Barnes
Chairman of the Board
and President

As Southwestern Bell Telephone Company closed out one era and opened the door to another, it did so on a successful note.

Total operating revenues in 1983 were $7.9 billion, a 2.5 percent increase over the previous year. This was achieved despite an almost flat volume of long-distance calls and the loss of terminal equipment revenue due to a federal ruling preventing the company from selling equipment beyond its year-end 1982 inventory.

Net income in 1983 was $892.7 million, an increase of 3.3 percent over 1982. This gain was limited by the judgment in an antitrust suit by Litton Industries, Inc., against the Bell System. The liability was shared by AT&T and each of the former Bell System operating companies. Southwestern Bell's share of the settlement, including interest, was $34.4 million before taxes, which reduced the company's net income by $18.2 million.

Return to equity was 12.16 percent, up from 12.05 percent the previous year.

Total operating expenses were slightly over $5.3 billion, up only 1.4 percent from 1982. This small increase was due, in part, to force control during 1983. Total employees declined by nearly 8,000 people, including 2,700 who transferred to AT&T. On January 1, 1984, another 18,000 employees were shifted to AT&T.

Districts 6 and 12 of the Communications Workers of America represent virtually all Southwestern Bell Telephone Company non-management employees. The union and the company negotiated a new three-year contract in August, 1983.

During 1983, Southwestern Bell Telephone was granted net rate awards of

$693 million, representing 62 percent of the amount requested.

Revenue Factors

The telephone company increased its revenues through a combination of access-line growth, strategic use of technology, increased productivity and regulatory relief. Those same factors will continue to be important to the company in its environment as a regulated subsidiary of Southwestern Bell Corporation.

Local Service

Southwestern Bell Telephone currently serves eight million customers in 1,190 cities and towns in its 542,000-square-mile region.

Access lines in the territory increased by 205,000 lines in 1983. The company

currently provides telecommunications links to 80 percent of the homes and businesses in its five-state territory.

Local service revenue per access line showed a moderate increase in 1983. At the same time, the number of employees needed to provide service decreased.

Southwestern Bell Telephone Company's service remains top quality based on both internal and external indicators. At the end of 1983, the company had met or exceeded internal service standards for 28 consecutive months.

The Network

The telephone company's state-of-the-art network puts it in a unique position to capitalize on the opportunities of the Information Age. The network links homes and businesses throughout the service region. It includes some of the most advanced electronic, digital and fiber-optic technology.

For instance, electronic switching systems serve 70 percent of all customers in our territory, significantly higher than the 55 percent average for the former Bell System. In metropolitan areas where the need for such innovative systems is greatest, 90 percent of the telephone company's access lines are served by electronic switching. Electronic switching is the best, fastest and least expensive method in use today for handling telecommunications traffic.

Another use of technology has been in the area of local digital switching. A total of nine major local digital switching projects were completed in 1983. Increased utilization of digital switching will allow the network to handle the ever-increasing amounts of data being transmitted by customers.

Repair technicians work throughout the night to restore service. This "spirit of service" remains a trademark of the telephone company.

Zane E. Barnes, far left, serves as the primary spokesman for the organization on telecommunications issues in his dual role as Corporation chairman and president of Southwestern Bell Telephone Company.

Figure 4·6 (continued)

Southwestern Bell Telephone Company
Continued

Companywide, the high-volume circuits — called trunks — between switching offices were 70 percent digital by the end of 1983. Trunks in metropolitan areas approached 100 percent digital. Southwestern Bell Telephone continues to be a leader in the deployment of intercity digital microwave technology.

Upgrading the network with optical fiber transmission systems continued in 1983, with several lightwave projects either completed or under construction. A total of 100 additional lightwave projects are in the planning stage. Optical fiber circuitry will bring revolutionary increases in call carrying capacity to the network, while reducing costs for handling this additional traffic.

Network Opportunities

Although the total network constantly is being upgraded, Southwestern Bell Telephone's philosophy of technological deployment has been to implement the most sophisticated equipment on a strategic basis. Technologically superior equipment is deployed in locations where the need for it is greatest and where profit potential is highest.

The overall excellence of the network also has spawned other opportunities in the areas of usage, telemarketing and long-distance calling.

Long-distance traffic represents just one of the opportunities for revenue growth from the local network. Among the others, for example, the company continues to explore marketing opportunities such as Custom Calling Services, WATS/800 Service, public telephones and central-office-based customer switching systems such as Centrex.

Electronic switching systems (ESS) are state-of-the-art for distributing telecommunications traffic, as well as a key to handling data and image transmission in the future.

Telephone company technicians, far right, splice lightguide cable. Fiber-optic transmission systems are an example of technology used by the company to upgrade its local network.

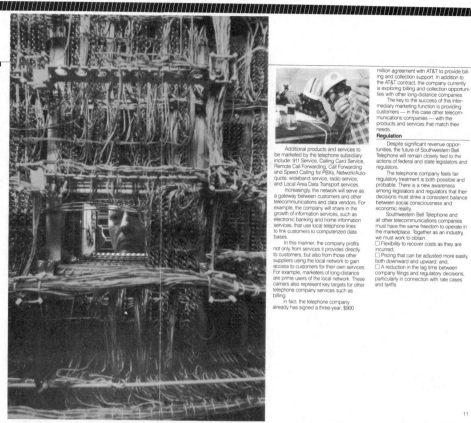

Additional products and services to be marketed by the telephone subsidiary include: 911 Service, Calling Card Service, Remote Call Forwarding, Call Forwarding and Speed Calling for PBXs, Network/Autoquote, wideband service, radio service, and Local Area Data Transport service.

Increasingly, the network will serve as a gateway between customers and other telecommunications and data vendors. For example, the company will share in the growth of information services, such as electronic banking and home information services, that use local telephone lines to link customers to computerized data bases.

In this manner, the company profits not only from services it provides directly to customers, but also from those other suppliers using the local network to gain access to customers for their own services. For example, marketers of long-distance are prime users of the local network. These carriers also represent key targets for other telephone company services such as billing.

In fact, the telephone company already has signed a three-year, $900

million agreement with AT&T to provide billing and collection support. In addition to the AT&T contract, the company currently is exploring billing and collection opportunities with other long-distance companies.

The key to the success of this intermediary marketing function is providing customers — in this case telecommunications companies — with the products and services that match their needs.

Regulation

Despite significant revenue opportunities, the future of Southwestern Bell Telephone will remain closely tied to the actions of federal and state legislators and regulators.

The telephone company feels fair regulatory treatment is both possible and probable. There is a new awareness among legislators and regulators that their decisions must strike a consistent balance between social consciousness and economic reality.

Southwestern Bell Telephone and all other telecommunications companies must have the same freedom to operate in the marketplace. Together as an industry, we must work to obtain:
☐ Flexibility to recover costs as they are incurred;
☐ Pricing that can be adjusted more easily, both downward and upward; and,
☐ A reduction in the lag time between company filings and regulatory decisions, particularly in connection with rate cases and tariffs.

10

11

(b)

NEWSPAPERS AND TABLOIDS

The newspaper format has an inherent immediacy and an informal honesty that come from its basic function. It is presently particularly popular because of the economics of its production. A tabloid is half the size of a daily newspaper and consists of subject matter of a more specialized nature. Often it is inserted directly into a daily newspaper. It, too, is inherently economical: The paper is inexpensive, the printing is fast, the binding is simple, and it is ready for distribution at the time it leaves the press.

Other products also utilize the daily-newspaper format: community newspapers, store catalogs, special sports, fashion, and seasonal tabloids. Their quality of reproduction can equal brochure and magazine standards, providing their budgets allow for sufficient design and production costs.

A grid layout system is essential to newspapers because of the abundant material that must generally be accounted for within a very short production schedule. Because the sheet is large, and because it must accommodate a sizable assemblage of copy, headings, photos, diagrams, and/or maps with little room for white space, exceptional skill in typographic layout and design is required or the contents will disintegrate into a collage of competitive confusion. It is important to note, however, that at times the suggestion of "busyness" or visual density is used purposefully to suggest variety and economy.

BOOKS

Books potentially have such diverse formats that they are considered among the most personally rewarding opportunities for graphic designers. They also represent the oldest form of the graphic-communication tradition. Of all the objects we design, books become

Figure 4·7
Product information must be well organized and inviting for sales impact and reference convenience. The ski catalog (a) and the lighting catalog (b) display complex technical details without boring the reader. Notice that both layouts, planned from grids, incorporate generous areas of white space.

If you could compare cross country ski equipment development to the human evolutionary process, you would have seen skis, boots and bindings still swinging in the trees ten years ago.

Until recently, cross country ski equipment was more similar to that of our ancestors than it was like the equipment available today. Skis were generally stiff, heavy and required arduous base preparation before use. Cross country ski boots tended to be uncomfortable variations of hiking boots. And bindings had the effect of restricting the skier's forward motion. People have been cross country skiing for hundreds of years, but the most dramatic development of cross country equipment has taken place only in the last decade.

Modern Ski Evolution

In 1970 we were one of the first to broadly introduce a cross country ski with a polyethylene base. This material had been used successfully in the alpine ski industry because it glides well compared to wood, requires no prior base preparation, and can be easily repaired if damaged. But more fundamental than improving the material which cross country ski bases were made of was the issue of waxing. At the time, the major technological hurdle to overcome was the necessity for complicated waxes and waxing procedures.

Waxing Revisited

All snow is crystalline and is, therefore, microscopically textured. A snow's texture changes as temperature and moisture content change. To get grip or purchase, a ski must be able to grab or hold the edges of snow crystals. And because weather conditions are always changing, a ski must be adaptable to different snow textures.

Traditionally, this had been accomplished by waxing the base of the ski. Wax will allow the crystalline edges of snowflakes to penetrate, giving grip or purchase. But because snow has a variety of textures, many different waxes are required. If a wax is too hard, snowflakes can't penetrate and the ski will slip. If a wax is too soft, snow will penetrate the wax too easily, and stay there so that the ski won't slide.

The Waxless Revolution

As a result, cross country skiers have been searching for alternatives to wax almost as long as the sport has existed. The first waxless concept was climbing skins, originally seal skins strapped to the bottoms of skis so that the fur would rise and catch if the ski slipped backward but would lie flat as the ski moved forward. Unfortunately, they were heavy, restricted forward glide, and would ice up in wet snow conditions.

Hundreds of years passed until the first modern, and ultimately successful, waxless concept was developed. In 1971 we began the "waxless revolution" by introducing the first cross country ski with the patented Fishscale Nowax base.

Since that time hundreds of thousands of skiers worldwide have started and continued cross country skiing because of the simplicity of the concept and the ease it introduced to this sport.

The Trak Fishscale Nowax base is a series of semi-circular protuberances which are heat molded into very hard polyethylene. When climbing or kicking, the edges of the protuberances dig into the snow to give firm

Continuous Fishscale

grip, yet their rearward slope permits easy forward glide.

Trak's first skis were made with the Fishscale base along the entire bottom, from tip to tail. On-snow research proved that sufficient kick was provided by placing the Fishscale area in the midsection of the ski only, and so the next generation of Trak skis had smooth tip and tail areas to permit better glide.

In 1975 the concept was advanced further with the development of the Variable Depth Fishscale Nowax Base. This new base has three different levels compared with the earlier models with constant depth protuberances. Following the smooth tip area on the base, the protuberances gradually increase in depth, reaching maximum depth under the foot (where the kick is most strongly exerted), and then fade out again toward the tail, which is also smooth. The graduated positioning of these levels continues to give Trak skis excellent kick as well as improved forward glide.

The Variable Depth concept was again improved with the introduction of the convex or domed protuberance. In this new configuration, the height of the kicking edges are increased, giving even greater kick and the top portions have been gently rounded so that the effective glide surface is increased as well.

Mid-Section Fishscale   Variable Depth Fishscale   Convex Fishscale

The New Omnitrak Base

Our most recent on-snow research has proved that changes in the shape as well as the depth of the protuberances have a significant effect on a ski's kick and glide. As a result, our new base has separate levels and configurations which compositely contribute to improved overall ski performance. Different glide and different kicking configurations are joined to give excellent kick and remarkably improved forward glide.

The New Omnitrak Base

Modern Ski Construction

Until recently, cross country skis were made entirely of wood, a material that limits the durability, flex and lightness of the finished product. With the introduction of fiberglass as a major structural material, ski construction underwent a revolution.

Fiberglass—glass filaments imbedded and locked together in a plastic resin—is one of the strongest yet lightest materials available today. When used as the top and bottom layers in a cross country ski, it becomes possible to produce a remarkably durable ski with increased "life" and flexibility at a much lower weight than has been possible before.

Because fiberglass now carries the structural burden in a cross country ski, the ski's core does not have to have the structural significance it had before. Ski cores of laminated wood are still popular because of their resilience, but they generally have air or foam channels in them to reduce weight.

Polyurethane or "PU" foam is the newest cross country ski core material. The foam is injected in liquid form into a mold between two layers of fiberglass where it expands to a controlled density. The higher the density of the foam, the greater the foam's strength. As a result, PU core skis weigh about the same as solid wood core skis, but have significantly more flexibility and durability.

After answering these questions, you should be able to decide the kind of cross country skiing you're going to be doing and the general type of equipment appropriate for your use. Types of cross country equipment break down into three basic usage categories.

Recreational Equipment

Recreational equipment is designed for all-around use, for performance in a variety of snow conditions for skiers of all abilities, from the first time skier to the expert.

Recreational skis are constructed for maximum durability. They are wider for greater stability, provide good flotation in unbroken snow, yet will function well in prepared ski tracks.

Recreational boots are designed for functional comfort. They offer all-around performance and are constructed of durable materials to meet the demands of both on and off the track use. Recreational boots are available both in Norm 75 models and in the new Norm 50, a concept which offers easier sole flex and increased ski control.

Recreational poles and bindings are designed to combine maximum strength with general all-around performance

Performance Equipment

Performance equipment is designed to meet the needs of advanced, more athletic or competitive cross country skiers.

Performance skis are designed for prepared track skiing. They are light and narrow, offering less resistance but requiring more technique and balance. Some performance skis are designed specifically for the expert skier and feature second camber construction.

Performance boots are lightweight Norm 50 models which offer increased torsional rigidity and greater ski control as well as reduced weight and drag in the track.

Performance poles and bindings are designed to combine maximum strength with minimum weight.

Special Equipment

Special equipment is designed to meet the rigors and demands of backcountry or wilderness skiing.

Special skis are designed for extra durability. They are wider for better flotation in unbroken snow and many models have metal edges for use on hard packed or glacial snow.

Special boots are designed for rugged backcountry use. They generally are constructed of warmer, heavier, tougher materials to stand up to the demands of wilderness skiing.

Fitting Your Equipment

Guidelines for fitting equipment are only general rules of thumb. Your height, weight, athletic experience and the kind of skiing you'll be doing all have to be taken into consideration when fitting your equipment.

Fitting Boots Like any athletic footwear, a cross country ski boot's performance depends on good fit. It should fit comfortably like a good walking shoe. The boot should be snug around the heel so that your foot doesn't lift out of the boot when kicking, and it should have adequate room in the toe area so that circulation is not impeded.

Everyone's body and skiing needs require a special and different fitting of equipment.

Fitting Skis With your feet flat on the floor, raise one arm straight up in the air. Generally, the pair of skis whose tips come closest to hitting the wrist of your upraised arm will be the right size for you. There are exceptions to the rule, though. If you are particularly light you will want a slightly shorter ski because you have less weight to be distributed on the ski. If you are heavier than is normal for your height, you will want a slightly longer ski to spread your weight over a longer ski surface.

If a ski is too long for you it will be hard to control; it will meander and roll in the track. If a ski is too short for you, the ski will tend to plow or dig in at the tip and be very slow.

Fitting Poles With your feet flat on the floor, raise one arm straight out from your body. The pair of poles that fits comfortably under your outstretched arm will be the right length for you. Cross country poles are longer than those used in downhill skiing because the arm motions are different. Cross country skiing technique relies in part upon propulsion from the arms. Longer poles are needed to provide this "push" throughout each full stride.

(a)

Courtesy Trak, Inc.

Figure 4·7 (continued)

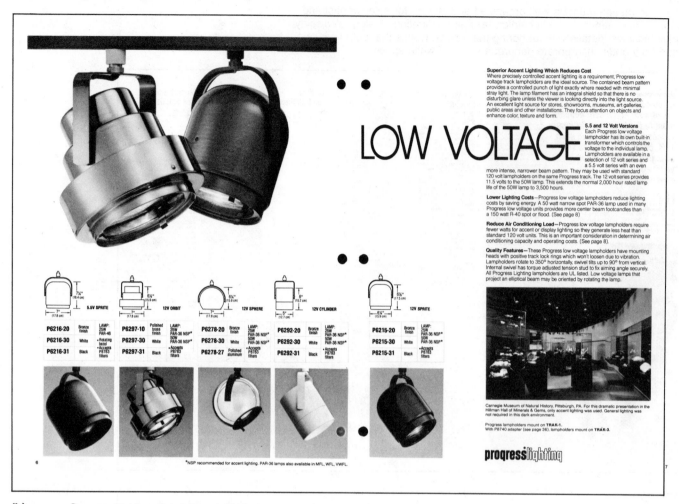

(b)   *Progress Lighting, Subsidiary of Kidde, Inc.*

the most valued examples, probably because of their permanence. In a sense, books have been the major vehicle for the shaping of education, the recording of history, and the interchange of information. The present development of computer systems and audio-visual/video media is currently challenging this. But in spite of these ongoing innovations and the universal application of radio, TV, and film, books will always have a convenience, authority, economy, intimacy, and enjoyable tactile presence that is not the case with electronic media.

Thick or thin, paper or hardcover, the book format

follows a traditional sequence. The cover or jacket is the "package wrapping" and introduces the subject matter through design, illustration, and texture. Half title, title page, contents, foreword, chapters (text), and index all follow in standard order. (See Figure 4.10) All elements are organized graphically through spacing and typography and they are related by a total design concept. The title page is often a variation of the cover. The chapter-opening pages are considered somewhat as graphic highlights. Books follow some system of grid or page layout. The more complex the contents, the more flexibility is accommodated by the grid.

SCARED SERIOUS

It's quiet on campus as the apprentice adults rehearse their futures

By Lisa Birnbach

I first met Alex in a poetry-writing seminar. You know the kind: brilliant, highly egocentric, raging professor entertains twelve devoted, almost sycophantic kids, all of whom take poetry more seriously than Teacher. I thought Alex was the most gifted in the group. Poetry consumed most of his energy, with marijuana taking second place in his priorities. There was nothing in between, and very little below. What he wore, when he ate, mattered little.

Alex graduated and I transferred to another school. I didn't see him again until two years later, in 1977, when I ran into him at New York's Penn Station. He

LISA BIRNBACH'S 'The Official Preppy Handbook' (Workman) is available in the religion section of the University of Washington bookstore.

was heading to his parents' home in Delaware for Thanksgiving dinner. He was wearing a suit and tie and carrying an attaché case. I was surprised by the way he looked, and shocked at what he was doing: selling ad space for a trade magazine. "Are you writing?" I asked. "I'm not," he said, avoiding my eyes. I asked him why he didn't take a part-time job so he could devote most of his time to poetry. "I like French food."

That's all it took. *Escargot* is not cheap. It no longer made sense for him to live in a garret and eat at coffee-shop counters while others, less deserving, snacked on *medaillons forestière*. Alex knew it was a sellout. He was embarrassed, and I felt rotten. Something strange was going on.

Things got even stranger during my senior year. The career-development office sent a constant tutti-frutti-colored stream of leaflets into my post-office box. I threw them out, unread. I didn't want a career; I wanted to

write. But suddenly, all the other earnest English majors knew what they were doing with the

rest of their lives: they were going into banking, retailing or law. I panicked. Was there something wrong with me? Did I miss an important lecture?

Winter 1981: I've been traveling around the country on a promotional tour for my new book, *The Official Preppy Handbook*. There's a school on the agenda almost every day — junior colleges, commuter schools, Big Ten and Ivy League. Feeling closer to the students than to the ladies who attend the book-and-author luncheons sponsored by department stores, I've been spending as much time as I can on campus. I've looked for signs of restlessness, for that edge, for proof that students are still kids, stalling any commitment to adulthood.

What I've found are apprentice grown-ups. They are carefully groomed, truly worthy of the terms *wholesome* and *clean-cut*. These days, everyone knows what everyone else's father does for a living, and it's discussed openly. They even understand how a mortgage is bankrolled. They rack up big dry-cleaning bills. They abuse their credit cards. They take summer jobs in brokerage

houses, and they take their beaus home to meet their parents.

The typical campus party is now an organized affair. Kids dress up like mummy and daddy. Men politely get drinks for their *dates*. When the party gets going, couples dance up a storm (swing is most popular), then they mop up themselves and the spilled liquor, shake hands and kiss goodbye.

College students are heavy drinkers. If drugs are a part of their lives, it is the cocaine they are offered at a party; marijuana is almost too pedestrian. Quaaludes are for kids with no ambition. Getting "wasted" is no longer a symbol of rebellion. It is done after studying or on weekends, perhaps in homage to daddy, who celebrates the end of a tough week on the crowded Friday-afternoon commuter train.

There's no indication that anything political is happening anymore. Occasionally, I've spotted a tattered notice re-

---

Figure 4.8
Rolling Stone magazine has pioneered some of the best, most energetic, freshest typography and layout. Although the layouts shown here are crowded, the material invites reading and is clearly separated by the lively use of rules, borders, and initial caps. *Design Director: Bea Feitter. Illustrations: Steven Singer & Bill Plympton. Art Director: Mary Shanalhan.*

Figure 4·8 (continued)

Jack Nicholson Is 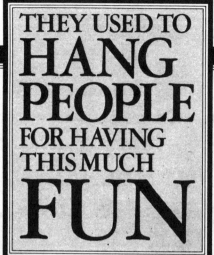 *Taking the Year Off*

The Outsider

HE THOUGHT OF HIMSELF AS a dark specter beyond the bathers. Most of the lifeguards at this particular New Jersey beach had opted for the image of Bronze Protector, but Jack Nicholson was different. He was a boat guard, and he enjoyed rowing out beyond the breakers. His job was to see that no swimmer strayed too far or got in too deep. It was the mid-Fifties, and Jack was the sort of older teenager who identified with Holden Caulfield, that sad, neurotic hero of J.D. Salinger's novel whose only dream was to stand in a field of rye where children were playing and to catch them before they fell off the cliff.

Jack stood as he rowed, and he was good with the boat. He wore a black lifeguard jacket, a World War II fatigue hat and mirror shades. His nose and lips were white with sunscreening zinc. He worked hard at the symbology of separateness.

The day that Jack Nicholson made the local papers for the first time was a bad one at the beach. There was a hurricane far out in the Atlantic, and it was kicking up heavy waves. The surf was too high for boats, and the guards were keeping swimmers in close. There was a jetty to the south and a separate beach below. That beach had its own crew of lifeguards, and it was there that eleven bathers were somehow carried out to sea by a vicious rip current.

Jack sprinted down to the beach, ready to help. There was no way to row the boats out through all that windwhipped surf. The strongest swimmer among the guards had strapped himself into a harness attached to a long rope. He would plunge out through the surf, grab as many of the endangered swimmers as possible, and the other guards would pull him back in. But there were too many drowning people out there, and one guard couldn't hope to save them all. A lot of them were going to die.

Nicholson ran back to his own beach, where the surf was not quite as high. Although the other guards doubted it could be done, Jack thought he might be able to muscle a boat out. He pulled through five-foot-high waves, waves so steep that sometimes it seemed as if the boat were moving in a vertical plane. Exhausted, he pulled out beyond the breakers, into the chop and swell, and made his way around the jetty, finally picking up the last five swimmers.

Everyone on both beaches was watching, and a news photographer got a nice shot of the boat topping the crest of a huge wave, bow pointing into the sky. That photo made the paper.

"You can't really see my face," Nicholson told me, "but the caption said I had risked hurricane surf to rescue five. Something like that. What they didn't mention is that as soon as I beached the boat, I puked my guts out in front of about 40,000 people."

Nicholson told me this story on a ski lift one day. I myself had been a lifeguard, and we were swapping tales of heroic rescues, as former lifeguards tend to do. What struck me most in the telling of this story was the way Nicholson described himself as a loner, an outsider. Lifeguards, I know from experience, tend to be gregarious. The strong young

Contributing editor TIM CAHILL *last reported on Jack Nicholson in 1975 (RS 201).*

THEY USED TO HANG PEOPLE FOR HAVING THIS MUCH FUN

people I worked with years ago were not being entirely facetious when they referred to themselves as "sun gods." Your average sun god does not like boat duty. He prefers to strut about the beach so that mere mortals may worship.

After a week of hanging around with him, skiing and talking about painters and authors, talking about basketball and film, it occurred to me that, despite his success, despite an Oscar, despite all the producers and directors and other actors who would love to work with him, Jack Nicholson still views himself as an outsider.

The Killer Instinct

THE WORST CELEBRITY INTERviews are conducted over lunch in some chic restaurant with the waiter interrupting a prize anecdote to ask who had the fettuccine while the public-relations person across the table is saying, "What Bobby really meant to say here was..." Some are held in a mobile home on a movie set. Others happen in desperate motel rooms around the world. Still others are held in the star's home after the cleaning lady has left. This interview was conducted on skis, over a period of several days. It was set up by mutual friends, and Jack called me at home to confirm the date. This is not the way these things are usually done in Hollywood, but it's the way Jack Nicholson seems to do them.

"Do you ski?" he asked.

"Not for several years," I said, "and then not very well."

"You'll do okay."

A few days later, I joined the Crack of Noon Club, an amorphous and informal group that convenes at a certain restaurant near Aspen's Buttermilk Mountain almost every day the snow is good. The restaurant serves good coffee, fresh-squeezed orange juice and the kind of enormous breakfast you want before hitting the slopes at the crack of noon. Membership in the club varies according to who feels like skiing on any particular day. Jack and his longtime companion, Anjelica Huston, are usually present. Sometimes Jimmy and Jane Buffett join them, or producer Lou Adler, or director Bob Rafelson might be there. I met a few instructors, a local racer, one of Jack's buddies who shares his

love of basketball and skiing, and Ed Bradley of CBS News, who was taking a short ski vacation.

"Jack," Bradley told me over his third order of sausage, "is of the *fugit* school. Here's the top of the mountain. There's the bottom. *Fugit*, let's go."

"Is he good?"

"Pretty good. I'd say his style depends largely on courage."

Promptly at half past the crack of noon, we hit the lifts. When the last of the group arrived at the top of the hill, the Crack of Noon Club suddenly became the Thundering Herd. They all simply took off down the slope like crazed Comanches, whooping for joy and leaving me gasping behind as I executed a large number of cowardly traverses.

Over the next few days, I managed to regain my snow legs to the point that I never completely lost sight of the Thundering Herd. Nicholson congratulated me on my perseverance, if not my technique. Small shows of courage went a long way with the Herd.

Jack himself was not the best technical skier in the group, but I seldom saw him anywhere but in the lead. Occasionally a hotshot would shoot by us, but in general, the rule was "No one passes the Thundering Herd." Nicholson obviously preferred the sides of the runs, where the bumps were fewer and smaller. Moguls annoyed him. He was after speed, and he seldom turned: "Slows you down," he explained.

He would often wait for me at the lift line, and we'd put in twenty minutes of interview time on the chair.

"You have a, uh, unique style," I said.

"Yeah. I'd describe it as massive poetry in motion," Jack said seriously, "though others say it looks like a dogfight rolling down the hill."

"Anjelica is a good athlete. Good technique."

Nicholson graced me with one of his perfect homicidal grins. "Yeah. But she lacks...the killer instinct." Some time later, I relayed the comment to Anjelica, and she replied with a vigorous masturbatory gesture.

Two things became very apparent, very quickly. One, Jack loved to ski the narrow, raggedy line that divides control from total disaster. Two, he enjoyed skiing with others. He took time out to help Bradley and me, the two weakest skiers in the group. Bradley hadn't skied in years, but he was improving hourly, and Jack, through word and deed, would caution him against the danger and delay of excessive caution.

Late one afternoon, on the hairiest run the Herd had yet negotiated, Bradley caught an edge, took a header and went bouncing ass over teakettle halfway down the mountain. His parka was ripped, he had a hard time breathing, and he lay there in pain for several minutes. When he finally did get up, he thought it wise to have me check him over for broken bones.

A spill like that can shatter your confidence, and Jack, mindful of this, set a slower pace and led us down the easier slopes. When we got to the lift, Bradley said he wanted to go back to the slope on which he'd crashed and burned. "Gotta get right back on the horse that threw you," he said. Now this is exactly what you might expect from a man like Bradley. In one of the most famous filmed reports to come out of the Vietnam War, Bradley was wounded, on camera. What is less well known is that, immediately upon being released from the hospital, Bradley made his way back to the front lines.

"We don't have to take the same run," Jack said, reasonably enough.

"Got to," Bradley replied.

B Y   T I M   C A H I L L

Figure 4·8 (continued)

College 1981

MURDER IN THE COMPUTER LAB

The game students play

By George Stein

KILLER AS AN ORGANIZED SPORT

Richard Baltin sleeps by day on a narrow mattress, a James Bond poster on the wall above his head. At night, he is awake, surrounded in his apartment by nineteen telephones, a blinking pinball machine and a video recorder playing James Bond spy thrillers. His Bond collection is almost complete. So is his collection of newspaper and magazine stories about his organization, KAOS (Killer As an Organized Sport). KAOS administers the playing of a game of pursuit and assassination called Killer. It's become the latest college fad, supplanting panty raids, streaking and toga parties.

At the University of Florida at Gainesville, Baltin is known as the master of make-believe murder. For weeks on end, KAOS members hunt each other down, making "kills" (with toy guns) until only one player is left "alive." Deceit, stealth and treachery triumph.

"The bottom line is that it's fun," says Baltin, a twenty-three-year-old graduate student from Miami Beach. "It's just an elaborate game of tag."

But Killer (most call it that) is much more than tag.

The game is now a nationwide — and controversial — campus craze. This is the fifth

GEORGE STEIN is a writer for the 'Miami Herald.'

consecutive quarter Killer has been played at the University of Florida, and it shows no signs of fading. All of the attention it has received — from concerned school authorities, scholars of social behavior and law-enforcement officials—only seems to draw more players.

In late January, the sixty-three students playing the game this term gathered in silence for the indoctrination session that kicks off each new round of Killer. Most disguised themselves, fearful of revealing their identities to a potential assassin. They wore stocking masks, ski masks, burnooses, sunglasses. Lurid greasepaint obscured the faces of two. One came as a grinning Halloween monster. Others simply wore brown paper bags with eyeholes over their heads.

Each player received a seventy-nine-cent toy pistol that shot rubber-tipped darts. Each also received a dossier on his first "victim": height, weight, eye color, hair color, class schedule, address, telephone number, hangouts, make of car and a recent photograph.

The rules require a kill in one week.

The origins of Killer go back to 1953, when science-fiction writer Robert Sheckley published a short story, "The Seventh Victim," in which he'd invented just such a game. In 1965, the game moved from magazine to screen in Carlos Ponti's *The*

91

Figure 4.9
Even though books may have a varying number of section titles, the sequence rarely changes.

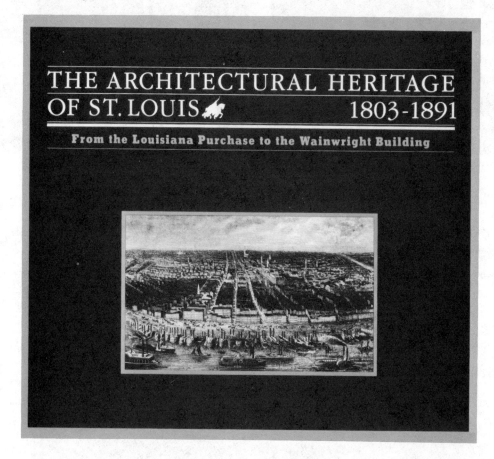

COVER

Figure 4.9 (continued)

THE ARCHITECTURAL HERITAGE OF ST. LOUIS

HALF TITLE

THE ARCHITECTURAL HERITAGE
OF ST. LOUIS 🐗 1803-1891
From the Louisiana Purchase to the Wainwright Building

Lawrence Lowic

Washington University Gallery of Art   St. Louis, Missouri   January 20–March 14, 1982

TITLE

Figure 4·9   **(continued)**

Designer: Robert Smith
Production: Charles Harmon, Mazlan Said
Printer: Jefferson Printing Co.
Typesetting: Adrian Typography, Inc.

Copyright ©1982 by The Washington
University Gallery of Art
St. Louis, Missouri. All rights reserved.
Library of Congress Card Catalog
Number 81-71595; ISBN: 0-936316-02-0

CREDITS

CONTENTS

CONTENTS

Figure 4·9 (continued)

FOREWORD

From the gleaming, stainless steel arch to the muscular stone and iron Eads Bridge and cast iron warehouse district immediately adjacent, the physical presence of St. Louis manifests more than two centuries of civic ideals, aspirations and achievements. During the nineteenth century the skyline and panorama of St. Louis underwent several distinct transformations, and at times the buildings symbolized a unified chorus of shared civic and domestic values. But today the city's architectural history eludes its citizens who confront vacuous spaces and the malaise of dilapidation while traversing its streets. The citizen who seeks knowledge of what once occupied vacant blocks or a sense of the cohesiveness that once unified disparate monuments and neighborhoods will be frustrated by the inaccessibility of photographic and narrative presentations of the city's architectural history. Though a few limited studies exist, as well as a fine guidebook to extant monuments, to date no one has successfully recovered obscure materials and data and organized a history of the structural growth of St. Louis. No museum has attempted to exhibit a comprehensive story of the transition from the French settlement to the organic differentiation of parts of the city into commercial, mercantile, residential, civic and religious components. The aesthetic and technical achievements of nineteenth century St. Louis architecture have remained unknown, as have understanding and appreciation of their relation to national tastes and ideals. For many of us our pride in St. Louis' architectural heritage is yet to be awakened.

The Architectural Heritage of St. Louis, the fruitful result of Lawrence Lowic's pioneering research and synthetic study, fills many of the voids in St. Louis' recorded architectural history. Sponsored by the School of Architecture, the Department of Art History, and the Gallery of Art at Washington University, this work represents not only the joining of our departments and resources, but also the collaborative teamwork of scholars, students and community members coordinated by Professor Lowic. His study argues for recognition of St. Louis' architectural heritage within the context of nineteenth century American architecture and suggests the role the city played in manifesting and promoting the ideals of the Westward Expansion into and beyond the Mississippi Valley. Flood, fire, disease and economic panic periodically visited St. Louis; Professor Lowic details these catastrophic events and the resulting transformation of St. Louis. His thesis includes analysis of individual structures, identifying the taste of patrons and skill of architects in satisfying both utilitarian and aesthetic goals. Further, Professor Lowic interprets the symbolic meaning of the shape the city achieved through juxtaposition of buildings and their organization along axes. Thus, this publication and exhibition present the technical, aesthetic and symbolic achievements of nineteenth century St. Louis architecture, reinforce a pride in that history, review the lessons contained therein, and encourage St. Louisans to participate in solving the architectural dilemmas of today's city.

We thank the many institutions which have joined Washington University in this project. The Missouri Historical Society has

7

PREFACE

As readers of the following essay will quickly discover, I take the history of St. Louis' urban development and architecture to be of more than local interest. Whether its history is the most typically American in the nineteenth century is perhaps arguable. That it was highly significant and deserves far more attention than it has from historians nationally seems to me beyond doubt. Given the restrictions placed on a work such as this it was regretably necessary to be selective with respect to material discussed. This is by no means a definitive work, but I do hope it will stimulate others to pursue their own study of the city. The resources available for such research are rich, perhaps better than for many other major American cities.

This study and the exhibition which it accompanies would not have been possible without the cooperation and assistance of many individuals and institutions. The staff of the Library at the Old Courthouse, Jefferson National Expansion Memorial, greatly facilitated my access to the large quantities of unpublished research and photographic materials available there. I would especially like to thank Sharon Brown, Eric Underwood, and Steve Harrison for their help. I am also grateful to Raymond Pisney and his staff at the Missouri Historical Society for their substantial assistance in bringing this project to completion. I am particularly indebted to Judith Ciampoli and Kathleen Moenster, both of whom invariably met requests efficiently and cheerfully over a long period of time. The staffs of the Art Room, St. Louis Public Library, St. Louis University Library, and the Rare Book Room, Olin Library, and the Art Library, both at Washington University, were also most helpful.

Several of my students have also contributed research to this project. Michael Tammenga brought together valuable information on the early Episcopal churches of the city; Elizabeth Markus researched the early Jewish community and the Second Merchants' Exchange; and Kathy Korn helped to track down information on Presbyterian and Methodist churches. Reverend Charles Rehkopf of Christ Church gave generous assistance with questions relating to the early history of Episcopalian churches and Mrs. John D. Davidson provided information on the original St. George's Episcopal Church. Esley Hamilton was helpful in answering inquiries concerning Pilgrim Congregational Church.

I am most indebted to Buford Pickens for his reading of the entire manuscript except for the Epilogue. His criticisms and suggestions have vastly improved it. Likewise, Frances Hurd Stadler was a demanding and knowledgeable editor whose comments and questions contributed materially to the final product. Doris Suits typed several drafts of the manuscript, often laboring under nearly impossible conditions.

Long ago Henry Lowenhaupt forcefully impressed upon me the virtues of St. Louis and its past. Later Charles and Rosalyn Lowenhaupt provided encouragement and help without which this essay and exhibition would likely never have been realized. At various times Glen Holt, Norris Kelly Smith and Constantine E. Michaelides have given support when it was needed the most. I am also very appreciative of the kindness and cooperation extended to this project by Eric Newman and David Mesker.

I wish to thank Gerald Bolas and his staff at the Washington University Gallery of Art; Catherine Burns, Jonathan Edwards, and Lisa Hirsh, who all assisted in bringing this essay to press and mounting the exhibition which it accompanies.

Finally, and most importantly, I owe a very special debt of gratitude to Mary M. Stiritz, certainly one of the most skillful researchers currently working on the city's architectural past, who has given freely of her knowledge of St. Louis and on numerous occasions pointed out the errors of my ways.

Lawrence Lowic,
Department of Art History

9

Figure 4·9 (continued)

In 1904 Henry Adams most reluctantly traveled west from Washington to visit the Louisiana Purchase Exposition in St. Louis. As he tells us in *The Education of Henry Adams,* he regarded the Exposition as the first creation in the twentieth century of the new American, child of steam, brother of the dynamo, and servant of the powerhouse. He was transfixed by the image which he discovered: in his opinion the world had never witnessed so marvelous a phantasm; long lines of white palaces, illuminated by thousands of electric lights, soft, rich, and shadowy in their profound solitude (Fig. 1). He enjoyed the Exposition with "iniquitous rapture, not because of exhibits but rather because of their want." Here he found paradox, "for had there been no exhibits at all, and no visitors, one would have enjoyed it only the more." At the end of a decade long period of search and "re-education" he could only wonder whether the extravagance of the Exposition reflected the past or imaged the future. Was it a creation of the old America or a promise of the new one?

Of St. Louis itself he had absolutely no doubts. It was for him a third rate town without history, education, unity, or art, and with very little capital. It was devoid of natural interest except for the river which it had regrettably turned its back on. This new social conglomeration with no social unity save its steam power had, according to Adams, thrown away thirty to forty million dollars on a pageant which was ephemeral as a stage set.

Undoubtedly measured by the standards of the Paris and London which he knew so well there is some small justice in Adams' evaluation of St. Louis. But on the whole it distorts or ignores more than it reveals. In reality the St. Louis which he visited in 1904 was the nation's fourth largest city, exceeded in population only by New York, Chicago, and Philadelphia. It was a city with a rather long history not without its significance and accomplishments. Far from being a raw unformed industrial slage heap in the wilderness, it possessed a wide variety of cultural institutions including two major universities. Its achievements in educational

innovation, social legislation, and as the source of nationally important intellectual movements such as its Hegelian revival, were all noteworthy. In many important ways it had been during the second half of the nineteenth century one of the nation's leading cities.

For St. Louis, no less than for Henry Adams, the Louisiana Exposition was, in the final analysis, a paradoxical event. On the one hand in mounting the largest exposition ever held, the city demonstrated to itself, if not to the nation at large, that it was still capable of significant achievements; that its future might still hold promise of renewed growth and vitality. And on the other hand the Exposition was a summing up of all that the city had been in the nineteenth century. The gleaming white classically inspired buildings of the Exposition were a logical continuation, a reaffirmation, of the values which had shaped St. Louis architecture for almost a century. The exhibitions which these buildings housed celebrating technology, science, art, and agriculture were integral to the image of itself which the city had promoted for decades. In the end rather tragically Adams' perception of the Exposition as ephemeral proved all too true. Rather than laying the foundation for a new era of growth in the city as its organizers hoped, it became in the light of history but a final, momentary effusion of the ebbing energies of a grand era of achievement which had all but passed. In the decades after the Exposition, slowly at first and then ever more rapidly after the Second World War, St. Louis began to decline.

Today the population of St. Louis is far smaller than it was in 1904, although its physical limits remain the same. Much of the urban fabric which existed then is also gone; a significant portion of the remainder threatened. Beyond the facts of economic and social deterioration which have categorized much of its recent decline (and may only now be reversing itself), there also lies a far reaching, if elusive to describe, loss of identity, of a comprehensible urban image, of historic meanings and continuities.

11

INTRODUCTION

Figure 3. Gabriel Cerre House, 1770. Drawing by Clarence Hoblitzelle.

Figure 4·9 (continued)

THE FRENCH CITY

On March 10, 1804, Captain Amos Stoddard, on behalf of the United States government, took possession of a relatively small settlement on the banks of the Mississippi whose origin and history were deeply rooted in the French and Spanish colonial experience in North America. More than a hundred years before, in 1673, Father Jacques Marquette and Louis Joliet had descended the Mississippi River as far as the Arkansas River. While their hope of finding a water passage to the "Red" or "California" Sea had been thwarted, they nevertheless had begun the process of French exploration of the then uncharted vastness of the North American interior. Some nine years later Rene Robert Cavalier, Sieur de la Salle, inspired by their effort, but intent on claiming the great interior valley which they had explored for France rather than finding a passage to the Pacific, succeeded in reaching the mouth of the Mississippi. He claimed the entire territory which he had transversed for Louis XIV.

From the very beginning the valley of the Mississippi was a potential source of conflict among rival European powers. Beyond its strategic importance in the struggle for empire, for the French it was also regarded initially as a possible source of wealth equal to that discovered by the Spanish in their new world colonies to the south. The early years of French exploration and colonization were therefore motivated by the hope of discovering gold and silver. Indeed, it was precisely this prospect which allowed the celebrated John Law to perpetuate his infamous Louisiana Bubble in the early eighteenth century, the collapse of which was to plunge France into a financial panic and thoroughly sour general perceptions of the valley's potential as a colony.

Despite the bad climate of opinion created by the collapse of Law's Bubble, colonization proceeded by fits and starts. Under Pierre Lemoyne, Sieur d'Iberville, and his brother, Jean Baptiste Lemoyne, Sieur di Bienville, from 1698 to 1722 France emerged as a major rival of Spain in the lower Mississippi Valley. From the founding of Mobile in 1702 to the establishment of New Orleans in 1722 French settlements sprang up along the Gulf coast and far into the interior at such places as Cahokia, St. Genevieve, Kaskaskia and Fort de Chartres in the Illinois Country.

While some of the first French settlers in southern Missouri and Illinois were attracted to exploration and mining of the mineral wealth of the region, others were no doubt attracted from Canada, in particular, by an image of the other natural resources and opportunities offered by the valley. Even such earlier skeptics as Voltaire had come to see this region as potentially the finest area of future settlement for the tens of thousands of his countrymen whose cramped conditions in France would eventually be alleviated by the bounteous wilderness of the North American interior. For many observers its prospects were truly Edenic: a temperate climate with almost continual spring, absence of disease, fertile soil, bountiful crops without ever having to plow, and mineral wealth, all of which made it a "Frenchman's Paradise."

Moreover, at least for the average French colonial of Canada

15

CHAPTER

The new surge in downtown building activity which had begun in the mid 1880's continued into the 1890's, although abated somewhat by the financial panic which swept the nation in 1893. A younger generation of St. Louis architects including Isaac Taylor, William Albert Swasey, and the partnership of Charles Ames and Thomas Young were among those who contributed to the new downtown image, created by the appearance of tall office buildings, which began to emerge between 1890 and 1914. This downtown building activity was accompanied by an equally impressive development of the city's central westend where such prestigious private streets as Portland Place, Westminster Place Washington Terrace, and Kingsbury Place provided a final refuge from the rapid change and blighting already occuring as far west as Grand Avenue and the area surrounding Vandeventer Place. In both the southwest and northwest sections of the city middle and working class neighborhoods spread rapidly towards the city limits.

Within the downtown several long standing city needs were finally satisfied. Shortly after the formation of the Terminal Railroad Association in 1889, plans were initiated for a new and larger Union Station which would consolidate rail connections within the city and provide it with an impressive gateway commensurate with the railroad's importance as the primary means by which most visitors now entered it. The site of the new station, between Eighteenth and Twentieth Streets on Market Street, selected over the strong objections of some downtown business interests, was considerably west of the central business district. Designed by Theodore Link, the new Romanesque Union Station, completed by 1894, was undoubtedly one of the largest and most lavish train stations constructed in the nineteenth century. Also completed at the same time and augmenting the passenger facilities of the Union Station, the Cupples Station, a complex of eighteen buildings located in the area bounded by Seventh, Eleventh, Poplar, and Spruce Streets, made possible as never before the rapid handling and transfering of freight on a large scale. Beyond their revolutionary functional efficiency, these cubical brick Romanesque warehouses designed by Ames and Young, although they derived some of their details from Richardson's Harrison Avenue Ames Store, nevertheless have been categorized recently as being of the superior quality in design and execution, comparable to the best wall-bearing, commercial architecture in nineteenth century America.

Following the usual intrigue and controversy surrounding municipal projects, a new City Hall designed by Eckel and Mann was opened in 1896, although work continued on it until 1904. A sumptuous French Chateau, the new building was constructed at the corner of Twelfth and Market Streets. With its completion the city finally obtained a municipal government building worthy of its status as one of the nation's leading urban centers. Its position west of Twelfth Street, along with the siting of the new Union Station, was expressive of an optimism in the minds of many who hoped for the continued growth and development of the central business district west of Twelfth Street in the coming decades. After the turn of the century, inspired by the vision of the Louisiana Purchase Exposition of 1904 and the enthusiasm generated by the City Beautiful movement, several attempts were made to create a monumental civic plaza west of Twelfth Street and running parallel to it in a north–south direction. These schemes were based on the new location of the City Hall and eventually came to include a connection with the Union Station. None were ever more than partially realized nor did the central business district ever effectively cross the great divide of Twelfth Street. Today St. Louis still lives with the remnants of its turn of the century dreams and the largely unsatisfactory consequences of its failure to realize them.

Within the heart of the central business district on Seventh Street another dream, also tragically destined to failure, began to take shape starting in 1890. It was on the corner of Seventh and

145

EPILOGUE

Figure 4·10
Because most books have a longer life than advertising and promotional graphics, their design becomes a more serious challenge. Here, the *Nautical Quarterly* beautifully merges the dynamics of magazine layout with the clarity and permanence of book design. *Design: Marilyn Rose*

THE FIRST YACHTS

AND YACHTSMEN

BY JOHN ROUSMANIERE

One of the fascinations of studying the history of yachting is discovering how, and sometimes why, people have justified spending impressive sums of money on small interludes of leisure. The classic explanation for the enjoyment of yachts, and for many other forms of what he called "conspicuous consumption," was given by Thorstein Veblen in *The Theory of the Leisure Class*, still the definitive critique of the mores of the wealthy eighty-three years after its publication in 1899. Conspicuous leisure and consumption, Veblen argued, are tools used to win the world's esteem, "for esteem is awarded only on evidence." So conspicuous has been American consumption of leisure in its various forms that it has even created a counter-culture among people who could well afford to join in. "Who do you think we are—Vanderbilts?" a Rockefeller once snapped when asked why his family didn't go in for big yachts. Unfortunately, Veblen did not apply his keen, sardonic intelligence to the social functions of such display, to those qualities of conspicuous consumption that have always seemed to patch up rips in the social fabric. Although the rich are different from you and me because they have more money, as Ernest Hemingway once assured Scott Fitzgerald (who knew more about it), almost everybody—rich and you and me alike—would be disappointed if the reassuring evidence of wealth and privilege were hidden behind brownstones and tweeds. Today, there are plenty of ways to satisfy this expectation: buy a baseball team, run for the Senate, allow your love life to be dissected in the pages of People magazine. Or (most tastefully) purchase a Swan 65; for, since the day 5000 years ago when a Mesopotamian scribe signified "nobleman" with a glyph showing a man in the bow of a reed boat, command of a sailing vessel has been a sign of wealth and privilege.

The earliest royal vessel not used for politics or transportation and therefore the first true royal yacht—may have been the first Queen Elizabeth's Rat o' Wight, reportedly built at Cowes in 1588.

Yachting, seafaring's youngest babe, was created three hundred years ago by the wealthy ruling classes of two nations, one bourgeois and the other monarchist. Each class built and conspicuously used its vessels of pleasure partly for enjoyment and partly as instruments of the state. Like present-day yachtsmen boasting over the yacht club bar about bigger engines, longer hulls and more enduring jibs, the Dutch and English pleasure sailors of the 17th century engaged in not-so-subtle tests of manliness and consuming power. The major difference was that sailing then was intimately bound with people's serious lives ashore, with commerce and religion, politics and science. In his great study of the ideology of mercantilism, *The Protestant Ethic and the Spirit of Capitalism*, Max Weber identified the bond between faith and worldly business that grew out of the Reformation in Protestant countries such as the Netherlands and England. Writing in 1904—five years after Veblen—Weber contrasted this holistic vision with the fragmentation of Gilded Age America. "In the field of its highest development, in the United States," the German sociologist observed, "the pursuit of wealth, stripped of its religious and ethical meaning, tends to become associated with purely mundane passions, which often actually give it the character of sport." Or, to put it another way, the game-playing of making money for money's sake.

To return to the waterfront from sociology, the many definitions of the word "yacht" show how times have changed. Today, a yacht is simply a boat used for pleasure. But when William Falconer wrote his *Universal Dictionary of the Marine* in 1789, he defined the word in three ways. First,

Two Dutch yachts pass close aboard in a contemporary engraving. The first is a Staten Jacht with spritsail rig, the other is a Convoyer, more burdensome and with genuine firepower. Both are likely vessels of the India Companies.

it was a state vessel "usually employed to convey princes, ambassadors, or other great personages from one kingdom to another" (their version of Air Force I). By that definition, there were yachts as far back as 2600 B.C., when a swoop-sheered cedar barge was disassembled and buried in the Great Pyramid for the purpose of delivering her master, the Pharaoh Cheops, on his voyage to the afterlife. The Egyptians deeply respected the image of the ship as a symbol of rebirth, believing that every morning the Sun God Ra rose out of the sea in a reed boat to sail across the sky. Later, the Greek Ptolemies who ruled Egypt kept as many as eight hundred *thalamegoi*, "cabin carriers," moored at Alexandria to convey officials on their work and pleasure rounds. One of Ptolemy IV's *thalamegoi*, built around 220 B.C., was said to be a huge catamaran three hundred feet long and a towering sixty feet high. The down-to-earth Romans were not fooled by the official status of these big galleys; they called them *lusoriae*, "used for pleasure." The poet Horace wrote of them, with the cynicism of a Veblen:

*They change their sky, not their soul,
Who run across the sea.
We work hard at doing nothing;
We seek happiness in yachts.*

Falconer next specified a special kind of yacht, a royal boat or ship "reserved for the sovereign" and "nobly ornamented with sculpture." These vessels did not have to sail very far. Cleopatra's famous barge was such an elegant boat. With paddles sheathed in silver and a stern layered with gold, the celebrated barge carried the queen to her seduction of Marc Antony in 42 B.C., up the Cydnus River. Like most ancient and medieval royal yachts, this barge flew sails colored purple (some scholars say crimson) with Tyrian dye made from ground mollusks. For the next 1600 years kings and princes luxuriated, sailed to battles, and sometimes were buried in such regal little ships as Caligula's barges, the Norwegian longship of Queen Asa, Richard I's *Trench le Mer*, and Henry V's *Trinity Royal*. So valuable were these vessels that monarchs used them as bribes when negotiating treaties.

The earliest royal vessel not used for politics or transportation—and therefore the first true yacht—may have been the first Queen Elizabeth's *Rat o' Wight*, which reportedly was built in Cowes in 1588 to celebrate the English victory over the Spanish Armada. So insignificant (or apocryphal) was *Rat o' Wight* that she is not mentioned by either of the two primary authorities on early yachting history: C.M. Gavin, whose *Royal Yachts*, printed in a limited edition in 1932, is (with *The Lawson History of the America's Cup*) one of the two most beautiful and informative books of yachting history; and Captain Arthur H. Clark, whose scholarly *The History of Yachting, 1600-1815*, has been a major source for all yachting historians since the New York Yacht Club

William Falconer's definition that comes closest to our own is his third: a yacht is a smaller vessel used either by government officials or "as pleasure vessels by private gentlemen."

commissioned its publication in 1904.

The first boat to meet Falconer's second definition that we know anything about is *Disdain*, a miniature of the warship *Ark Royal* that King James I commissioned from the shipwright Phineas Pett in 1604. Pett wrote that she was built for James' ten-year-old eldest son, Prince Henry, "to disport himself in about London Bridge and acquaint his Grace with shipping and the manner of that element." Only twenty-eight feet long "by the keel," *Disdain* was "garnished with painting and carving, both within board and without, very curiously, according to his Lordship's directions." Since "curiously" meant "carefully" in Stuart English, Pett found nothing strange about the woodwork. Henry died eight years later, leaving his brother Charles heir to the throne, and *Disdain* disappeared from the Navy List in 1618. We don't know if his training program was a success; we do know that he sailed frequently and that a larger royal ship was being built for him at the time of his death. (All lengths in this article are "by the keel"—the length of the keel; overall lengths are about ten percent greater.)

Falconer's definition that comes closest to our own is his third: a yacht is a smaller vessel used either by government officials or "as pleasure-vessels by private gentlemen." This is how the first yachts were used on the Ij River in Amsterdam by thousands of middle-class burghers, back in the extraordinary Golden Age of the Dutch Republic. The 17th century was the century of Rembrandt, Spinoza, independence from Spain, and the creation of the first great capitalist state—all on a damp fringe of Europe that had been painfully won from the North Sea. Centuries of struggle against the sea and invaders had made the Dutch a serious, independent people who proved immediately receptive to the harsh theology of the radical Reformation. Sir William Petty, the English scientist, described the Dutch as "for the most part thinking, sober men, and such as believe that Labour and Industry is their duty towards God." Although it was sometimes difficult to distinguish the focus of their piety—"Voilà vôtre religion" ("This is your religion") Sweden's King Charles X once lectured a Dutch diplomat, holding up a coin—the Netherlanders could not be accused of practicing conspicuous consumption. As an English visitor observed: "never any country traded so much, and consumed so little: they buy infinitely, but 'tis to sell again, either upon improvement of the commodity, or at a better market. They are the great masters of the Indian spices, and of the Persian silks; but wear plain woolens, and feed upon their own cloth to France, and buy coarse out of England for their own wear."

By 1662, some two million people, many of them Jewish and Protestant refugees from the Inquisition and other pogroms, were packed into the seven United Provinces of the Netherlands at a density of about one hundred and thirty-five people a square mile (one and one-half times the

Figure 4.10 (continued)

Figure 4·10 (continued)

It was only the other day that I heard of your being in Paris, and it gave me pleasure to ascertain the fact, because I wanted to give my notions about the yacht "America," which has beaten John Bull so badly, and I know that by furnishing them to you, I can reach that class of my fellow countrymen who above all others will be delighted with the admirable performances of our clipper; I allude to boat builders and men connected with navigation. It was my lot to commence "following the sea" after the death of my father, who had me educated for a learned profession, but died while I was young and left me no estate. I have served in all kinds of vessels, and in all stations, so that I know the ropes about as well as the average run of seafaring folks, and fortunately I am now owner and captain of a trim brig, which may one of these days give me the means of laying up in some comfortable little harbor, when I am no longer seaworthy.

I happened to be at Havre when the news came of the preparations making for the Regatta at Cowes, and determined when the America got amongst them to be on hand, for I knew all about her and her builder—I had heard a good deal about the Messrs. Stevens—and I was certain that the Yankees would never send a boat all the way across the big pond to be beaten by anything afloat. The challenge given by the America was just about the sauciest thing ever done. She bid defiance to a fleet of nearly seven hundred yachts, whose supposed speed had long been a national boast with England, and to do up her work in the most gallant manner, she sent word that she would meet her competitors on their own cruising ground. Mr. Bull liked this "pluck" very well, for it resembled his own, but he thought there was a little more of the braggadocia in the challenge than there was discretion. No wonder! for in the *Yacht List* of England for 1851 it was stated that "Yacht building was an art in which England was unrivalled, and that she was distinguished pre-eminently and alone for the perfection of science in handling them." When that entry was made in the log the writer had'nt much of an idea that he was so far out in his reckoning. He thought that White, Camper, and Batsey, and others in England, were unrivalled as builders, and never heard of such a man as Steers.

When the yachtmen and their admirers—the builders—the people all along shore—the old salts and the young—the regular sailor and the amateur, heard that a "long black schooner" had crossed the Atlantic, and would soon be off Cowes, prepared to race with all the yachts of the squadron, they were all in a flutter, as chickens might be when a hawk was hovering over them. And when her sharp bow was seen cutting through English waters, the folks took a long look at her rakish build, and began to exchange opinions about her, some of which were very amusing I assure you. Most of the Englishmen, after inspecting her through their spyglasses, declared that she was "h'ugly"—and that though she should prove to be fast, she could never claim to be "'andsome." But there were many knowing ones who saw in a moment that she would certainly show her stern to any vessel in England, and that setting anything to chase her was, as one of them said in my hearing, like starting a bull dog after a hare. These fellows had seen our clipper ships and steamers, and knew that for getting along fast through the water nothing had touched us on the ocean. But it amazed even some of them to think that the solid English build with bluff bows was to be proved wrong by the performances of a wedge-fashioned craft with a long bow, sharp as a knife. They had always thought it the best indication of a vessel's rapidity when the water piled up in foam around her cutwater, and she was "carrying a bone in her teeth." They were surprised to find that the Yankee had done his utmost to avoid that unnecessary fuss, and pared himself away forward so as to cut the water as noiselessly and smoothly as possible—not pushing any load ahead of her like the old Jackass brigs down east, which make high tide wherever they go, but actually glancing through the water, and turning on each side a sheet of unbroken water as if she were quietly propelled through glass.

It was sometime before the America's rig was understood. The English had never tied their mainsail down on the boom, but let it flow and belly even when going dead to windward. When they saw the America's laced every where as tight as it could be got, they didn't feel sure whether that was going to work well or not, but when they saw some of her operations with the sheets chock aft, and watched her skimming along in the wind's eye, they began to think that flat sails were about right. The first time she got under way, those who saw her start thought she was not quickly handled, and consoled themselves with the idea that though the boat might beat, her men were not equal to the English tars in handling such a craft. This amused me a good deal I can tell you, for I had seen the men aboard, and knew that they could be as quick as cats if they chose. But when they were not in a hurry it was of no use to get along fast, particularly as a little show of dullness might tempt the squadron into a match with hopes of success founded on their superior management. But they were shy—very shy, and it was not until after they had been told that it would be an actual skulk not to give the America a chance, that at last Mr. Stephenson, owner of the Titania, took up the challenge. She was considered a fast boat, and her owner did all he could for

30

the honor of the squadron and his country.

Well, to ball off my yarn a little quicker, let us run direct to the first regatta, when all the people that could get there assembled at Cowes to see the strange sea-bird spread her wings and fly. I was "around all the time," as the boys say at home, and heard a good deal of queer talk about the America. One old salt, who took me for an Englishman, said he'd be blowed if he didn't think that 'ere rakish lookin' craft was just as sartin' to beat the whole ruck of 'em goin' to wind'ard—just so sure as she started. He said he'd been long a tellin' of 'em that it wouldn't do to thump an' hammer at the water like a Dutch galliot, when you could go through it like a sharp knife in a Cheshire cheese, and he added that it took the Yankees to find that out as they had done long ago. I hav'nt seen that 'ere boat go yet—he continued—but if she stands up and don't bury for'ad, she's agoin to make them yacht chaps open their eyes wider han they ever did afore.

When the gun was fired, all the vessels set their sails except the America. She waited a little to give the others a start so as not to get crowded amongst them, and to pass them where she liked when she got fairly off. By and by up went her mainsail, and may be it didn't set right—as flat as a board and as big as it could be made. Then to show what she could do when she was in a hurry, she spread her foresail, jib and gaff topsail about as quick as a bird could stretch his pinions. "My h'eyes!" said the old salt, "them's the slow chaps you were tellin' us about." There was a light breeze from W. S. W.—the Beatrice led, then came the Arrow, then the Volante, then the America. In just about half a minute every body saw that the trial was what we call "a soft match." Why the English yachts didn't seem to move—the America just walked up to them, and passed along as the Alida would slip past a Jersey ferry boat. She passed them one after another until off Oldcastle point, when people began to speculate as to what would be the fate of the yachts when they came to beat round the island. Oh Lord! When the America trimmed her sheets aft, what consternation there was in the crowd around me.

"It's all up with 'em," said one.

"Pshaw!" exclaimed another, "she beats the steamboat."

"It's *blarsted* queer, any'ow, to see 'ow she does 'er work," said another.

"Why there isn't a show at all," said my friend the old salt. "She's got 'em every way, h'on the wind or h'off. Them 'ere yachts can 'ang up their fiddles."

This was a right good fellow, and it took him but a very short time to see that Old England was no match for Young America, "this hitch." Off a place called Brading Water, our yacht took the lead, and from that time until the end of the race she did no other business but running away from the whole batch of vessels in the race or out of it, who tried their hand with her. I suppose my old friends in New York—the builders and boatmen of all sorts—will be particularly delighted to know that her Majesty the Queen, and her husband, and the Royal children too—think of that—all these had a chance to see our little America excel her competitors, as I hope the greater America will do throughout all time, but although I took considerable pains to find out what the "Royal children" thought or said of the feat they witnessed, I was so unfortunate as not to obtain any satisfactory intelligence

"It's all up with 'em," said one. "Pshaw!" exclaimed another, "she beats the steamboat." "It's *blarsted* queer, any'ow . . ." said another.

on this momentous question. It is rumored that the young Prince declared in specific terms that the America was "one of 'em," and his sister said she was "a bird," but the rumor "needs confirmation," as you editors say, and I don't like to compromise the royal family by attributing any remark to either of them which they are not positively *known* to have uttered.

The beat was so awfully bad that folks wanted some grain of consolation, and they got up a story that the America had forfeited her right to the prize by going inside instead of outside the Nab. I thought it wasn't of much consequence how she *nabbed* them, for she had them fast enough and bad enough, to show them that they never had had what our boys call a "look," or a "living chance." It's very hard for them to give up their old notions and models, but our English friends must make their vessels sharper, and stretch their sails flatter. Then they may regain some of the reputation which their squadron has just lost. A protest was made against giving the America the prize for the reasons I have mentioned, but it was withdrawn, and Mr. Stevens received what he had so handsomely won. It was remarked in an English paper that "while the cutters were thrashing through the water, sending the spray over their bows, and the schooners were wet up to the foot of the foremast, the America was dry as a bone," and the account added, "her superiority was so decided, that several of the yachts wore, and went back to Cowes in despair." There was one very funny response given to a

31

For more than 130 years, the America's Cup has been the subject of sporting attention from the masses and from millionaires; it has been the subject of a sort of yachting chauvinism; it has been the subject of tempest-in-a-teapot controversies; it has been the subject of journalism and gossip. And it has been the subject of art. ☐ On the next ten pages we present artists' interpretations of boats and scenes from America's Cup contests. Most of these works are from the last century, when the racing action was easier to capture on canvas than to freeze for a photograph. Our selection has been made from a single private collection, the owner of which wishes to remain anonymous. We chose them for their diversity—of style, of medium, of quality—and simply because we liked them. ☐ The skills of the artists run the gamut from one-step-away-from-amateur to proficient professional. They are from both sides of the Atlantic, presumably from both sides of the fence. Some portray a particular moment of a particular race. Others are less dynamic in mood; they are portraits of defenders and challengers. Their styles reflect contemporary artistic movements—luminism, impressionism, realism. The mediums they represent are varied—oils, lithographs,

34

NAUTICAL QUARTERLY

An America's Cup Gallery

BY REBECCA SMITH

even silk thread and cloth. ☐ It is no coincidence that, of the seven works by Americans, the five that can be identified are by artists living and working in the environs of New York City, the center of American yachting in the nineteenth century with its easy accessibility to the lower harbor and Sandy Hook, the venue of the America's Cup before 1930. ☐ But who were the men behind the paints, the silk, the lithographer's stone? We are fortunate that the recent renewal of interest in marine painting has focused some attention on the artists themselves. We offer here what we could find out about them, for their stories are as distinctive as their works. One was a yacht designer turned yacht painter turned yacht designer again. Another was painter to an English King. Two were prolific printmakers. One is unknown; another is known to us only by his name. These artists have preserved for posterity a boat, a moment, a canvas of wind and drama from the history of this great yachting event. Posterity—that's us! That's you, that's me, landlubber and sailor alike, who can turn these pages and enjoy scenes from America's Cup contests we were never able to witness. We invite you to turn—but lingeringly—these pages.

35

Books require a lengthy production period. The time involved, and the consequent expense, allow for refinement not possible in other design forms. Indeed, some of the finest layouts and typography (including photography and illustration) have been created for books. The book has long been appreciated as an art form by serious collectors. Some artists even use typography or the book form as their creative medium to express a purely visual-tactile concept rather than a literate one. Such works can be found in rare book collections.

MAGAZINES AND PERIODICALS

Magazines are also called journals when they are produced for special interests—usually for scientific, educational, or professional readers. A magazine consists of: (1) *editorial content*—stories, reports, reviews, articles, departments, photos, illustrations, diagrams, and so on; (2) *advertising matter* related to the type of reader the publication serves.

Magazines use layout grids for convenience and ease of assembly, and to establish a unique graphic organization or identity. The individual character of these layouts is obvious: If you separate some pages from various publications, you can most likely identify the sources correctly by the typography layouts only. Generally the layout in a particular magazine will either follow a uniform typographical style regardless of the subjects in the articles, or each article will be designed independently to reflect its content. Advertising layouts must also be balanced with editorial matter, either divided into separate areas or distributed in extended alternate areas.

Thousands of magazines are available on every subject imaginable. Some of the best graphic examples are not, unfortunately, magazine-stand, general-interest products, so they are not readily accessible. Library periodical racks or special magazine shops are economical sources of information, reference, and inspiration. Old magazines and advertising are currently enjoying historical and simply curious interest among collectors. (See Figures 1.11, 1.12.) Search them out; they offer abundant research material for serious firsthand study.

Figure 4.11a
Currently, experimental publishing and typography are attracting increasing interest. Often, design ideas can be adapted for practical application from these activities. Paper companies frequently produce promotional pieces that look like purely creative works, as the example from E. I. duPont de Nemours and Company (Inc.) illustrates.

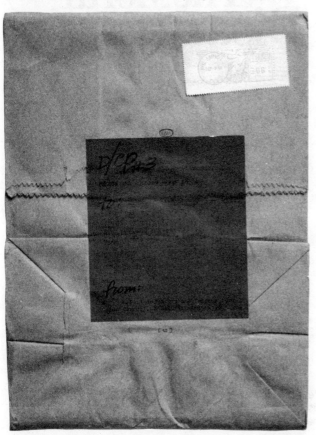

Figure 4.11b
In the world of literature, "concrete poetry" plays with words, letters, and visual form. This poetic announcement, designed by composer Bill Patterson is also reminiscent of Dada poetry, but here it was produced by a computer.

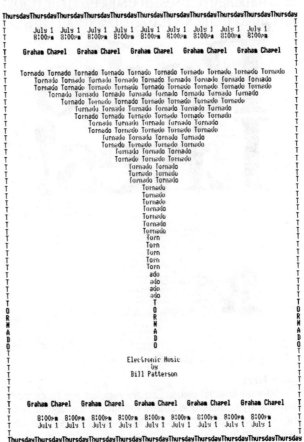

Figure 4.12a

In its 50-year special issue, *Esquire* repeats the typography. Yet, because of extensive style, size, and space variations, the layout looks fresh and contemporary. This technique encourages browsing through the marginal material.

Reprinted with permission from Esquire. Copyright © 1983 by Esquire Associates.

HEARTBURN: A DIAGNOSIS It's funny— no mean contribution to a genre whose natural form of expression is the whine" BY JUDITH MARTIN

Two major influences on literary women of a certain age:

1. Ernest Hemingway in *Fathers and Sons*, 1933, explaining Nick Adams' method of curing domestic injury: "If he wrote it he could get rid of it. He had gotten rid of many things by writing them."

2. Countless college boys, circa 1945-1965, breaking up with female liberal-arts majors

When a celebrity couple splits up in the limelight, when a husband is unfaithful and a wife cries for six weeks—in the right hands, believe it or not, that's entertainment. And that's Heartburn, Nora Ephron's first novel — for all those who've never seen the hilarious side of heartache

(whom they had seduced with the argument, "If you don't experience life, how do you expect to be an artist?": "If you haven't suffered, how do you expect to be an artist?"

From the resulting deluge of novels, essays, articles, diaries, unrhymed poems, and assorted other *belles lettres* documenting suffering on the occasion of the break-up, one assumes that many artistic souls who have truly lived feel

Nora Ephron: four points of view by photographer David Seidner.

better now. Whether their readers do is another question.

Nora Ephron's heroine in *Heartburn*, a writer suffering a marital break-up, is a second-generation believer in the Nick Adams School of Literary Catharsis who knows that her dead mother's sole advice and comfort to her in this crisis would have been "Take notes."

But she has slipped something extra into the standard list of motivations for entertaining others with one's history, recited here as "Because if I tell the story, I control the version. Because if I tell the story, I can make you laugh, and I would rather have you laugh at me than feel sorry for me. Because if I tell the story, it doesn't hurt as much. Because if I tell the story, I can get on with it."

Did you catch that? "I can make you laugh." Along with four advantages to the teller, there is one for the listener.

And, indeed, *Heartburn* is funny—no mean contribution to a genre whose natural form of expression is the whine. What is more, it contains fourteen recipes (three of them for potatoes), a classic version of the Kreplach Joke, an original skit on the Jewish Prince Routine, and a story line parallel to that of the author's last marital break-up as chronicled in the popular press but with juicier details ("Perhaps you are wondering whether we had sex?")

Miss Ephron has a marvelous eye for the mundane details that shake people's worlds. Betrayal is a husband's having secret joint therapy with his mistress "at the family rate!" Rejection is being able to identify your mugger because you had been wondering whether he were "single and a college graduate and straight."

(Continued on page 349)

SOME THINGS ABOUT NORA EPHRON . . . and betrayal, marriage, romantic illusions, and dinner parties in Washington, DC, and New York — an interview by Amy Gross

Nora Ephron is the author of *Heartburn*, the funniest novel of this year or any other year in modern history, which began in 1963. It's a book that makes people laugh out loud, get teary in places, and you can cook from it too. There's one recipe—for lima beans and pears—that narrator Rachel Samstat attributes to her mother, but I happen to know it came from Nora's friend Lee Bailey, and so will you if you turn to page 293 of this issue of Vogue.

Rachel Samstat is a cookbook author who is married to the well-known Washington, DC, columnist Mark Feldman. They have one child, Sam, and Rachel is seven months pregnant when she finds out that Mark is having an affair with Thelma Rice. Mark and Thelma are not only having an affair together—they're in joint therapy with Thelma's husband and a Guatemalan shrink "who looks like Carmen Miranda and has a dog named Pepito." Rachel has basically graduated from therapy, but under the circumstances, she shuttles with Sam home to New York and her therapy group, led by the wonderful celebrity shrink, Vera.

I told them a little about Thelma. I said she had a nose as long as a thumb and walked like a penguin; that made me feel better. I said Mark was a schmuck; that made me feel even better. I told the part about all three of them going to see the Central American charlatan and her dwarf dog, and I said how unfair it was that I couldn't even date.

"She must be feeling better," said Ellis. "She's making jokes."

"She makes jokes even when she's feel-

ing terrible," said Vera. "Don't let her fool you."

"Why do you have to make everything into a joke?" asked Diana.

"I don't have to make everything into a joke," I said. "I have to make everything into a story. Remember?"

"How do you feel?" asked Eve.

"Hurt. Angry. Stupid. Miserable." I thought for a minute. "And guilty."

"You didn't do this," said Eve. "He did."

"But I picked him," I said.

"Anyone would have picked Mark Feldman," said Vanessa.

"No last names in group," said Vera. . . .

"What do you want?" said Vanessa. "Mark is going to turn up, and you have to know what you want when he does."

I thought about it.

"I want him back," I said.

"What do you want him back for?" said Dan. "You just said he was a schmuck."

"I want him back so I can yell at him and tell him he's a schmuck," I said. "Anyway, he's my schmuck." I paused. "And I want him to stop seeing her. I want him to say he never really loved her. I want him to say he must have been crazy. I want her to die. I want him to die, too."

"I thought you said you wanted him back," said Ellis.

"I do," I said, "but I want him back dead."

Nora Ephron is the daughter of people who wrote snappy dialogue for Spencer Tracy and Katharine Hepburn (*Desk Set*) among others. In an interview years ago, Nora told me, "Most *(Continued on page 346)*

Figure 4.12b

Vogue follows another trend: Its informal, exploding typography exudes a break-the-rules approach. Some clarity is sacrificed, but the style conveys a dynamic, changing energy consistent with up-to-date fashion. *Art Director: Roger Schoening. Designer: Ron Kajiwara. Courtesy Vogue. Copyright © 1983 by The Conde Nast Publications, Inc.*

Three-Dimensional Forms

PACKAGING

Packaging is a very complex design area. It can be considered a combination of printed matter, a three-dimensional object, and a form of cover or "product jacket." A package can be a sturdy appliance shipping carton or a sculptural specialty container. Today's package does more than hold the contents: It is part of a sales program to induce purchasing of the product. It represents the manufacturer and it must compete fiercely when it holds a shelved retail product. It must also be serviceable, legible, and incorporate packaging regulations. When it is shown in advertising it should be attractive and memorable.

The choice of packaging materials is complex: Cardboard, paper, foil, metal, and plastic are only some of the possibilities. There is a parallel complexity of special manufacturing, printing, and displaying processes. Any supermarket, hardware store, or pharmacy is a potential encyclopedia of the packaging industry, and is thus worth studying. The construction of packages is in itself fascinating: Unravel a few packages, such as cigarette hard packs or beverage cardboard six packs, to study their designs and appreciate the logic and economy involved.

Figure 4.13a
The L'eggs container is now a classic in packaging forms. It is a fine example that an unconventional solution can be successful in the consumer market. *Courtesy L'eggs, Inc.*

Figure 4.13b
At the other extreme, popcorn really "pops" when you get enough packages together. The boxes are conventional shapes, so the graphics must do the work.

Packaging does present some special formal design problems: the integrity of the design must be maintained across all surfaces; one package that is part of a multiple pack must relate to others in the pack. The shape of the surface is also vital—what works well on a flat box is not the same as what is funtional on a cylindrical metal can. Another consideration is the categories of products. Cereal boxes and their graphics are quite different in a collective sense than packages and graphics for toilet articles, beer, or detergents: Cereal graphics are usually somewhat playful; those for toilet articles are more refined.

POINT-OF-PURCHASE DISPLAYS

Point-of-purchase displays are similar to packages: They are essentially three dimensional and are made of mostly the same materials. They can be in the form of

Figure 4.14
Packaging is taken for granted; it seems to just come along with the product. But an extraordinary amount of research and design study go into it. The sales of a product depend on its packaging. The examples here contrast a range of products in totally different containers. *Courtesy Overlock Howe Consulting Group, Inc.*

105

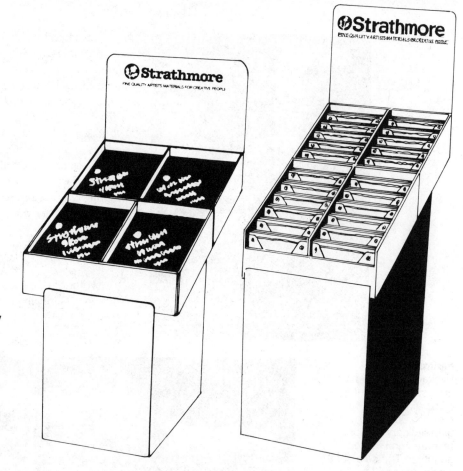

Figure 4.15
Point-of-purchase designs usually promote specials, bargains, or new products. The Strathmore displays shown here are actually folded out of their shipping containers or connected to parts contained along with the products. The economic advantage of this kind of design solution is obvious. *Designer: Kurt R. Schaefer.*

card racks placed on counters or of end-of-aisle stands in retail stores; they can be hanging banners, tags, or other three-dimensional devices that call attention to product specials or store events. They may be complex enough to include moving parts and lighting.

Often the shipping container for a product converts into the display for the product. Because such a display is an important part of the consumer marketing program for its product, it is usually bright and bold graphically.

TRADE-SHOW OR CONVENTION EXHIBITS

Conventions have become a major means of communicating new products and services to a specialized audience. The fields of education, business, science, and manufacturing, for example, conduct periodical meetings during which exhibits survey for attendees, in a short span of time, current new services and products in their areas. Exhibits generally take place in light, somewhat social environments (hotels, convention halls) and can be graphically quite stimulating.

Such environments, however, also comprise complicated design situations: Competition is tight for attention. The displays themselves become the reference material for the exhibitors' representatives or technical experts and sales staff. The information must be exceptionally concise, convincing, and visually compelling.

The graphics usually reflect the corporate identity of the exhibitor as well as their exhibited products. The graphic design problems may include coordinating lighting, audio-visual presentations, photography, illustration, typography, manufacturing demonstrations, entertainment, and a staff in attendance with their accompanying data material, conference area, samples, phones, storage, and so on.

Like packages and point-of-purchase displays, trade exhibits are mostly produced by designers who specialize in this area. Displays can be more permanent—for example, in museums, where special exhibits may last weeks, months, or even be permanently installed. Corporations also may develop exhibit areas in their lobbies or in specially constructed facilities at their headquarters to graphically explain their processes or history.

Electronic Media and Film

TELEVISION

Commercials originate with concepts visualized on paper in a story-board format, which resembles a comic strip. Then follow the numerous details of producing the commercial, which includes the supervision of a design staff. The skills needed for such productions

(a)

(b)

Figure 4.16
A trade show is an exciting, competitive event of which the display exhibits are an integral part. Designing exhibits requires many design skills as well as a good feeling for actual space. Also, the salespeople themselves must always fit into the design display structure. Exhibits are expensive to construct, even if they are as simple as the OCTOPUS example (b) shown here, which was designed by Malcolm Grear. *Malcolm Grear Designers, Inc.*

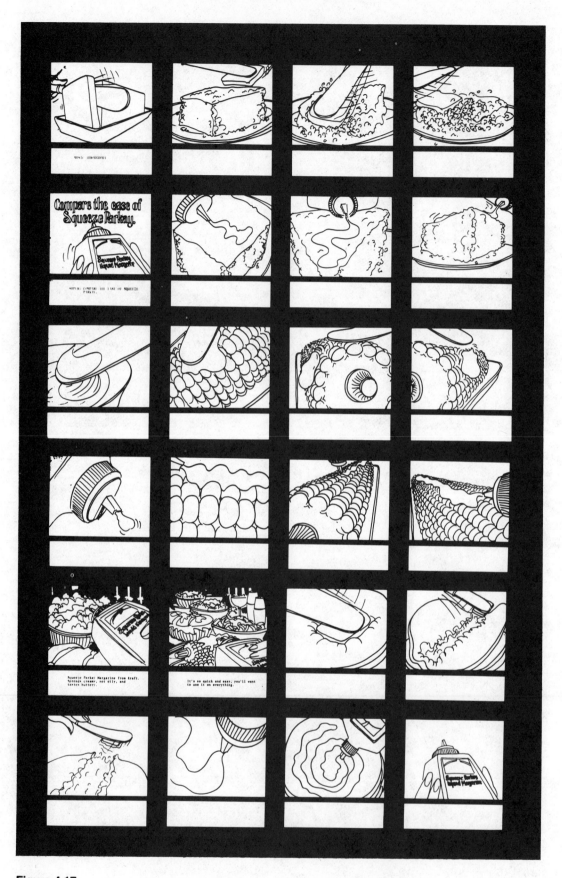

Figure 4.17
TV story boards, which highlight the proposed action, have much of the look of comic strips or sketches of a metamorphosis, and the design problems they face are similar. Story boards for TV are probably the most complex of all graphics to create, because they need to convincingly represent movement, sound, and time.
Gene Hoefel, Art Director.

reach beyond layout and typography. A designer in TV must have the ability to design and think sequentially, a feeling for sound, movement, timing, and drama, plus general graphic-design skills. The ability to conceptualize, however, is more important than sketching perfection.

Filmmaking and audio-visual presentations require similar experience. These are growing media that offer wide opportunities for the graphic designer. Computer-generated graphics are also related to the new developments in video and film.

The function of the designer in TV is not always obvious, but all video producers and stations use graphics for special presentations and on-air identification, and to produce their promotional print material.

Corporate Identity

Larger companies or institutions coordinate their graphic material with a master plan: The design of the business cards, the name on products, and even the company airplane are potential bearers of graphic de-

tails. The design problem is not only to create the logo itself, but also to consider where and how it will be applied. The typography and color of every aspect must also be planned. This is a lengthy, expensive process because the basic plans are usually used for many years. Because of this, the identity program must be flexible enough so it can apply to future unknown forms and uses. Frequently, the decided-on program is presented in a Graphic Standards Manual to the company personnel. Sometimes a logo is so complex that it needs to be adapted to subdivisions or additional sections of a corporation.

Diverse Applications

Graphic design is applied in a diverse spectrum of occupations and media that do not fit easily into simple definitions and categories. By considering such products as calendars, greeting cards, t-shirts, party favors, novelties, labels, tags, bags, buttons, coupons, menus, match covers, bumper stickers, toys, and games, you can see that creative opportunities for graphic designers are indeed extensive and varied.

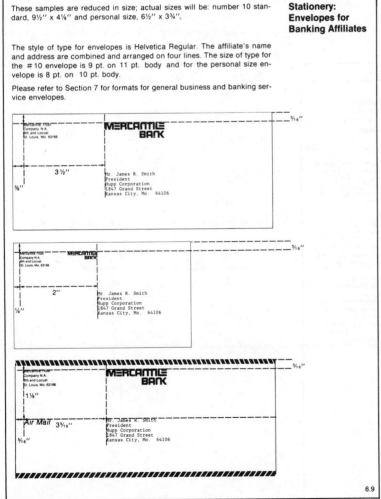

These samples are reduced in size; actual sizes will be: number 10 standard, 9½″ x 4⅛″ and personal size, 6½″ x 3¾″.

The style of type for envelopes is Helvetica Regular. The affiliate's name and address are combined and arranged on four lines. The size of type for the #10 envelope is 9 pt. on 11 pt. body and for the personal size envelope is 8 pt. on 10 pt. body.

Please refer to Section 7 for formats for general business and banking service envelopes.

**Stationery:
Envelopes for
Banking Affiliates**

Figure 4.18
These examples from a Graphic Standards Manual show extensive directions and measurements accompanying the graphics. Because the range of people referring to such a manual is potentially very wide, the instructions must be clear and concise. *Logo design: Lippincott & Margulis. Graphic Standards Manual: Obata Design.*

Figure 4.18 (continued)

This sample is reduced in size; the actual letterhead is 8½" x 11".

The style of type for letterheads is Helvetica Regular. The affiliate name is arranged in caps and lower case in three lines, as is the corresponding address and telephone number and the size of type is 9 pt. on 11 pt. body. The address block is centered between the affiliate name and logotype as illustrated on the sample letterheads in this section.

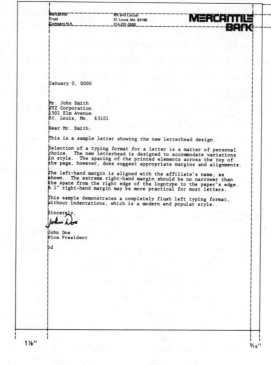

The letterheads are designed to accommodate variations in individual style of typing format. The left-hand margin is aligned with the legal name as indicated. Very short letters may require a margin adjustment.

Carbon Duplicate Sheets:
The standard size letterhead can be printed on tissue for carbon duplicate sheets.

Second Sheets:
A letterhead sheet with only the logotype as positioned and printed in this sample should be provided for correspondence that requires a second page.

6.2

The directional system shown is compatible with the high-visibility signage. System drawings are available for directional signage and detail construction features, lighted and unlighted versions and recommended wording for a variety of site situations.

**Signage:
External
Directional
System**

The directional signage system is a post and panel design. The signs may vary in size, height, and may be double post or single post.

The construction is fabricated aluminum. The finish is baked enamel. The color is Mercantile Blue, Pantone # 286 for the panels and matte black for the posts.

All lettering is white and is Helvetica Medium.

The panels may be non-illuminated with silk screened lettering or internally illuminated with routed, plastic backed letters.

9.4

110

Figure 4·18 (continued)

Accurate logotype reproduction sheets are included in the appendix of this manual. To insure quality in reproduction, these authorized copies should be used for all original art work. Should a size be required which is between two on the sheet, you should reduce photostatically from the larger size. Do not photostatically enlarge the logotype or use previously printed ones. Do not rephotostat a copy because each generation will cause variations and loss of sharpness.

The design is effective when used quite small or very large. However, the logic of good communication and the technical limitations of printing suggest that the logotype not be used smaller than one half inch wide.

It is unnecessary to impose a maximum size limit. A grid scale to insure accurate reproduction for unusually large size logos, such as required for signage, is provided in this manual.

MERCANTILE BANK

MERCANTILE BANK

MERCANTILE BANK

MERCANTILE BANK

½

It is incorrect to use Mercantile Bank logotype smaller than one-half (½) inch wide.

2.1

Figure 4.19
Environmental graphics, such as banners, flags, and wall graphics, have brought design into the public area more as an art form than as pure advertising. Such graphics are widely accepted and add to the visual excitement of any city.

111

PRODUCTION

5

of production and its supervision are an extension of the creative process, and form the basis for the construction of the resulting product. Production techniques are the designer's tools and implements as much as are pencils, brushes, and markers.

Printing production includes decisions about layout, illustration, typesetting, photography, retouching, lettering, printing, paper, inks, binding, and die cutting, among others. The more you learn of the production stages, the more design options you will have available.

The preparation of materials for reproduction or construction of most graphic work is surprisingly similar, although the manufacturing processes will differ. Once you understand the basic skills, you can adjust them to whatever special requirements may occur. If you can assemble and produce material for brochures, you can learn to adapt the same skills to specify the plans for a corporate signage system or package. The "feel" for applying color, scale, shape, and form has universal value but the most necessary ingredient is a creative, open-minded, investigative attitude.

For greatest impact, most of the production information in this book has been reduced to the essentials. Although not comprehensive, the following data, specifications, and terminology are universal and dependable. They should give the beginning designer enough latitude to produce capable, effective graphic works even with modest budgets and when using limited resources.

Production Responsibilities

Production is the process that transforms a graphic concept into a reproducible or tangible product. Basic production skills and knowledge are expected from all designers at entry-level positions. Later, when the creative responsibilities of the designer or art director are more demanding, much of the production detail is provided by other staff members who specialize in this area. The execution of the production steps, however, is always subject to the designer's standards. The mechanics

Layout Method

For printed matter, designers first develop thumbnail sketches—roughs or comprehensive layouts. Once these are approved, the subsequent mechanical steps are carried out in coordination with other skilled graphic-industry specialists. (See Figure 2.3.) Copy, text, and headlines are written, typed, and typeset. Photographs, drawings, and diagrams are executed; paper and printers are selected. A production schedule is planned and followed. The assembly steps probably occur as shown. (See box)

When sketching rough layouts, designers draw the larger type in pencil, marker, or pen ensuring that the style, size and weights are clear: Large type must be legible. They then rough in body copy or small type with graphic "shorthand" techniques that indicate the area, general size, and heading weights or "color."

At this stage, photographs, charts, and illustrations are also sketched in actual size and approximate color or value with enough detail to generally represent the image. In many instances, especially for packaging or book jackets, the design is not roughed in but is carefully rendered so that it looks remarkably close to a finished product. This is called a "comp" or comprehensive ren-

---

STEPS FOR A SIMPLE PRINTING PROJECT

1. Meet client (take notes):
   Outline the *purpose* of the piece: For whom? To do what?
   Study copy (typed).
   Determine the size, format (folded or unfolded), need for envelopes.
   Decide quantity. Budget.
   Decide colors: one, two?
   Assess need for drawings, photos from other sources.
   Compare samples of previous pieces.
   Choose date for mailing or distribution (check mailing regulations).
2. Make rough layouts or dummy.
3. Consider cost (estimates) for:
   Design and production time;
   Paper (and its availability);
   Printing (and schedule);
   Type (and schedule);
   Photostats;
   Photos, illustrations;
   Art supplies (for layout and paste-up).
4. Get purchase order.
5. Get client approval of design, production estimates.
6. Redesign to new specifications if cost is too high.
7. Produce mechanical art.
8. Check proofs and press samples.
9. Bill client. Keep track of *all* expenses and time records.
10. Save samples and file all other notes, roughs, and so on.

PRODUCTION OF PRINTED MATTER

(advertising, brochures, catalogs, stationery)

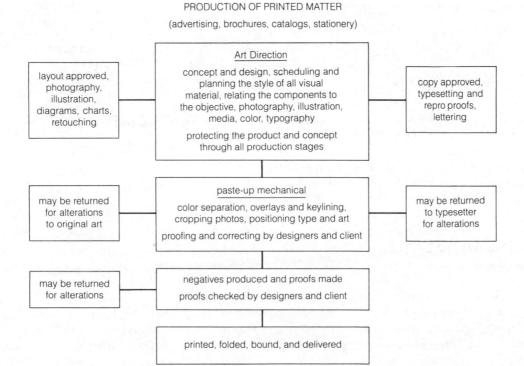

Figure 5.1
Copy lines can be ruled with a pencil or marker. The illustration here shows the most common techniques for doing this. Type larger than 14 point is usually roughed in with words, often using gray markers. Sheets of fake "Greek" press type are also available; applying pressure transfers the letters from the sheets to the rough. Some designers also use copy from clippings and stat this into layout position.

dering. All designers require much practice to acquire reasonable professional-quality rough and comp techniques. Some artists specialize in this work, but all beginners can expect to use these skills during the first steps in their design careers.

Printing Processes

A common design opportunity is to produce some type of letterhead, logo, flyer, poster, or brochure. Most printing of these products today is done by the offset-lithography process. Other techniques that are useful, especially for printing small quantities, utilize office copiers and screen-process (silk-screen) methods.

OFFICE COPIERS

Experimental work or trial layouts can be tested with fair success on a good office copier or on a copier at a "quick-printing" service. If the copier will accept alternate paper, then consider using colored paper to add an interesting contrast.

Office copiers can duplicate on an 8½″ × 11″ (letter-size) or 8½″ × 14″ (legal-size) sheet. A few can also copy on an 11″ × 17″ sheet and might have some reduction capacity. If your actual size paste-up is fairly clean, you can successfully produce a very low-cost brochure, small poster, or letterhead using both sides of the sheet and a colored paper in an office copier. Photographs do reproduce somewhat, but they often appear "filled in," resulting in a loss of detail. Frequently, however, this is a design fringe benefit because of the strong

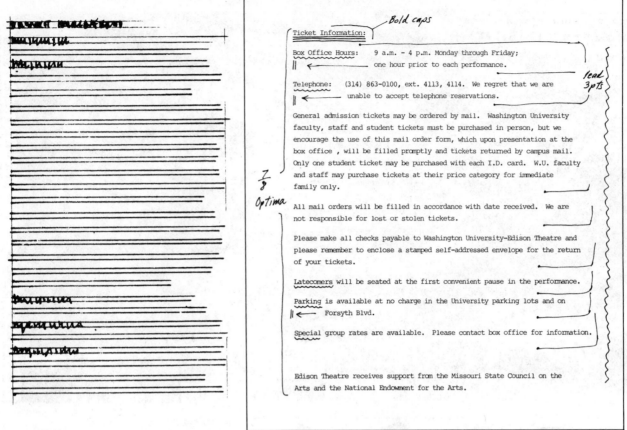

Figure 5.2a
Type can also be set to follow the layout. Specs on the original copy are more specific.

Figure 5.2b
This example includes the original copy to show the specifications.

simplified image that emerges: Most copiers do not reproduce large areas of solid black very well. But the feel of printing will result and anyone can be a publisher with a product ready for quick evaluation for only a few cents per copy. Office copiers are also very useful for producing inexpensive, rough layout sheets.

BLUEPRINTING

The blueprint process has great limitations for general printing. Blueprinting is mostly used by architects and engineers to duplicate drawings, but large posters can be produced in very small quantities, for a relatively low cost, using this technique. Blueprints today are usually not blue, but black, and they are thus called "black-line" prints. To make one, you draw on either a very translucent sheet of tracing paper with solid black ink or marker or on acetate. Because this is a positive process, to get black you draw in black.

You can enlarge any paste-up into a film for printing. You can also use the process as a means of duplicating large line illustrations or layouts.

SCREEN-PROCESS METHOD

The screen-process method is excellent to use to print large sizes, large areas of color, and small quantities. The results are best on relatively smooth paper.

Because photographs are reproduced with large dot screens that result in a lack of detail, it is best to avoid reproducing them using this method. The design options, fine detailing and registration accuracy, will depend on the skills and equipment capacity of the particular printer doing a job.

Mechanical art for photographic screen process is prepared similarly to that for offset printing. If the mechanical is produced on an acetate surface, actual size, it can be used as a film positive, but any white proof paper left on the acetate will hold back the light when the screen is exposed. This will result in ink appearing where the paper was placed because the screen would be open here.

Screen process is also used in conjunction with offset printing when a light color must be printed on a dark paper. It is the only method available for printing a pure white on a colored paper. The process is used extensively in the sign industry.

"QUICK-PRINTING" SERVICES

At their best, quick-printing services use offset presses that actually operate on the same principle as larger presses. The difference is that they have more quality and size limitations because of their simplicity. They are very reasonable to maintain, set up, and operate without extensive training. Their advantage is low

115

Figure 5.3
Inexpensive announcements can be
produced fast and distributed at little cost
using the collage technique and an office
copier. An immediate and honest expression
can result, in spite of the limitations of this
process. The examples shown here express
spontaneity and informality.

*Design: Samia A. Halaby and Kevin Hylton. "On
Trial: Yale School of Art."*

Figure 5.4
This poster, whose finished size was 17″ × 22″, was "blueprinted" from a film produced from a paste-up. Such prints fade eventually, but if kept from strong light they can remain stable for a long period of time.

cost, speed, and wide availability; the plates are made quickly and inexpensively with paper and plastic. The artwork must be actual size and everything must be pasted on one surface, with no overlays. Halftones must be prescreened and positioned. They can reproduce reasonably well if the screen is not too fine and appropriate care and skill are used.

Practical sizes for quick printing are 8½″ × 11″ and 8½″ × 14″. Some of these presses can also print up to 11″ × 17″. Most offset and bond papers, in a variety of textures and weights, are acceptable stock. Unlike office copiers, quick-printing presses can vary the ink colors but each color requires extra press-cleaning charges. Some equipment cannot successfully print large areas of color. Coated (enamel or glossy) papers may not work well either. Investigate the capacity of the particular printer at hand before planning a design. Using special colors, papers, and photos all add time and cost to the work, so plan ahead by understanding the limitations.

OFFSET PRINTING

Offset printing offers the designer the most extensive range of sizes, detail, quality, colors, and so on. The printers (or lithographers) are able to reproduce everything from stationery and business cards to full-color magazines and books. The limitations are mostly time and budget. Mechanical art can be complex, comprising several overlays and requiring special instructions to the printer about positioning of photos, reductions, reverses, tints, and the like.

Proofs, which show the location of all design elements for a particular product in actual size, are available in offset printing. In most work proofs are not made from plates which are used on the press for printing, but from the negatives, which are made by photographing the paste-up. Proofs are very economical; they are thus used to make a dummy, or mock-up of a design.

Figure 5.5
This 8½″ × 14″ folder was assembled from office-copier clippings from old book illustrations. By including borders and decorative initials with a small amount of type and printing on a colored paper, a modest but unique piece of community publicity was produced.

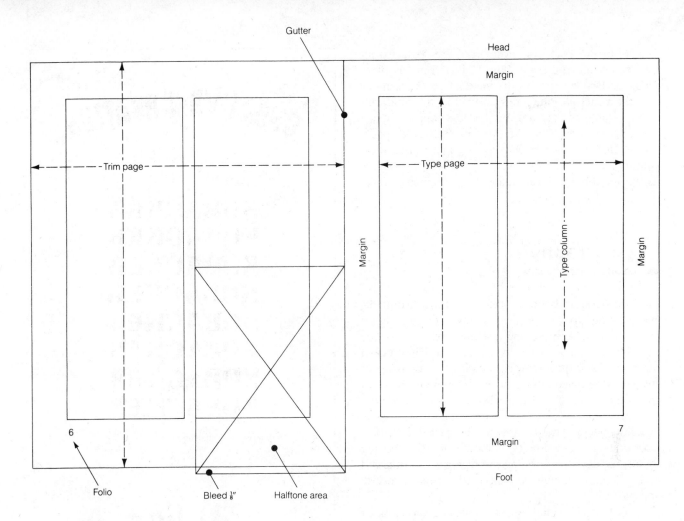

Figure 5.6a
This is a typical example of the organization of a two-page spread in a brochure.

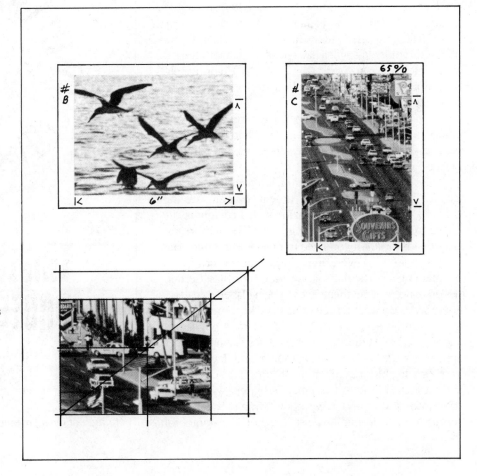

Figure 5.6b
Photo sizes are marked at the edges of the prints. If the print is valuable, the marks can be made on a tissue overlay. Be sure to key the photos to the layout for quick identification. You can indicate the percentage of enlargement or reduction instead of the actual dimension. A diagonal line through the desired layout size can quickly allow proportional accuracy when cropping.

A "brown print" or silver proof is a contact print on a blueprint-type paper. Proofs also come as blueprints or Dialux. The brown material provides more contrast, which is sometimes preferable; the blueprint is more stable and accurate but has less contrast, hence less apparent detail. Color-Key® is a more complex proof because it is in color. Each color is contact printed on a film with a transparent dye. When layered, the films show everything in location and in approximate color.

Typography

Typography is the process of setting, arranging, and printing type. Today type is almost universally set by photographic typesetting machines, which have the capacity to enlarge or reduce a "font" or full alphabet extensively and thus allow extremely tight control over spacing. Most machines can set from 6-point to 36-point type; others can set as large as 72-point type. When the layout requires large sizes (36-point type plus) a special headline machine can be used to photographically produce one letter at a time from about $\frac{1}{4}''$ to $1\frac{1}{2}''$ in height. By further photo processing the type can be enlarged to any dimension, outlined, shadowed, repeated, curved, and more.

Type is described by style name and variations of size and weight. Some common styles are Roman, Gothic, Square, and Script. With the advent of photo- and computer-designing processes, variations of styles have proliferated rapidly. All styles have product names—for example, Helios, Avant Garde, Cairo, Palatino. Unfortunately, several identical styles are called different names by different manufacturers.

Designing with type depends on very careful attention to detail. (See Figures 4.10, 5.9 and 5.16.) Good concepts with equally good design layout can fall apart because of weak typography.

Typography, like illustration, is affected by stylistic trends. This is especially noticeable if you compare the contents of a 10-year-old magazine with a current issue. These trends can be interesting to analyze and are especially important if you need to produce an up-to-date look. Beware, however, of the hazard of acquiring and maintaining a particular stylistic pattern or bias: Certain design concepts lend themselves to being labeled "dated." Some styles do weather the trends and become "classic" in a common sense. Types such as Garamond, Times Roman, Caslon, Futura, and Helvetica, for example, never appear to wear out but remain popular and dependable. They are legible, readily available in many variations, and have stood the test of time. Designers with imagination can always find new ways to arrange them. Conservatism in choosing a type style is not a guarantee of

Curved

Step and repeat, with weight changes

Full circle

Perspective

Figure 5.7a
There are very few limitations to the phototype process.

ABCDEFGHIJKLMN
Inline

AABCCCDDEEEFFF
Outline

ABCDEFGHI
Drop Shadow

ABCDEFGHIJKL
Shadow

AABCDEFGHIJKLLM
Open Shadow

AAABBCDDEEF
Swash

ABCDEFGHIJ
Decorative

Figure 5.7b
Some styles are difficult to read if the statement is long. These variations can be useful for logos or product names.

quality, but it is a safe policy to first acquire experience in legible, straightforward typography and use of good functional type styles before attempting more daring variations. Notice that some older layouts still hold up very well alongside contemporary work.

Because there are thousands of styles of alphabets and type available, inexperienced designers can understandably be confused with the seemingly unlimited choices. A good method to begin with is to select one readily available style that comes in several variations: light, medium, bold, italics, and so on. Then solve typographical problems by relying on variations of size, space, weights, and color contrast. (See Figure 5.16.) Soon the possibilities within one style will not seem as limited, and you will begin to "think" in type somewhat like a musical composer who senses the structure of a score mentally or "hears" the notes. Eventually you can introduce other styles and develop unique combinations among them for particular applications.

There are many photo-typesetting processes. It is best to ask about the capabilities of the machines at the type source before deciding on a particular typesetter. Much of the quality of a typesetting product remains dependent on the skill of the operator and on the quality control of the firm.

A manuscript to be typeset is first marked with standard specification terms that translate into style, size, length of lines, leading, and spacing. What may seem like a simple block of copy requires a surprising number of directions. The designer can either give rather tight layout instructions to the typesetters, or the designer can simply specify the style and size and let the typesetters interpret the space and weights as best as they can. In the latter case, the designer can make adjustments later by altering the proofs. However, not all typesetters use terms or codes in the same manner; also, ambiguity can result due to inexperience or carelessness. Clarify your markings with the typesetter before

121

Light

Medium (also called "regular")

Bold

Extra Bold

Condensed

Italics (all the above come with italics)

Abcdefghijklm
Abcdefghijklm
Abcdefghijklm
ABCDEFGHIJKLM
ABCDEFGHIJKLM
ABCDEFGHIJKLM

base to base

Helvetica
Helios
Claro
Megaron

same style,
different names

ABCDEFG | abcdefg

body of lower case
or lower case x height

type size in points

Figure 5.8
Many of the terms we use in typography today are holdovers from the days of metal type.

Figure 5.9
This spread from *Parade Magazine* relies heavily on typography. The photographs are not exceptional, but within the lively variety of initial caps, subheadings, rules, and white space, they take their place in a well-balanced layout. Not only is the visual activity of the type attractive, but it also invites easy reading. *Art Directors and Designers: Ira Yoffe and Christopher Austopchuk.*

Young Olympians must give their all for what they get

The Price of Being The Best
BY BUD GREENSPAN

BEFORE Willie Banks starts his dash down the triple-jump runway, he smiles broadly and waves to the crowd. Then he begins a rhythmic dance to his own finger-snapping cadence that is quickly picked up by the spectators in the stands. Soon, throughout the stadium, a roaring chant falls in sync with Willie's finger-snapping dance.

With the roaring crowd, Banks' body seems to electrify, much like the fiery burn before a spaceship takeoff.

When his emotional and physical pitch reach takeoff time, Willie's face loses its smile and is transfixed as he concentrates on the runway. Then he roars off with a sprinter's speed and a pole-vaulter's power. On landing, it is evident that Banks is one of the strongest contenders in an event that has not been won by an American since the St. Louis Olympic Games of 1904.

Banks, 27, is one of the world's best triple-jumpers and, barring injury, is certain to make the 1984 United States Olympic team. He is one of three of the nation's brightest hopes for the 1984 Olympics interviewed by PARADE. All are reaching for gold medals after years of stringent personal and financial sacrifices in countries where their training is government-subsidized.

A high price is paid by U.S. athletes who strive for Olympic gold medals—to be recognized as the best there is. Most of us would deem the price too high, yet they are willing to pay it.

Banks was one of the favorites to win a medal at the 1980 Moscow Olympics, but the United States boycott kept him out of the competition.

The most noteworthy item at Moscow in the triple-jump competition (formerly called the "hop, step and jump") was the fact that 35-year-old Viktor Saneyev of the Soviet Union was attempting to win his fourth successive gold medal in the event. He set the Olympic record of 57 feet, 3/4 inch in 1968 but had to settle for the silver medal at Moscow when he was beaten by a Soviet teammate. But the fact that Saneyev, with government subsidization, was still competing as an "old man accentuates the plight of Willie Banks, 11 years his junior and faced with the prospect of earning a living.

One year after the Moscow Games, Banks was ranked first in the world, but then, with the educational and financial constraints that were placed upon him, he dropped from his premier ranking.

Banks was a second-year law student pressured with finding enough time somewhere in the day to train without losing ground in school. His grueling daily schedule went something like this: 8 a.m., breakfast; 9 a.m.-3 p.m., law school (including lunch); 3-6 p.m., track training; 6-7 p.m., dinner; 7-11 p.m., library study; 11 p.m., sleep.

But the worst soon will be over for Willie Banks.

"I finish law school this summer, and those other people better look out!" he says. "Last year was a mess for me because I couldn't train properly. But I'll have a whole year of preparation before the 1984 Los Angeles Games."

Banks has the third-longest triple-jump in history with his U.S. record of 57 feet, 7½ inches, but his athletic ability provides only half the excitement. In competition, Banks creates his own dramatic atmosphere that, win or lose, is certain to make him a worldwide television personality. He brings glamour to an event that formerly had as much excitement as the 35-pound weight throw.

A second U.S. contender is 27-year-old American super heavyweight boxer Tyrell Biggs. Biggs has fewer problems than most U.S. Olympic hopefuls.

The 6-foot-4, 218-pound athlete has decided to postpone a professional boxing career in the hope that he will gain greater glory by following in the paths of Floyd Patterson, Muhammad Ali and Joe Frazier, Olympic gold medal-winners who went on to the professional world heavyweight championship.

Last summer, Biggs was riding high after winning the world super heavy-weight amateur championship in Munich, Montreal and Moscow. His loss to Damiani heralded a new era, and Biggs became the logical contender for the throne.

However, in a dual matchup a few months later between Cuban and U.S. teams, Stevenson knocked out Biggs. The aging but still powerful Stevenson let it be known that he still yearns to become the only man in history to win four Olympic gold medals in boxing.

Biggs, however, is convinced that his loss to Stevenson was a fluke. He is one of the few U.S. Olympic hopefuls whose goal seems unmarred by financial, social and emotional obligations. As a boxer, Biggs' training is subsidized by the United States Olympic Committee, and when he's not involved with competition around the world, he can be found either at the Olympic training center in Colorado Springs or at Joe Frazier's gymnasium in Philadelphia. His dedication to training is absolute, and he has all but given up his friends until after the Los Angeles Games.

His father, James Biggs, a former fighter, sums up the family attitude: "When you fight, all your friends will be watching you, but it will be you who's in the ring."

The preparation and the sacrifices required of aspiring Olympians are made day in and day out, year in and year out. The discipline is monumental, ever-present and sometimes oppressive.

"I guess most American teens would feel my life isn't much fun," says 17-year-old Julianne McNamara, who is one of our country's best hopes in the women's gymnastic competition at the 1984 Los Angeles Games, "but I have my whole life in front of me to enjoy those things I miss now."

Her incentive is great: If victorious, she will become the first U.S. athlete ever to win an Olympic gold medal for women's gymnastics.

McNamara is enthusiastic when she talks about her daily schedule, which most U.S. teenagers would regard as cruel and unusual punishment. For example, in order to get the daily training she needs, McNamara has had to live apart from her own family for three and a half years. Although her family lived in Danville, Calif., near Sacramento, she spent three years in Eugene, Ore., training with Dick Mulvihill of the National Academy of Artistic Gymnastics. Most recently, she lived in Huntington Beach, Calif., with Claudia and Richard McGann and their daughter Allison, who is also a gymnast, to train daily with the Southern California Acro team, her sponsor. McNamara's daily training schedule, her 15 competitions a year—and a tight budget—allowed for only Christmas visits and two weeks each summer with her family.

"I missed my parents a lot," says McNamara. "I'd call them and write them every day."

Her mother since has taken an apartment in Huntington Beach, and her father plans to commute from Danville on weekends to see them. McNamara trains each day after she finishes at Marina High School in Huntington Beach. She's in her senior year and has maintained a straight-A average despite having attended three high schools in four years.

"I go to school in the morning, then I train from l p.m. to 6 p.m., Monday through Friday," McNamara says. "I'm so tired at the end of the day that it's difficult to do homework and impossible to have a social life. Boyfriends will have to wait until after the 1984 Olympics."

Why does McNamara do it? Travel is one reward: "I've been to China, Russia, Yugoslavia, Hungary—how many 17-year-olds get to go to all those places? And," she adds, "I consider myself lucky to have a goal, to have friends and coaches committed to me. I believe that the discipline, hard work, organization and goal-orientation that are part of my life now will also help me in my later life. Of course, sometimes I do get depressed—usually when I'm exhausted—that's when I can lose sight of these benefits. But I love what I'm doing, and my sacrifices are shared by all those I compete with, and that always pulls me through."

For more than three decades, women's Olympic gymnastics has been dominated by the Soviet Union and Eastern Bloc countries. At the 1984 Los Angeles Games, this dominance will, for the first time, be challenged by young women from the United States and China.

McNamara will face heavy competition from athletes whose countries fully support them financially and who began training as infants. Says her coach, Don Peters, of the Southern California Acro Team, "Julianne's training is one large, tiring block each day, whereas the East Germans, who go to sports schools, train twice a day for shorter intervals and attend school at the same facility. They have this advantage of coordination of the two programs and support throughout the school.

"It's tough," says McNamara. "Before I became world-class and was able to get some sponsors, my training used to cost my parents between $5000 and $10,000 a year."

American Olympic aspirants are just beginning to get the coaching and financial support given Soviet and East European athletes.

continued

Among the nation's brightest hopes for the 1984 Olympics, also shown on the cover, are (l-r): Tyrell Biggs, boxer; Tom Jager and Tiffany Cohen, swimmers; Florence Griffith, sprinter; Willie Banks, triple-jumper; Peter Vidmar, gymnast; and John Crist, decathlete.

Julianne McNamara, 17, could be the first ever to win the U.S. an Olympic gold medal for women's gymnastics.

Years of hard work— for that one brief moment

Super heavyweight Tyrell Biggs and coach Larry Middleton.

'I have my whole life in front of me to enjoy things I miss now'
—JULIANNE McNAMARA

COVER PHOTOGRAPH BY AARON RAPAPORT

Roman

Caslon
ABCDEFGHIJKLMNOPQRSTUVWXYZ
abcdefghijklmnopqrstuvwxyz

Baskerville
ABCDEFGHIJKLMNOPQRSTUVWXYZ
abcdefghijklmnopqrstuvwxyz

Bodoni
ABCDEFGHIJKLMNOPQRSTUVWXYZ
abcdefghijklmnopqrstuvwxyz

Century
ABCDEFGHIJKLMNOPQRSTUVWXYZ
abcdefghijklmnopqrstuvwxyz

Garamond
ABCDEFGHIJKLMNOPQRSTUVWXYZ
abcdefghijklmnopqrstuvwxyz

Times Roman
ABCDEFGHIJKLMNOPQRSTUVWXYZ
abcdefghijklmnopqrstuvwxyz

Gothic

Avant Garde
ABCDEFGHIJKLMNOPQRSTUVWXYZ
abcdefghijklmnopqrstuvwxyz

Futura
ABCDEFGHIJKLMNOPQRSTUVWXYZ
abcdefghijklmnopqrstuvwxyz

Helvetica
ABCDEFGHIJKLMNOPQRSTUVWXYZ
abcdefghijklmnopqrstuvwxyz

Optima
ABCDEFGHIJKLMNOPQRSTUVWXYZ
abcdefghijklmnopqrstuvwxyz

Square serif

Lubalin Graph
ABCDEFGHIJKLMNOPQRSTUVWXYZ
abcdefghijklmnopqrstuvwxyz

Stymie (light)
ABCDEFGHIJKLMNOPQRSTUVWXYZ
abcdefghijklmnopqrstuvwxyz

Figure 5.10
These styles are readily available and are used often.

It's easy to recognize the latest in adding machines. Just look for the extra set of keys. One set on an adding machine means it's obsolete. Two sets means it's an "addo-x" 2341E. We call it an Automatic Multiplier because it is so much more than an adding machine. It has everything an adding machine has plus fully automatic multiplication. It does percentages in a flash. Invoicing, job costing, inventorying, and many other computations are done as fast as you can push the keys. With all its advanced money-saving features, "addo-x" costs no more than conventional adding machines. Test one, without obligation, alongside your present machines. Call your dealer or write: "addo-x" 300 Park Ave, NY 22

Figure 5.11a
This 1952 ad for Addox, by Ladislav Sutnar, characterized by its opposing diagonal and the use of ample line spacing in the copy, has held up well over the years. *Designer: Ladislav Sutnar.*

Figure 5.11b
This 30-year-old layout for Upjohn by Will Burtin also retains a contemporary energy. *Designer: Will Burtin.*

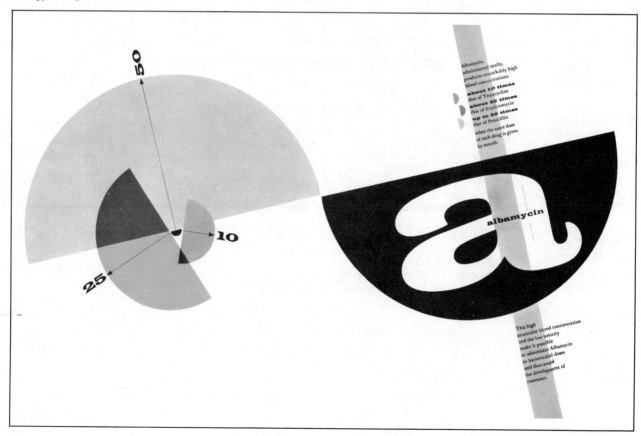

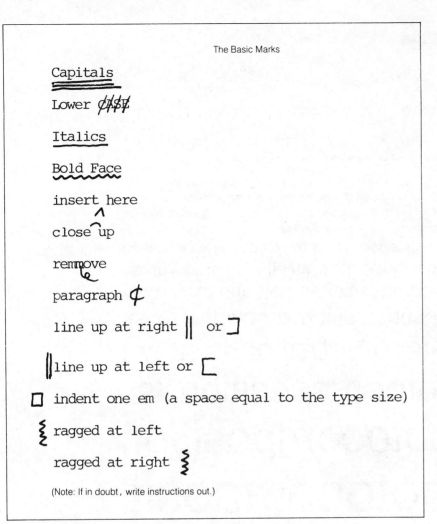

The Basic Marks

Capitals

Lower CASE

Italics

Bold Face

insert here

close up

remove

paragraph ¢

line up at right ‖ or ⌉

‖line up at left or ⌊

☐ indent one em (a space equal to the type size)

ragged at left

ragged at right

(Note: If in doubt, write instructions out.)

Figure 5.12
These are common specification marks. They should be in a color for clarity.

typesetting is done to avoid extra cost and confusion. When marking complex copy, use colored pens (red, blue, or green) to clarify and separate instructions from the copy. The text or body copy is composed in a continuous column of type (galley) with paragraphs, line spaces (leading), and variations of style, size, and weight. If too large for the machine doing the composition, the larger type or headlines will be set one letter at a time by a headline-setting machine. Most equipment requires type sizes to be photographically enlarged or reduced.

The type styles shown in Figure 5.10 are common and accessible. Type variations of a particular style can be regular, italic, condensed, extended, or open, to name a few. The weights can be light, medium, bold, or extra bold. Sizes are based on the *pica* system (12 points equal 1 pica, 72 points equal 1 inch). From 6 to 14 points is considered body copy size (text or composition). Larger sizes are used as headings or headlines. Sizes larger than 72 points (1 inch) are indicated by inches. The spacing and length of lines are indicated by points and picas. The line length is sometimes called the measure. Thickness of bars or rules is measured in points.

Before you specify body copy or text size, you must first convert the typewritten manuscript mathematically to the size of the proposed machine-produced type, to determine how much space to allow and if the manuscript will fit in the predetermined area. There are several methods of doing this. The most common is to multiply the number of characters-per-pica figures, which is furnished for all type sizes by the typesetters or the manufacturers. These figures are usually printed on the type sample sheets.

Fitting the copy to layout areas can also be a simple process of counting and multiplying, if you have a sample of the type available. Just count the number of characters of type in the size required (including spaces and periods) that fit into the line length in your layout. Then count the same number of letter and spaces on a line of your manuscript. Draw a vertical line on the page at this point. Count the copy lines to the left of the vertical line in each paragraph, then add the leftover letters to the right of the vertical line, counting one line when the number of letters equals the proper letter count (character count) for a typeset line. Remember that any last letters that do not equal the number for a line will still comprise a line, although a short one. The total number of lines multiplied by the point size plus the points between the lines (leading) will give you the depth of the manuscript when coverted to type (72 points or 6 picas equal 1 inch).

125

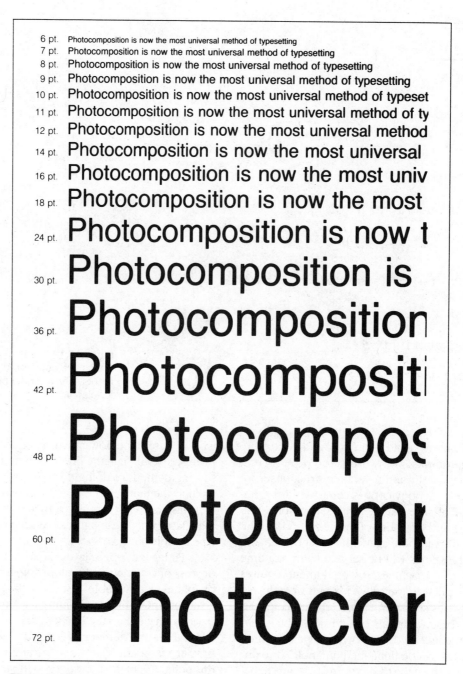

Figure 5.13a
These are traditional sizes from the days of metal type, but the phototypesetting process allows for in-between sizes.

RULES

Hairline

Half pt.

One pt.

One and a half pt.

Two pt.

Two and a half pt.

Three pt.

Four pt.

Five pt.

Six pt.

Seven pt.

Eight pt.

Nine pt.

Ten pt.

Eleven pt.

Twelve pt.

Fourteen pt.

Sixteen pt.

Eighteen pt.

Twenty pt.

Twenty-four pt.

Thirty pt.

Thirty-six pt.

Figure 5.13b
Rules are easy to use in layout since they can be produced by the typesetter.

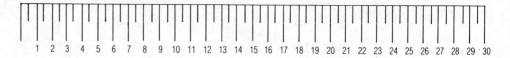

pica scale (12 points)

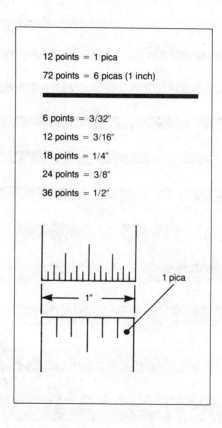

12 points = 1 pica

72 points = 6 picas (1 inch)

6 points = 3/32″

12 points = 3/16″

18 points = 1/4″

24 points = 3/8″

36 points = 1/2″

1 pica

1″

Figure 5.13c
You can improvise a bit with
a ruler if you don't have a
pica scale.

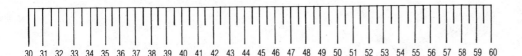

30 31 32 33 34 35 36 37 38 39 40 41 42 43 44 45 46 47 48 49 50 51 52 53 54 55 56 57 58 59 60

Points for vertical measurements   Line Counting Guide

7	8	9	10	11	13	14	15
A		B		C		D	

Slit the opening between the numbers.

A B C D

Figure 5.13d
This Line Counting Guide and Pica Scale can be copied with an office copier. Slit the open areas. When you place the chart over the layout, the numbers in one of the columns should line up with the copy lines. If the copy is leaded, the numbers in the column will include the leading. For example, 8-pt type leaded 2 pts will line up in the 10-pt column. The Pica Scale is used for 12-pt type.

129

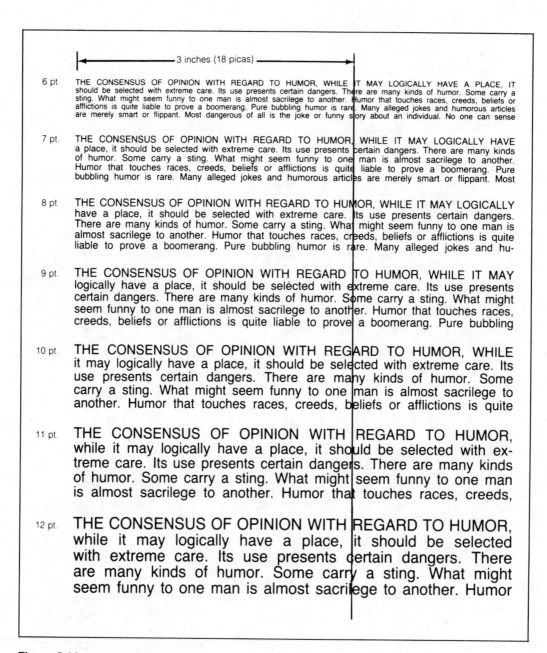

← 3 inches (18 picas) →

6 pt. THE CONSENSUS OF OPINION WITH REGARD TO HUMOR, WHILE IT MAY LOGICALLY HAVE A PLACE, IT should be selected with extreme care. Its use presents certain dangers. There are many kinds of humor. Some carry a sting. What might seem funny to one man is almost sacrilege to another. Humor that touches races, creeds, beliefs or afflictions is quite liable to prove a boomerang. Pure bubbling humor is rare. Many alleged jokes and humorous articles are merely smart or flippant. Most dangerous of all is the joke or funny story about an individual. No one can sense

7 pt. THE CONSENSUS OF OPINION WITH REGARD TO HUMOR, WHILE IT MAY LOGICALLY HAVE a place, it should be selected with extreme care. Its use presents certain dangers. There are many kinds of humor. Some carry a sting. What might seem funny to one man is almost sacrilege to another. Humor that touches races, creeds, beliefs or afflictions is quite liable to prove a boomerang. Pure bubbling humor is rare. Many alleged jokes and humorous articles are merely smart or flippant. Most

8 pt. THE CONSENSUS OF OPINION WITH REGARD TO HUMOR, WHILE IT MAY LOGICALLY have a place, it should be selected with extreme care. Its use presents certain dangers. There are many kinds of humor. Some carry a sting. What might seem funny to one man is almost sacrilege to another. Humor that touches races, creeds, beliefs or afflictions is quite liable to prove a boomerang. Pure bubbling humor is rare. Many alleged jokes and hu-

9 pt. THE CONSENSUS OF OPINION WITH REGARD TO HUMOR, WHILE IT MAY logically have a place, it should be selected with extreme care. Its use presents certain dangers. There are many kinds of humor. Some carry a sting. What might seem funny to one man is almost sacrilege to another. Humor that touches races, creeds, beliefs or afflictions is quite liable to prove a boomerang. Pure bubbling

10 pt. THE CONSENSUS OF OPINION WITH REGARD TO HUMOR, WHILE it may logically have a place, it should be selected with extreme care. Its use presents certain dangers. There are many kinds of humor. Some carry a sting. What might seem funny to one man is almost sacrilege to another. Humor that touches races, creeds, beliefs or afflictions is quite

11 pt. THE CONSENSUS OF OPINION WITH REGARD TO HUMOR, while it may logically have a place, it should be selected with extreme care. Its use presents certain dangers. There are many kinds of humor. Some carry a sting. What might seem funny to one man is almost sacrilege to another. Humor that touches races, creeds,

12 pt. THE CONSENSUS OF OPINION WITH REGARD TO HUMOR, while it may logically have a place, it should be selected with extreme care. Its use presents certain dangers. There are many kinds of humor. Some carry a sting. What might seem funny to one man is almost sacrilege to another. Humor

Figure 5.14
Notice that there are roughly seventy-five letters (characters) in 6-pt type within 3 inches, about fifty-nine in 7 pt, about fifty-six in 8 pt, and about fifty-three in 9 pt. If you use the 9-pt type, the typewritten copy will fit almost in the same number of lines. Paragraph four will possibly fit into five lines, making a total of thirty-three lines of type. If we add 1-pt leading to the type and 6 pts between the paragraphs, we have 33 × 10 pts = 330 pts plus 6 × 6 pts = 36 pts for a total of 366 pts. Because there are 12 pts in a pica and 366 ÷ 12 = 30.5 picas. 6 picas in an inch will make the depth of the copy about 5 3/32".

Figure 5.14 (continued)

← —————————————— 53 characters —————————————— →

By anticipating regulatory changes, Plus Chain
has been able to capitalize on new opportunities   3
through innovative marketing strategies.

The now-famous "Grant" ads (shown at right) distinguished
Plus Chain from its competition and dramatically
increased overall awareness of the Company in its   4
markets.

When regulatory changes shifted emphasis to the
development of new products, Plus Chain was ready,
bringing these products to the marketplace first   5
and supporting them with creative advertising,
public relations and sales efforts.

The Plus Chain 50 Plus Club is typical of one
of the marketing strategies developed to attract
a specific target group. Seminars, travel opportunities,
merchandise discounts and personalized service have
made 50 Plus the largest senior citizen program of   5
its kind.

A series of television ads featuring Joe Roberts
(shown at right), President of Plus Chain Caldwell
Bank, N.A., offered clear and concise introductions   4
of many new consumer products.

In the series, Plus Chain became one of the first
financial institutions to take a mass market, retail
approach to Money Market Certificates of Deposit.
Reaching a broader audience and alerting it to   6
weekly fluctuations in interest rates created one
of the most successful campaigns in company history.

The tradition of reaching the marketplace first with
unique products continued in 1983 when Plus Chain
became the first major bank in Illinois to introduce   6
the exclusive Visa Gold Card. Customer response to
this prestigious card has been enthusiastic and
continues to grow.

_____

33 lines

If all you have is a word count, use an average of seven letters per word (which includes the space between words) to estimate original copy length. The most common design problem is miscalculating and having too much copy for the space. If in doubt, when the fit seems close, it is better to figure on the cautious side. There can be a 15 percent variable in type counting, even when using the best methods of estimating, so taking chances with extra tight specifications can result in serious oversetting and cost/time loss. To avoid problems resulting from poor character-count estimates, try to design layouts that are flexible. Also, if you are not confident about measuring, spend a few minutes with the typesetter to clarify your confusion.

Designing with type is mostly a matter of spacing and sizing as well as selecting styles, but you should always keep legibility in mind. Occasionally, it might be appropriate to sacrifice legibility a bit for special headlines, titles, or unique logos. Be careful, however, not to create difficulty in reading columns of copy or text or you will lose readers (and clients, too, maybe). Legibility can be a problem: when lines are set too long for the point size (research on legibility indicates that the maximum should be 10 words or about 55 characters per line; when the type is too small or too large; when the type is reversed in large quantity; when the type is printed in a light color or with minimal value contrast. Of course, bad printing, poor repro proofs, or careless paste-up can also affect clarity.

Helvetica, which is widely available, has become almost a universal style of our times; some designers feel it is overused. However, it is a good basic style, it is legible, its letters are comparatively large, it comes in many weights and variations, and it is relatively easy to draw or sketch in layouts. Also, Helvetica is available in extra light, regular, medium, bold, extra bold, italics, condensed, extended, and outlined variations.

A typewriter can produce a surprisingly useful type product with considerable savings in cost. Letters typed on a good electric typewriter are quite clear, even reduced about 25 percent on an office copier. The "immediacy" of a typewriter's face also makes it look especially informal and personal. Results can be excellent, too, if you combine typewriter with pressure type. Some well known designers, such as Paul Rand and Saul Bass, have used the typewriter with memorable results.

Figure 5.15
The typography in this Free Press ad is integrated with drawings and photos which partially cover the words. But in a repeat like this or when there are enough letters open to read, total legibility really is not a big problem.
Dave Munch, Promotion Manager.

We're a brand new, brand name way to shop.
You can jump for joy at the savings, breathe a sigh of relief, shop with a smile for names you can trust, and give a gift that's bigger and better and still pay less. Because at Outlet Square the savings are big, the names are famous and 98% of the fashions and home furnishings are first quality. And the few seconds you'll find are clearly marked.

The Outlets in Outlet Square save you money not by offering you last year's looks, but by buying better, selling bigger volume and using every clean modern inch efficiently. There's a simple, contemporary look to the whole place. Not luxurious, but pure pleasure to shop in. We're a brand new concept in shopping and that gives you a brand name way to save.

That's what shopping in the '80's is all about.

Jewelers Outlet
Diamonds up to half price less! 14 karat gold chains, earrings, bracelets, rings. All up to half price off! Men's and ladies' watches at enormous savings. Classic and contemporary designs. Major investments at major savings.

Dansk Factory Outlet
Save 58% on Kobenstyle 2 qt. casserole with lid. Save 50% on Gustave bar glasses, highball and lowball. Save 69% on classic china, a 4-piece placesetting with a platinum or gold band. And more from one of the world's best-known names in dinnerware.

Burlington Coat Factory Warehouse
The #1 factory outlet in the whole U.S.A. with clothes for the whole family from the top manufacturers. Save 30% to 60% on kids' clothes, men's slacks, suits and sport coats, dress and sport shirts. Women's blazers, skirts, pants, suits, dresses, sweaters. Winter coats for everyone. Even fun furs and jeans. Big savings on the best things for your whole family.

Linens 'N Things
Beautiful things for bed, bath, closet and your table. All the finest makers of linens are stocked here with prints and solid sheets, towels, blankets, bed spreads and lush comforters. Placemats and table cloths for the formal or casual table. And a vast array of bath-room accessories, soaps, closet organizers. Top designers' designs to dress up your home for less.

Plumm's
A store for career-minded misses' sizes to dress for success in designer fashions at outrageous savings. Velour lounging suits, classic suits and separates, luxurious accessories, finest costume jewelry, splendid belts and scarves with designer names. This place is a real plum.

Crystal & Glass Outlet
A gleaming paradise of exquisite things at down-to-earth prices. The finest manufacturers of leaded crystal and glassware are represented here in beautiful gifts, cut crystal and brass lamps, sparkling serving pieces for your holiday table. Save also on silk flowers, brass things, wicker ware, picture frames, oriental rugs, porcelain figurines, decorative candles.

Hit Or Miss
High fashion from the big names. The very latest in junior and misses' skirts, slacks, designer jeans, tops of all kinds. Country tweeds or metallic leathers. This store has the latest and best. Save on hosiery, jewelry and perfume sets too.

Burlington Shoes and Handbags
Famous brand leather shoes from Europe and America. Soft, supple leather handbags, all styles', all sizes. Casual shoes, running shoes, strappy heels, smart pumps for daywear, glittery designer shoes for dinner and evening wear. Plus big savings on the finest leather accessories to have and to give.

Off The Rax
Wool slacks in this-minute colors, suits, tops, skirts, blazers, the very latest designs from the very famous manufacturers that you read about in magazines. All for the junior and misses sizes with an eye for fashion and an eye for saving. Hosiery and accessories too.

Relax with a snack
Spend the day at Outlet Square. Come often, stay long. We change all the time. And while you're saving, take a break at one of the 4 quick and casual places to eat. Then, refreshed and renewed, resume your saving.

Opening Thursday, October 15th

East Independence Boulevard & Kings Drive. Hours: Monday-Saturday 10:00 AM to 9:00 PM; Sunday 1:00 to 6:00 PM

Figure 5.16
This ad, for the Rouse Company in Boston uses Helvetica, a typeface with many variations. The designer gets right to the point with informality and clarity, while using up much of the available space. This example shows clearly that good copy and layout can be reinforced by basic, simple typography. *Art Director: Rick Horton.*

Figure 5.17
The layouts for the American Institute of Graphic Arts (a) and the Graphic Artists Guild Newsletter (b) look clean and ordered and not cheapened by typewriter type. (c) Paul Rand also uses typewriter type masterfully in this 1942 brochure. (d) The Simplicity ad, also an older example, even includes rubber stamps in a fresh, informal concept. (e) The Hunter College poster shows the maximum punch that is possible with very expedient materials.

aiganewsletter

THE AMERICAN INSTITUTE OF GRAPHIC ARTS 1059 THIRD AVENUE, NEW YORK CITY 10021 VOLUME TWO, NO 1 APRIL 1979
AIGA IS A NATIONAL NON-PROFIT MEMBERSHIP ORGANIZATION, FOUNDED IN 1914, WHICH PROMOTES EXCELLENCE IN GRAPHIC DESIGN

Sixtieth AIGA Medalist to be Chosen

The AIGA Medalist is chosen each year, subject to approval by the Board of Directors, by a small committee whose duty it is to consider which persons among the leaders in each segment of Institute activity or interest are worthy of receiving the award. Nominees, whose names are submitted by members (see form enclosed for members in this issue), are considered for their long-term contributions to graphics.

This year, the AIGA celebrates its sixtieth year of awarding this honor. Since 1920, individual recipients have made distinguished contributions to the historical development of graphic arts. The earliest Medals were frequently given for achievements in typography and book design that represented technological innovations. During the first half of the century, creative handling of the new printing processes generated popular interest in visual communications, and Medalists included typographers such as F.W. Goudy (1927) and W.A. Dwiggins (1929), designers of "Goudy Modern" and "Caledonia," who served to inspire the new graphic language.

Other Medalists include Mehemed Fehmy Agha (1957), awarded for the "revolutionary effect on American magazine design" which resulted when he discarded restrictive visual boundaries that prevailed in layout and typography. Saul Steinberg (1963), famous for his New Yorker covers, was cited for the eloquence and precision of his work. Medals also have gone to architects, painters, and photographers (Richard Avedon, Philip Johnson, and Robert Rauschenberg). Milton Glaser (1972) was cited for "graphic design of beauty, vitality, invention and humanity." The most recent recipient, Lou Dorfsman, was cited as a major innovative force in the development of CBS visual communications. Nominations for the 1979 Medalist should be completed by early May.

Leipzig Book Fair

"The Best-Designed Books from all over the World," 1979, will be presented in Leipzig and Berlin, Germany, from September to November. The exhibition, sponsored by UNESCO, will include a special section, "World Literature for Young Readers," children's books that appeared from 1974 to 1978.
Notification of entry should be made by May 15th. The deadline for receipt of exhibits is June 30th. Applications are available from: Börsenverein der Deutschen Buchhändler zu Leipzig, Ausstellung, Schönste Bücher aus aller Welt 1979, DDR-701 Leipzig, Postfach 146, Germany. There is no charge for participation.

Books Clinics Successful

"It was our intention to show the complete scope of publishing, from author to bookstore, giving equal time to all," commented Lidia Ferrara, Chairwoman of the AIGA Book Clinics and Art Director at Alfred A. Knopf. "We wanted different points of view and were pleased that the series was successful." The series of five panel discussions, which was sold out at the Grolier Club, focused on the key individuals involved in publishing a book: authors, editors, art directors, production managers, and sales directors. For quotes on the publishing process, see the Comment section on page 3. Cassette tapes of each session are available at AIGA.

Two Surveys in Progress

Two questionnaires should aid AIGA in compiling useful information for those in graphic design. The first, a demographic survey of our membership, will help define the profession and result in a directory of names and addresses. The second, sent to 1000 educational institutions, will result in a list of schools giving courses in graphic design on a variety of levels. The list will be available for students and professionals, and will answer questions concerning programs and degrees. The questionnaire was prepared by George Sadek, Dean at Cooper Union, and David Levy, Dean at Parsons School of Design.

(a)

Designer: Ellen Shapiro.

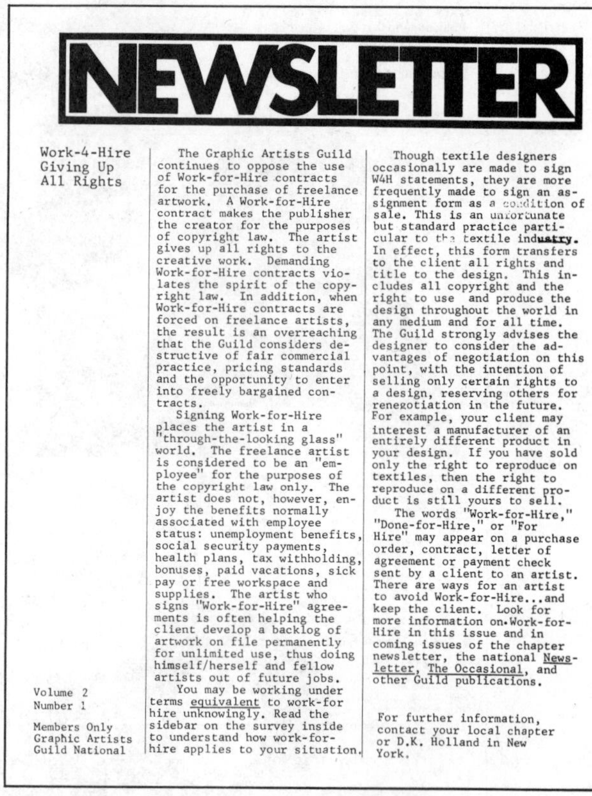

NEWSLETTER

Work-4-Hire
Giving Up
All Rights

The Graphic Artists Guild continues to oppose the use of Work-for-Hire contracts for the purchase of freelance artwork. A Work-for-Hire contract makes the publisher the creator for the purposes of copyright law. The artist gives up all rights to the creative work. Demanding Work-for-Hire contracts violates the spirit of the copyright law. In addition, when Work-for-Hire contracts are forced on freelance artists, the result is an overreaching that the Guild considers destructive of fair commercial practice, pricing standards and the opportunity to enter into freely bargained contracts.

Signing Work-for-Hire places the artist in a "through-the-looking glass" world. The freelance artist is considered to be an "employee" for the purposes of the copyright law only. The artist does not, however, enjoy the benefits normally associated with employee status: unemployment benefits, social security payments, health plans, tax withholding, bonuses, paid vacations, sick pay or free workspace and supplies. The artist who signs "Work-for-Hire" agreements is often helping the client develop a backlog of artwork on file permanently for unlimited use, thus doing himself/herself and fellow artists out of future jobs.

You may be working under terms equivalent to work-for hire unknowingly. Read the sidebar on the survey inside to understand how work-for-hire applies to your situation.

Though textile designers occasionally are made to sign W4H statements, they are more frequently made to sign an assignment form as a condition of sale. This is an unfortunate but standard practice particular to the textile industry. In effect, this form transfers to the client all rights and title to the design. This includes all copyright and the right to use and produce the design throughout the world in any medium and for all time. The Guild strongly advises the designer to consider the advantages of negotiation on this point, with the intention of selling only certain rights to a design, reserving others for renegotiation in the future. For example, your client may interest a manufacturer of an entirely different product in your design. If you have sold only the right to reproduce on textiles, then the right to reproduce on a different product is still yours to sell.

The words "Work-for-Hire," "Done-for-Hire," or "For Hire" may appear on a purchase order, contract, letter of agreement or payment check sent by a client to an artist. There are ways for an artist to avoid Work-for-Hire...and keep the client. Look for more information on Work-for-Hire in this issue and in coming issues of the chapter newsletter, the national Newsletter, The Occasional, and other Guild publications.

For further information, contact your local chapter or D.K. Holland in New York.

Volume 2
Number 1

Members Only
Graphic Artists
Guild National

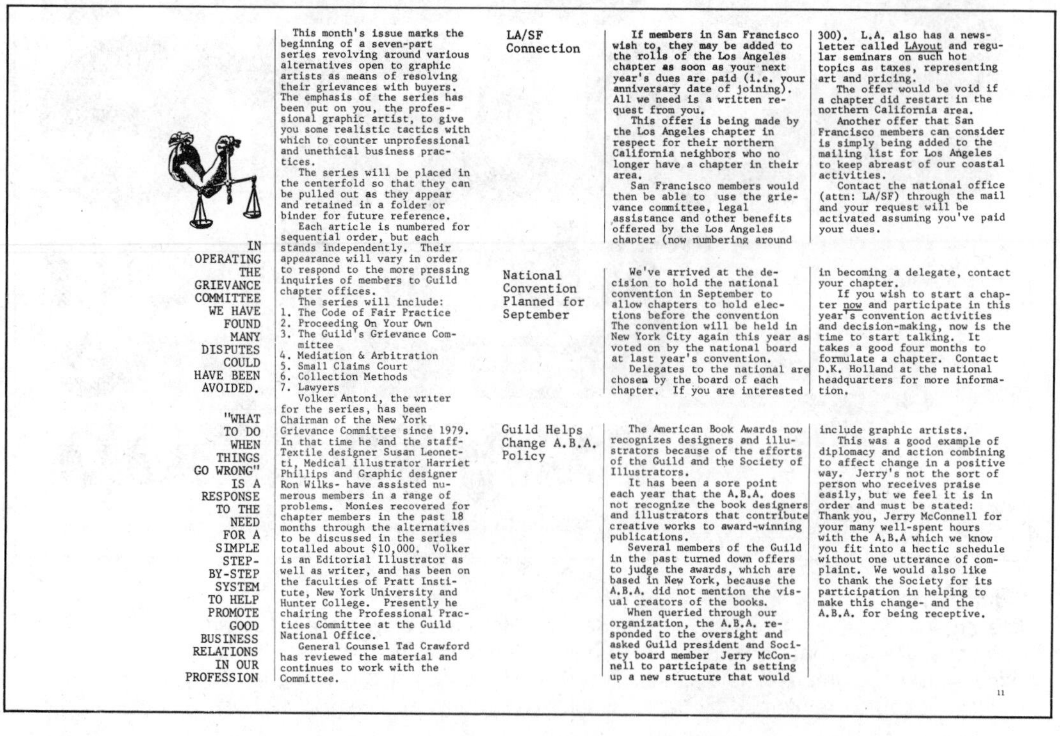

IN OPERATING THE GRIEVANCE COMMITTEE WE HAVE FOUND MANY DISPUTES COULD HAVE BEEN AVOIDED.

"WHAT TO DO WHEN THINGS GO WRONG" IS A RESPONSE TO THE NEED FOR A SIMPLE STEP-BY-STEP SYSTEM TO HELP PROMOTE GOOD BUSINESS RELATIONS IN OUR PROFESSION

This month's issue marks the beginning of a seven-part series revolving around various alternatives open to graphic artists as means of resolving their grievances with buyers. The emphasis of the series has been put on you, the professional graphic artist, to give you some realistic tactics with which to counter unprofessional and unethical business practices.

The series will be placed in the centerfold so that they can be pulled out as they appear and retained in a folder or binder for future reference.

Each article is numbered for sequential order, but each stands independently. Their appearance will vary in order to respond to the more pressing inquiries of members to Guild chapter offices.

The series will include:
1. The Code of Fair Practice
2. Proceeding On Your Own
3. The Guild's Grievance Committee
4. Mediation & Arbitration
5. Small Claims Court
6. Collection Methods
7. Lawyers

Volker Antoni, the writer for the series, has been Chairman of the New York Grievance Committee since 1979. In that time he and the staff- Textile designer Susan Leonetti, Medical illustrator Harriet Phillips and Graphic designer Ron Wilks- have assisted numerous members in a range of problems. Monies recovered for chapter members in the past 18 months through the alternatives to be discussed in the series totalled about $10,000. Volker is an Editorial Illustrator as well as writer, and has been on the faculties of Pratt Institute, New York University and Hunter College. Presently he chairing the Professional Practices Committee at the Guild National Office.

General Counsel Tad Crawford has reviewed the material and continues to work with the Committee.

LA/SF
Connection

If members in San Francisco wish to, they may be added to the rolls of the Los Angeles chapter as soon as your next year's dues are paid (i.e. your anniversary date of joining). All we need is a written request from you.

This offer is being made by the Los Angeles chapter in respect for their northern California neighbors who no longer have a chapter in their area.

San Francisco members would then be able to use the grievance committee, legal assistance and other benefits offered by the Los Angeles chapter (now numbering around 300). L.A. also has a newsletter called LAyout and regular seminars on such hot topics as taxes, representing art and pricing.

The offer would be void if a chapter did restart in the northern California area.

Another offer that San Francisco members can consider is simply being added to the mailing list for Los Angeles to keep abreast of our coastal activities.

Contact the national office (attn: LA/SF) through the mail and your request will be activated assuming you've paid your dues.

National
Convention
Planned for
September

We've arrived at the decision to hold the national convention in September to allow chapters to hold elections before the convention The convention will be held in New York City again this year as voted on by the national board at last year's convention.

Delegates to the national are chosen by the board of each chapter. If you are interested in becoming a delegate, contact your chapter.

If you wish to start a chapter now and participate in this year's convention activities and decision-making, now is the time to start talking. It takes a good four months to formulate a chapter. Contact D.K. Holland at the national headquarters for more information.

Guild Helps
Change A.B.A.
Policy

The American Book Awards now recognizes designers and illustrators because of the efforts of the Guild and the Society of Illustrators.

It has been a sore point each year that the A.B.A. does not recognize the book designers and illustrators that contribute creative works to award-winning publications.

Several members of the Guild in the past turned down offers to judge the awards, which are based in New York, because the A.B.A. did not mention the visual creators of the books.

When queried through our organization, the A.B.A. responded to the oversight and asked Guild president and Society board member Jerry McConnell to participate in setting up a new structure that would include graphic artists.

This was a good example of diplomacy and action combining to affect change in a positive way. Jerry's not the sort of person who receives praise easily, but we feel it is in order and must be stated: Thank you, Jerry McConnell for your many well-spent hours with the A.B.A which we know you fit into a hectic schedule without one utterance of complaint. We would also like to thank the Society for its participation in helping to make this change- and the A.B.A. for being receptive.

11

(b)

(c)

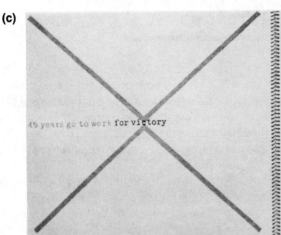

45 years go to work for victory

From its very inception in 1897 every Autocar activity has trained the Company for its vital role in the war program. For 45 years without interruption it has manufactured motor vehicles exclusively, concentrating in the last decade on heavy-duty trucks of 5 tons or over. For 45 years Autocar has pioneered the way, developing many history-making "firsts" in the industry: the first porcelain spark-plug; the first American shaft-driven automobile; the first double reduction gear drive; the first

circulating oil system. For 45 years Autocar insistence on mechanical perfection has wrought a tradition of precision that is honored by every one of its master workers. These are achievements that only time can win. The harvest of these years, of this vast experience, is at the service of our government. Autocar is meeting its tremendous responsibility to national defense by putting its 45 years' experience to work in helping to build for America a motorized armada such as the world has never seen.

Designer: Paul Rand.

(d)

AND SHE DID IT ALL BY HERSELF

Once there was a woman and she had the Christmas spirit. In fact, she had so much Christmas spirit, that her gift list grew longer and longer every year. Unfortunately, her bank balance didn't grow along with it.

She started her shopping earlier. She walked and she looked and she stopped and she thought. Then she sat down to rest. And there on the counter before her, was the key to her Christmas problem. Of all things, it was a large Simplicity Pattern Catalog.

She thumbed through the pages, she went down her list. There was a handsome robe for Dad, adorable doll clothes for Mimi, aprons galore for the "Aunts", even stuffed toys for the babies. She heaved a sigh of relief, bought three printed patterns, and fabric to match, and headed straight for home. That was how it began.

She hemmed and she pinked and she nodded. And as Christmas drew nearer, her pile of packages grew larger, and the spirit lived in her heart. What a wonderful thing, she thought, to put part of *yourself* in a gift... your work, your time, the touch of your hands. She'd *never* had so much fun!

And then it was Christmas morning--with gifts for all on her list. They Oh'd and they Ah'd and they kissed her. And she almost burst with pride. It was the merriest Christmas *any* of them ever had . . . because, you see, she did it all by herself -- with the help of Simplicity Printed Patterns.

Simplicity
PRINTED PATTERNS
FASHION'S PRIDE AND JOY

Courtesy Simplicity Pattern, Inc.

(e)

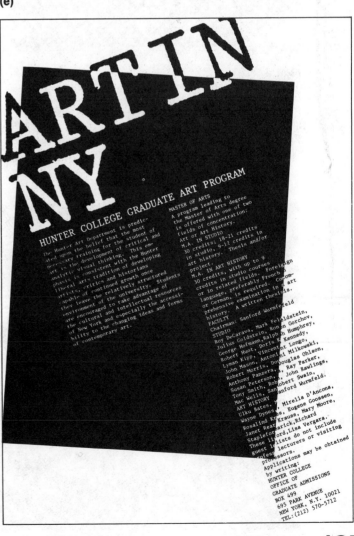

Design: Joseph Bednar.

135

Figure 5.18
This exaggerated screen shows the dot principle of reproducing photographs. The screens are labeled according to the number of rows of dots per inch—65 line, 100 line, 150 line, and so on. Notice that areas in the halftone that look like a checkerboard have a 50 percent proportion of dots per square inch.

Images

Photographs are converted into screen patterns called *halftones* to be reproducible on a printing press. Most photos use dot patterns but other types of screens are available; the most common are mezzotints, straight-line patterns, and posterizations. These require special camera techniques but are quite effective for reproducing photographs.

When using photographs in a layout, a designer first marks the dimensions or proportional percentage that the photographs will be on the printed piece. Crop marks—to indicate the outside edges—are marked along the edges or on tissue overlays. If the image in the photograph is to be silhouetted or outlined from the background, the designer must use a mask overlay to outline the image area on the photo. Designers can also specify to print photos very lightly, reduced, or with very high contrast.

Frequently, line illustrations or drawings, comprised of either solid shapes or thin black lines and thus called *line art,* are used in design. Line art is especially economical to reproduce because it does not need screens or dot patterns. Many illustrators use cross hatching or stipple-dot techniques to depict complex details.

Although line-art originals are drawn in black and white, they can be printed in any specified ink color. If an illustration is in full color, then it must be printed by the same four-color process as transparencies and prints. If an illustration is shaded with gradations, however—as in a wash drawing or airbrush painting—it must be treated the same as a photo—that is, it must be produced through the halftone process.

Figure 5.19
Special screen conversions such as those shown here can create effects with photos ranging from the hand drawn to the abstract. Many times these techniques can improve otherwise weak photos.

Figure 5.19

(continued)

EXAGGERATED DOT PATTERN–
APPROXIMATELY 20 LINE

LINE SHOT–HIGH CONTRAST LINE
CONVERSION

HALFTONE WITH HIGHLIGHTS
DROPPED OUT

LINE SHOT–SCREENED 30%

LINE SHOT COMBINED WITH
30% TINT

HORIZONTAL STRAIGHT LINE
HALFTONE

MEZZO TINT HALFTONE

HALFTONE WITH CONTRAST–
REDUCED 50%

Like our artist's rendition of an Art Director? Send for your free 19" x 27" color poster to: Design Typographers, Inc., 500 N. Dearborn St., Chicago, IL 60610. Please enclose $1 for postage. In Chicago, just call 329-9200 and ask.

Figure 5.20
Although this poster by Nancy Quinian reveals fine detail, it was mechanically reproduced as line art along with the type. The artwork is all in fine black lines, which suggest the modulation of a softer drawing material. This is a good example that line art is not limited to being contrasty, bold, black-and-white imagery. *Art Director: Jim Courtright. Illustrator: Nancy Quinian.*

Paste-up

If any publication—copy or art—is to be printed on both sides of one sheet, the material must be organized on separate areas of layout board, one for each side. Each color to be printed requires a *separation*—that is, an individual sheet for each color with everything placed very accurately. These sheets are usually acetate and are called overlays.

PASTE-UP OUTLINE

NOTE: There is more than one method of preparing art properly; each firm usually adopts its own variation. Although the following list outlines a common procedure, the safest approach for any specific project is for the paste-up person to consult the printer for suggestions.

1. Use a smooth bristol or illustration board base. Leave 2″ to 3″ around the layout.
2. Rule all dimensions, columns, and grid lines in very light nonreproducing pen or pencil.
3. Draw trim marks in black or red outside the layout area at the corners. Also draw fold marks at folds. Draw black lines around all color and photo (halftone) areas or use masking sheets (Paratone, Amberlith, Rubylith).
4. Position all type repros (if the repro sheets are not waxed, use rubber cement) of body copy, headlines, credits, and so on. Cut large type where letter spacing is needed.
   Note: Allow about 1/8″ around all type to minimize shadows and to protect the type.
5. Position any stats of logos, drawings, and other artwork.
6. Cut overlay masks and position art for separation on overlay.
7. Check dimensions and positions.
8. Attach a tissue overlay for spec information for artwork. Attach a cover sheet to protect artwork.
9. Indicate colors, quantity, paper, and so on, on boards and/or overlays.
10. Have client approve layout; then have printer go over layout and instructions.

The overlay is used where the colors touch or print over one another. (See color plate 18.) If they do not touch, this may not be necessary. Instructions for colors and folding must be clearly written around the paste-up and on tissue overlays when applicable. (See color plate 9.)

Brochures, catalogs, or any publication requiring binding is usually prepared as series of two-page layouts. These can be either facing page spreads (the way they will actually be seen) or pagination spreads (the way

they will appear on the press plates). Using facing-page spreads allows the designer to accurately visualize the "flow" and relationship of information as it will eventually appear. This method actually creates a bit more work for the printer, but it does keep the general layout visible and under total design control. Appropriate layout changes can be conceptualized and made because the size and placement of the material are immediately apparent; ensuring the integrity of the design thus outweighs the mechanical convenience of using a pagination layout. If the mechanical art is on a sheet of heavy bristol, then it can be cut and repositioned later if necessary. Always include a dummy of folding and assembly directions to help the printer locate the pieces conveniently for positioning.

In pagination layout, (also called bindery lay) pages are separated from their normal sequence. For example, in an eight-page booklet, page two would be across from page seven. This layout makes conversion to plates simpler and printing less costly; however, it can lead to confusion when proofing from the paste-up. Also, when any art extends over the middle of the page (gutter) paste-up should be in facing-page spreads to ensure accuracy.

Magazines have strict requirements for camera-ready art and generally supply the necessary technical information to the design studio or agency.

Inks

Inks for printing can be matte, gloss, transparent, opaque, or coated with varnish. Ink colors are specified by ink suppliers with color swatches or number systems, such as the popular Pantone Matching System.® (See box.)

To reproduce colored originals in full color, a special converting process called *four-color process printing* is used. (It is expensive to print small quantities using this method.) The image is separated through four photographic filters into four negatives, then onto four plates. Printing such a separation in a dot pattern with the four standard process colors—blue, yellow, magenta, black—appears to reproduce the original full-color image. However, even only using one or two colors, a remarkable range of color effects is possible if tints are used or if the two colors are carefully selected. (See Figure 5.21 and color plate 6.) For example, an orange and a purple become a brown when overprinted. If any color is converted into a tint (dot pattern), the result is the equivalent of adding white or the color of the paper. Such tints can also be overprinted to create other color effects.

Regardless of the printed color desired, all artwork must be provided in red or black for the camera film to receive it. It must also be drawn and measured very

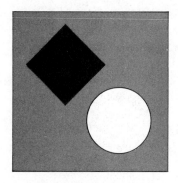  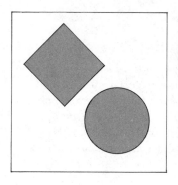 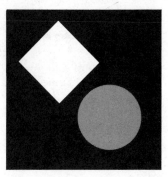

Figure 5.21
Black and white can be extended dramatically by using reverses and tint areas.

accurately in order for the colors to register properly. When the ink is to be printed up to the edge of the paper (to *bleed*), the mechanical art must overlap the edge of the trim lines by 1/8″. (Refer back to Figure 5.6)

The following "rules of thumb" can help determine the economics of printing:

1. Printing black ink on white paper has the lowest cost.
2. Printing black ink on colored paper has the next highest.
3. Printing colored ink on white paper has the next highest.
4. And printing colored ink on colored paper has the highest cost.

Using halftones, tints, heavy inking, and close registration adds printing costs and could make a black-on-white piece cost more than a "color on color" piece with only line art. An inexpensive piece might not be effective, however, so all the cost factors are relative to clarity of concept and attention value desired.

INK NOTES

1. *Black and white*

   Black ink may be gloss or matte. Varnish, plastic coat, or laminated plastic applied over the ink can also produce a shiny effect. (Varnish can also be matte or gloss.)

   White ink does not look as white as white paper; it looks milky (not a bad effect for the right purpose).

   Only screen-process printing produces a good white ink; otherwise, reverse printing is used to produce white.

2. *Color*

   Select colors from the Pantone Matching System®; note that ink colors print differently on coated versus uncoated surfaces.

   Inks can be *transparent* or *opaque*.

   Printers can match swatches.

   Art materials can match Pantone® inks.

   Offset press operators can control density of ink color by water-ink proportion.

   Colored ink on colored paper

   Paper color is "added" to the ink; allow for this.

   Textured paper adds some darkening.

   Most inks are somewhat transparent.

   Tints of red are pink.

   Halftones lose contrast and detail in light-valued colors.

   It is hard to read *thin type* printed in light colors, *reverse* type in light-value colors, or type in light colors printed on rough paper.

3. *One color and two color*

   Any ink is termed a color.

   Printing red ink on blue paper is a *one*-color job (called a "color-on-color" job).

   Printing black and red ink on white paper is a two-color job. If you use a tint of black to get a gray effect the job is still a *two*-color job.

   Printing "color on color" is an economical way to get a lively effect. Also, tints of one color are generally more reasonable to use than is a second ink.

4. *Special inking processes*

   Split fountain: Printing two colors at one time on one surface with a one-color press. The inking process is divided. The colors do not overlap, but are in separate areas. This is also the way to get a "rainbow effect": letting two colors blend in the inking system.

   Duotone: Two halftones of the same black-and-white photo each printed on top of the other in different colors, one usually black.

   Thermography: Raised-ink effect; ink is "baked" by heat.

   Metallic inks: Work best on white or dark colors on smooth, coated paper.

   Fluorescent: Glowing, vibrant colors; but fade faster.

   Stamping: Printing foil instead of ink; comes in gold, silver, copper, dull, gloss, and some colors.

Paper

Paper is available in standard sizes that are related to common publication sizes and printing-press sizes. A universal, practical paper size is 17″ × 22″ (and its division). Any smaller proportions are also practical (for example, 17″ × 17″, 16″ × 20″). These sizes fit conveniently on presses at almost all printers. Also, if the quantity of material to be printed is small, only some paper will be wasted in trimming. Thus, all papers come in this size or proportions that are close.

Paper thickness is called *weight* (or basis). The basis weight for a paper is the weight of a 500-sheet package of a specific size of that type of paper. Standard sizes and weights vary with the types of paper.

Specifying paper for a particular project requires cautious experience or dependable advice on such variables as what ink coverage, opacity, and detail can be expected. Not all colors, sizes, weights, and textures of paper that are manufactured are readily available. Paper distributors and printers can assist you in choosing appropriate paper for your particular needs; often they will give you actual samples of printing on most of the products they handle.

Printing firms always have some paper available "in-house" so it is usually an advantageous to inquire about what choices a particular firm offers before you specify your work. Sales representatives should be helpful in locating your selections, and in explaining the relative costs and quality options.

Sizes generally available in inches	17 × 22	17½ × 22½	19 × 25	23 × 29	23 × 35	25 × 38	26 × 40	20 × 26
Coated	●	●	●	●	●	●	●	●
Coated cover				●	●	●		
Uncoated	●	●	●	●	●	●	●	●
Uncoated cover				●	●	●		
*Bond	●	●				●		
Bristol				●			●	●
Text (book)					●	●		

*Bond also comes in 19 × 24 & 28 × 38.
Note: 17 × 22 can be conveniently cut from 23 × 35 or 25 × 38 sheets with little loss.

Figure 5.22
You avoid costly paper waste when you design material related to convenient paper sizes.

TYPES OF PAPER

Most firms have some white *bond* for letterheads; *offset paper* for general publication use; *cover* or *bristol*, a thicker weight paper for covers, posters, and cards; *coated* (enamel), which is very smooth and recommended for printing high-quality detail. Most paper distributors can also quickly respond to special paper requirements by filling orders from their extensively stocked supplies.

Bond comes in common weights of 20 and 24 lb., and common working sizes of 8½″ × 11″ and 17″ × 22″. **Bond** is a relatively thin paper, best printed on one side, such as for letterheads. It is available in pale colors and a few subtle textures: wove, cockle, linen, laid. Letter-size (#10) envelopes to match are generally available in white; colored envelopes are less accessible.

Offset paper comes in a large choice of sizes; check your source of supply for availability. Common weights for paper are 70, 80, and 100 lb. and for covers, 65 lb. Good working sizes are 17″ × 22″ and 23″ × 35″. The lighter (text) weights are good for brochures, fold-ers, posters, flyers; thicker cover weights are good for catalogs, brochure covers, and announcements.

Offset paper, probably the most available of the papers, has excellent opacity, which makes it suitable for printing on both sides or heavy ink coverage. It is available in many colors and with a variety of surface textures. Remember that white should always be in stock, but not necessarily all other colors.

Cover is the name of the heavy weights of paper in any category. Common cover size is 20″ × 26″. Bristol is also heavy and is good for menus, cards, heavy folders, and so on. Some colors of bristol match certain bonds; it is, however, available mostly in whites, creams, and off-whites. Many business cards are printed on bristol. The weights are comparable to cover weights. A common bristol size is 22½″ × 28½″. Cover stock must be scored to fold properly. (See later discussion of scoring.)

Coated (enamel) paper weights come in 60, 70, and 80 lb.; cover weights are 60 and 80 lb. The common size is 23″ × 35″. This paper has a special coating applied to create a very smooth surface, which can be extremely shiny or matte. It is excellent paper for printing high-detail illustrations or photographs. Colors printed on this paper tend to look more brilliant than on other papers. Both sides can be printed, although the cover weight may only be coated on one side. Coated paper is produced in colors, but may not be easily available as such.

Text paper commonly comes in a weight of 70 lb.; cover weight is 65 lb. The common size is 23″ × 35″. Although this paper is manufactured in a wide variety of textures and colors, its availability is limited by the economics of demand and inventories. It is very useful for high-quality brochures, booklets, and announcements. It should have excellent printing characteristics, but halftones do suffer some loss of detail.

DIE CUTTING

Die cutting means cutting a portion of the paper away. Cutting off a corner is a die cut, but a relatively inexpensive one. Making any straight cut or holes the size of notebook holes are also simple procedures. Most printers who die cut store used dies to reuse them; usually they have available a selection of circles, squares, ovals, stars, seals, or octagons. Because all die cutting requires an extra printing step and special equipment, it involves added cost. Reusing dies, however, can reduce this cost considerably.

SCORING

Scoring simply means adding a pressured indentation on a piece of paper along a line that will be folded. If you are making a dummy, you can simulate a score by running a blunt edge along the fold line. All heavy paper must be scored before folding. Note that paper, like wood, has a grain; when paper is to be folded against its grain it must also be scored.

█ Format Requirements

BOOKLETS AND FOLDERS

From *one* 17″ × 22″ sheet you can produce any of the following formats:

1-17″ × 22″ poster;

2-11″ × 17″ posters per sheet;

4-8½″ × 11″ flyers per sheet;

1-8½″ × 11″ folder with eight sections;

1-4¼″ × 11″ folder with sixteen sections (or eight sheets);

1-8½″ × 11″ booklet with eight pages;

1-4¼″ × 11″ booklet with sixteen pages;

1-5½″ × 8½″ folder with six sections (or three sheets);

1-5½″ × 8½″ booklet with sixteen pages;

1-7½″ × 8½″ folder with twelve sections (or six sheets);

1-7½″ × 8½″ booklet with twelve pages;

1-4¼″ × 7½″ folder with twenty-four (or twelve sheets);

1-4¼″ × 7½″ booklet with twelve pages.

142 These sizes do not include bleed or trim allowances.

Eight page booklet

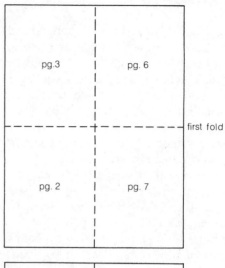

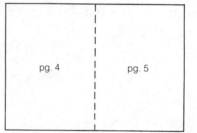

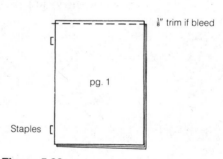

Figure 5.23
A sheet becomes an eight page "signature" when it is folded twice at right angles.

Booklets can be made by printing on both sides of a larger sheet, then folding, stitching, and trimming. Note that each trim means cutting ⅛″ off of the side being trimmed. If you also bleed the color, ¼″ total may be cut from that side because you add ⅛″ for the bleed.

ENVELOPES

Extensive stock formats of envelopes are available. However, envelopes can also be custom made if the quantity required is large enough and the time schedule permits. If an envelope is part of a design project, begin by planning the envelope, because its requirements might affect the entire design format. As is true of most paper products, white envelopes are more available than are envelopes with special colors.

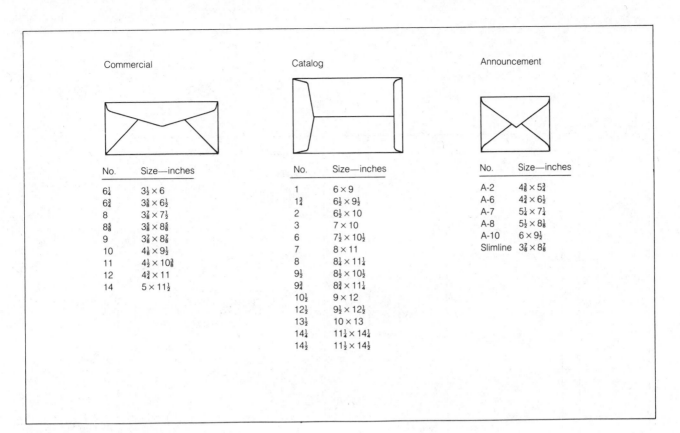

Commercial		Catalog		Announcement	
No.	Size—inches	No.	Size—inches	No.	Size—inches
6¼	3½ × 6	1	6 × 9	A-2	4⅜ × 5¾
6¾	3⅝ × 6½	1¾	6½ × 9½	A-6	4¾ × 6½
8	3⅞ × 7½	2	6½ × 10	A-7	5¼ × 7¼
8⅝	3⅝ × 8⅝	3	7 × 10	A-8	5½ × 8⅛
9	3⅞ × 8⅞	6	7½ × 10½	A-10	6 × 9½
10	4⅛ × 9½	7	8 × 11	Slimline	3⅞ × 8⅞
11	4½ × 10⅜	8	8¼ × 11¼		
12	4¾ × 11	9½	8½ × 10½		
14	5 × 11½	9¾	8¾ × 11¼		
		10½	9 × 12		
		12½	9½ × 12½		
		13½	10 × 13		
		14¼	11¼ × 14¼		
		14½	11½ × 14½		

Figure 5.24
These are the most available sizes and styles.

BOOKS AND PERIODICALS

Books and magazines are assembled in much the same way as catalogs and annual reports. Because they involve many pages, using preprinted layout paste-up grids or stats can ensure accuracy and save time. Also, presetting much of the copy can facilitate placing related material, such as photos that should appear adjacent to their copy references.

If you would like to design and construct a small book, you can hand bind it simply, while still ensuring a fairly professional look. Your results may not be as permanent or as professional as those specialists produce, but their "feel" can be similar enough that the personal effort involved will be worthwhile. Indeed, if you use covers and end sheets of different textures and colors than the text sheets, and print on them with a combination of typewriter type, pressure type, quick-printing services, and some hand coloring, you can produce a hand-designed and hand-bound book that is as complete a design product as one that is machine printed and bound.

NEWSPAPERS

Newspaper or tabloid layout is similar to book or periodical layout except that the time of assembly is comparatively fast paced. Such layouts always follow grid systems and specific typographic styles, which help accommodate their extreme schedule pressures. By planning special features not related to daily events well in advance, many papers are currently able to introduce welcome new vitality in design and illustration.

PACKAGING

Package-layout techniques and printing instructions are about the same as for brochures, books, and other publications. However, packaging formats generally require the printers to submit especially accurate dimensioned plans and to give careful instructions related to folding allowances of the die-cutting locations. For best results, the printers and the product manufacturers must cooperate in supplying each other complete information.

When learning to design box packaging, the easiest material to use for mock-ups or dummies is cardstock (bristol board, railroad board, etc.) or corrugated cardboard. A good way for you to learn the mechanics of folding is by examining boxes commonly found in retail stores. It is best to score the fold lines with pressure from a blunt edge rather than to cut into the material, which weakens it. If the material is thick, such as corrugated cardboard, then make a series of cuts like dashes to provide a good bend but leave some material for strength.

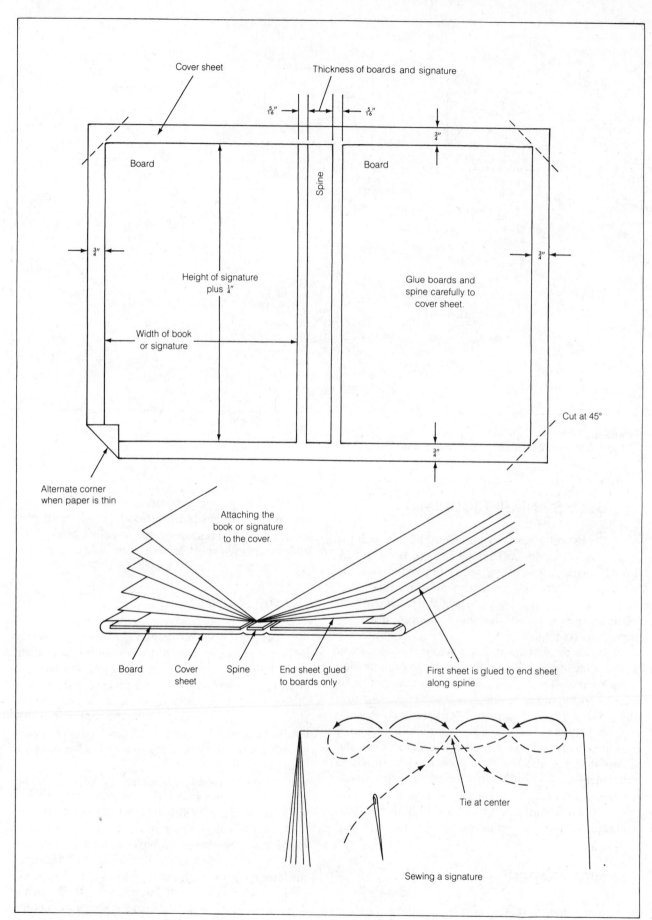

Figure 5.25a
These instructions will help you to construct a professional looking book dummy.

144

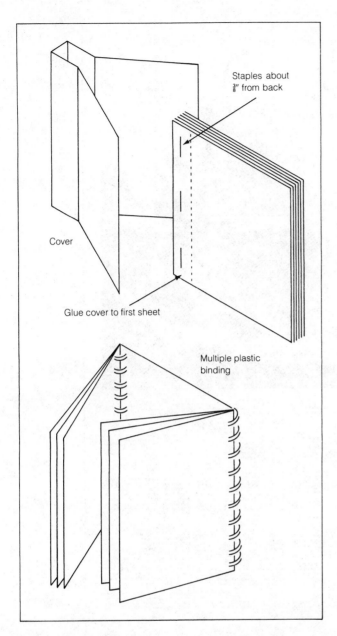

Staples about ⅜″ from back

Cover

Glue cover to first sheet

Multiple plastic binding

Figure 5.25b
These bindings allow you to assemble changes of paper or include other materials.

Figure 5.25c
You can assemble a book in very short time with this binding method.

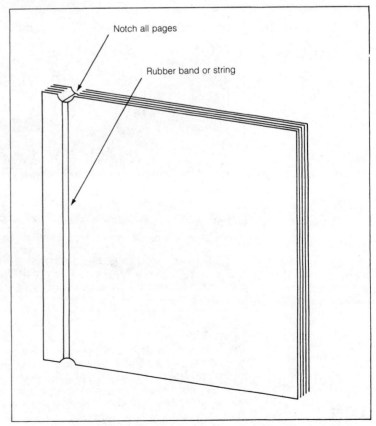

Notch all pages

Rubber band or string

Figure 5.26

The New York Times is a model of excellence in newspaper layout. The basic grid is apparent and the typography follows a design system which allows ample room for variety. The design adds up to great legibility with good potential for reader interest. Notice the subtle use of white space between copy and images. *Copyright © 1984 by The New York Times Company. Reprinted by permission. Copyright © 1984 by Louis Silverstein, Vice-President for Art & Design, the New York Times.*

Figure 5.26 (continued)

Appalachia's Pioneer Past

Walking into a world of make-do-or-do-without in a Tennessee museum

Replica of typical southern Appalachian country store at the museum.

By WILMA DYKEMAN

Early morning mist lifts slowly from the East Tennessee countryside, revealing a weathered rail fence that unites in giant cross-stitch patterns busy barnyards and assorted buildings of the Museum of Appalachia.

Museum? A peacock's cry shatters the stillness, goats bleat, guinea fowl chatter their old-fashioned "pot-a-rack, pot-a-rack," and there is the sound of an ax biting through tough red oak.

Museum? The bitter pungency of wood smoke drifts across the glistening fields, farmyard smells of cattle and sheep and chicken's dust-wallows blend with the occasional fragrance of herbs and posies growing inside a picket fence.

Museum? Doors to a primitive cabin, furnished in every detail as it might have been two centuries ago, stand wide as if the occupants had just stepped out to do the morning milking. The door to the log school house is open as if its pioneer boys and girls had run down to the spring to fetch fresh water in the worn old piggin before taking their places on the stiff wooden benches.

These sounds and smells and inviting sights of everyday living belong to a museum, yes — but one with a difference.

Midway on its north-south sweep from Detroit to Fort Lauderdale, Interstate Highway 75 slices through the heart of southern Appalachia. Midway in its passage across this rugged mountain country, the highway built for making time today provides access to a winding, two-lane Tennessee road inviting an ex-

WILMA DYKEMAN is a novelist and historian whose 14 books include "The French Broad," "The Tall Woman" and "Return the Innocent Earth."

perience of taking time to discover yesterday. One mile off the highway on a 75-acre farm of rolling meadows and upland woods near Norris is the Museum of Appalachia. Its 30-odd buildings and their surroundings preserve the past of a pioneer era, not so much as exhibits as an evocation of a way of life that once flourished in this country.

We are introduced into that earlier time of make-do-or-do-without through a large display barn. Here are many of the more than 200,000 objects that John Rice Irwin, the museum owner, has gathered during 20 years of searching through the region. Many of the objects were treasured family relics, some were discarded as worthless trash. Each article related to some aspect of mountain survival — its needs, its ingenuity, its progress. He furnished the cabins and other buildings with appropriate items — from cluttered mantels and pie safes to a sunbonnet hung over a bedpost and a homemade crutch leaning against the mud-daubed wall.

Other objects are assembled in the display barn. Here are massive millstones that were turned by mountain streams and rivers as settlers ground corn and wheat for bread. Nearby is a well-worn walking stick notched for votes counted long ago at a local election.

The spinning wheels and looms, guns and homemade musical instruments, baskets and crockery we might expect in such a collection are all here in abundance. Their variety testifies to the originality of a people who turned their daily necessities into personal experiences of creativity. Here, too, is a village post office with yellowed letters waiting in some of the pigeonholes. What messages did they carry of war and death and politics, crops and children? Nearby are a dentist's tools — wicked-looking iron tooth-pullers for those long-ago toothaches whose remedy was usually extraction. And along one wall of the balcony is an assortment of animal traps — ranging from powerful, steel-jawed bear

traps that could crush bone in their cruel grip to the intricate mechanics of a mouse-catcher devised by some patient inventor of the hills.

The display includes a cooper's shop with sturdy barrels for farm use and a meat trough fashioned from an immense poplar log in which a family's supply of meat, usually the favorite pork, was salted down. Here is a primitive cheese press and a broom press — one of the earliest pieces in the museum, dated about 1706 — for the frugal housewife who made her own brooms. And for the men who thrust roads through these hills and valleys, citizens often volunteering their time for certain days of "road working" and — later on — forced convict labor, there are the hammers that "busted stone." Knapping hammers, they were called; their slender hickory handles permitted a loose grip while delivering a heavy blow.

The man who amassed these artifacts also collected memorable details of their use. Mr. Irwin pauses before a display of primitive bee gums and points out why pioneer households prized beeswax (kept hanging in a bag from a rafter) as well as honey from their hives. String was coated with beeswax to make it stronger. Beeswax was used to coat a harness or a "smoothing iron" that

had been heated on the fireplace. Boiled with certain herbs it was used as medicine.

Whether he explains a cobbler's bench and tools ("Shoes are one of the hardest things to find now. People used to wear them out and there was nothing left to keep.") or an iron pot for making salt, a country jail cell or a fox-and-goose game board, Mr. Irwin follows the object into the lives of people.

Near the door to the display barn he pauses and kicks the toe of his boot against an anvil. "That anvil could have been useful to the Confederate Army. They needed horseshoes desperately. When Union soldiers came across this anvil on one of the farms around here it was too heavy for them to carry away, so they heated the horn of the anvil and cut it off, left it useless to the Confederates."

Beyond the display barn the museum opens before the visitor. We can go at a pace we choose through cabins that have been homes and are made to seem so today. We can explore a smokehouse where meat was cured and laid by; the corn crib where food for family and animals alike was stored; a blacksmith shop; gristmill; loom house, and the outdoor privy. A log church nestled on the hillside seems ready for a Sunday preaching and gospel singing, and in the schoolhouse a little higher along the path visiting teachers and students hold classes, bringing them closer to the local history.

Work goes on, according to the season, much as it has for generations. In the spring a horse and plough turn the earth for a garden that yields a summer harvest of peas and corn and beans, tomatoes, squash, cabbage, beets, potatoes, onions, lettuce and okra. In autumn long stalks of cane are ground on a mill powered by horse or mule, and the cane juice is boiled ("stirred off," in local jargon) on an outdoor furnace in long open pans. Apple butter, cooked in wide iron or copper kettles lends a spicy aroma to the crisp fall air.

When the moon is right, red oak shingles are rived for use on any building that may need roof repairs. "You have to put the shingles on in the dark of the moon," the old fellow using mallet and froe (a cleaving tool)

may tell you, "else they'll curl." The moon's sign played an important part in many pioneer activities from gardening to medicine.

Folk wisdom or superstition, call it what you will, is important to Mr. Irwin. Born a mountain man, serving for a while as superintendent of schools in his county, he has combined several kinds of knowledge in creating his museum. The museum is a discovery of a way of life and the resourcefulness, the courage, the wit and artistry of its people.

Each of the dwellings reflects aspects of that way of life. The Daniel Boone Cabin received its name when it was chosen by 20th Century-Fox to be the frontier home of the television series "Young Dan'l Boone." Its harsh authenticity strikes the visitor who steps onto the hard-packed red clay floor once swept by a sturdy wooden broom that leans in one corner. Crude beds constructed with poles in two corners of the room are covered with straw. A table with legs pegged into the top required no nails, which were scarce on the frontier. An iron kettle in the fireplace, a gourd for precious salt, a homemade wooden rake, two-pronged fork and other farm tools leaning against the wall, and a log fashioned into a mortar for pounding corn into hominy suggest the daily necessities met in this small room.

The Arnwine Cabin, also one-room, marks

Continued on Page 30

Minnie Black, a musician scheduled to perform at Fall Homecoming. Her fiddle is made from a home-grown gourd.

147

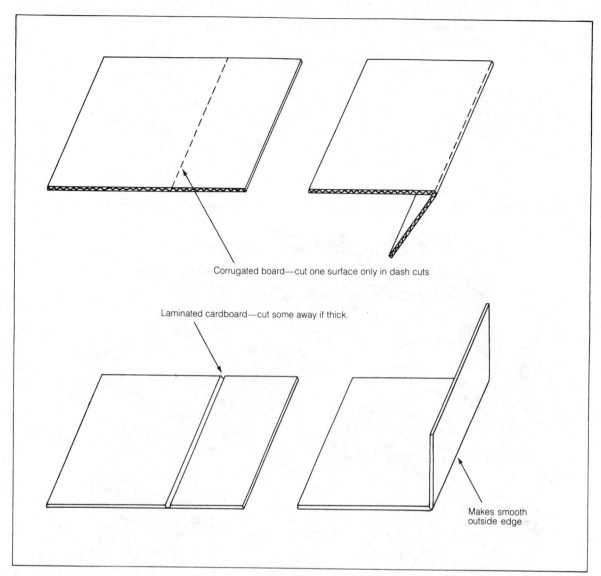

Corrugated board—cut one surface only in dash cuts

Laminated cardboard—cut some away if thick.

Makes smooth
outside edge.

Figure 5.27
A cardboard dummy will look more finished with rounded corners.

SIGNAGE

The term signage may refer to anything from a decal on a restroom to a logo on a water tower. From the design perspective, this field is thus extremely difficult due to the multitude of potential shapes and surfaces that can occur. For example, vehicle styles change yearly yet graphic identity must have built-in adaptability.

The process of planning signage systems for environmental or vehicle applications begin with thumbnail concepts and continues through various stages through to client presentations. Scale is an important consideration in this type of design so concept roughs should indicate the sizes relative to a human scale. The graphics should include actual dimensions displayed with the artwork. Contours, surface areas, and colors of the objects involved are drawn so as to show the relationships of the graphic elements.

Generally, a large-scaled paste-up with color swatches is submitted by the designer to the sign producers. If the design is to be printed by screen process it will proceed in much the same way as a mechanical for printed material. If the sign is to be hand painted, however, it can be projected either onto the actual surface or onto a paper surface, from which it is accurately transferred to the actual site, and then painted into the final design.

Manufacturers of signage materials offer design options within standard systems of structure, assembly, and letter forms. Such standardization is used extensively in complex architectural work: Individual project designers adapt the standard materials to provide special design services and products to the clients. (See *Sweets Architectural Catalog Service* at a library or architectural office for detailed examples.)

148

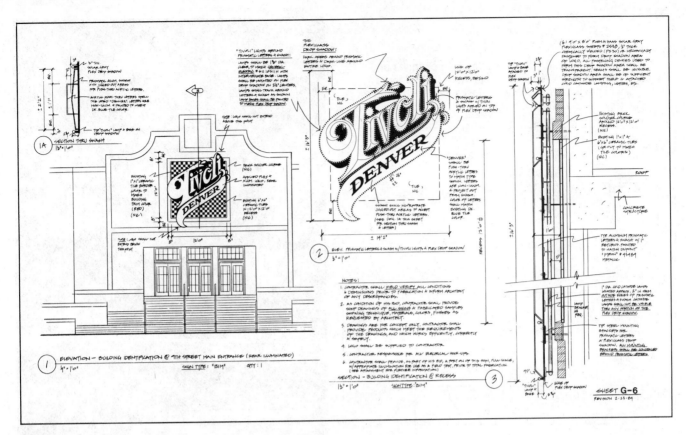

Figure 5.28
The Tivoli sign shows how many other considerations are involved besides the letter forms. This is a design area in which graphics, architecture, and engineering merge. *Architects: Hellmuth, Obata & Kassabaum, Inc.*

DISPLAYS AND EXHIBITS

Displays to be manufactured in quantity are designed much like packaging. The construction details of point-of-purchase displays are mostly designed by special engineers.

Exhibits are usually combinations of graphics screened or painted directly onto the exhibit surfaces and photos and other data attached to the exhibits mechanically or by adhesive materials. An exhibit design is similar to a construction plan drawn to scale and showing all sides and sections including dimensions. The details of any complex or special areas are planned on separate drawings. Much of the detail information is submitted in paste-up form in actual size if practical.

Rarely do two exhibits have the same problems, so the design procedures cannot be generalized easily. However, some universal hints do apply. For instance, cardboard and corrugated board are good materials for assembling mock-up models for most exhibits and accompanying signage. If you use model airplane cement to make these mock-ups, you can avoid the characteristic warping or staining of water-based glues. You can also design colors and graphics on separate surfaces, and then attach them using spray adhesives or adhesive transfer paper. If you are working on plastic or acetate surfaces, you can also use polymer paint; it will adhere if properly mixed. Mixing some polymer medium into the paint is helpful for smoothness.

TELEVISION

When designing for video, stage the concept in several drawings (story boards) to show the development of the activity (camera movement, subject movement, and color) in as few steps as necessary. The drawings do not need highly finished qualities, but they must concisely convey the images and their meanings within the sequence. (Refer back to Figure 2.8.) Along with the art position the copy related to each stage and comments about voice, action, music, sound, and so on. Because timing is crucial in this format, it must also be stated in the story board. Sometimes photographs are helpful, but usually explanatory drawings suffice, whether the final product is to be animated or a "live" action performance.

Because art directors' drawing skills vary, an illustrator adept at sketching story boards might be assigned to create the actual renderings to be shown to the client. For television design, however, remember that creative visual *concepts* are more valuable than illustration excellence per se.

149

Figure 5.29
Standardized signage facilitates making changes and
additions within reasonable costs, especially when a
project is extensive, such as a hospital or sports center.
Courtesy Adelphia Graphic Systems.

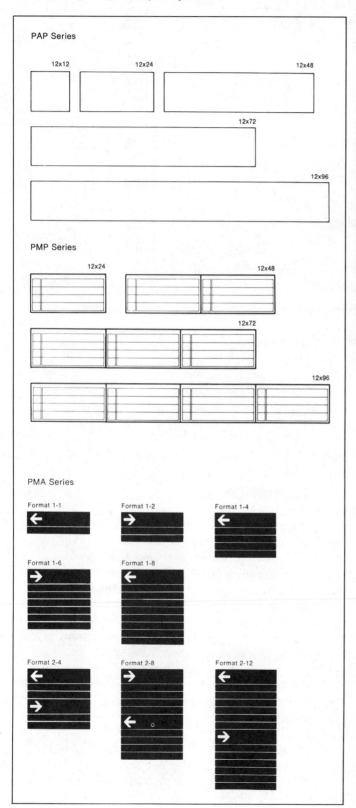

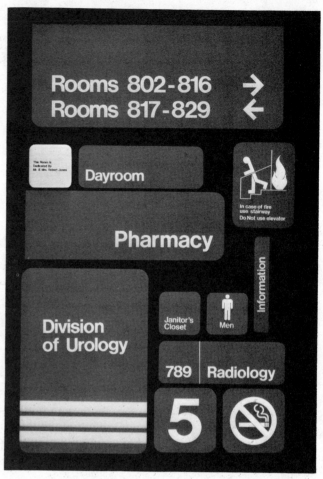

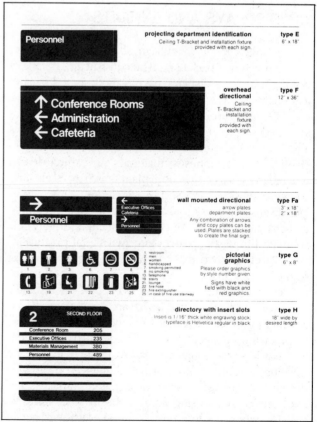

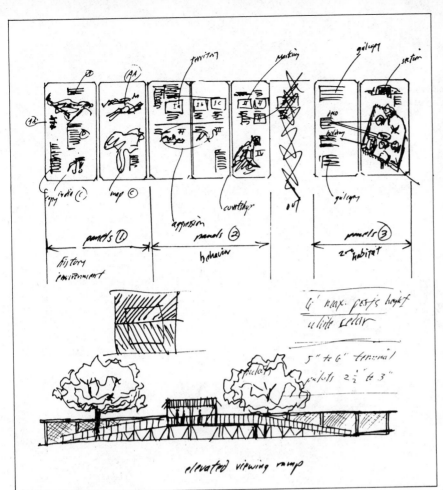

Figure 5.30
Constructing displays requires visualization of the sites and relative scales of the designs proposed. The concept-development process proceeds like that for printed matter, beginning with thumbnails, continuing with roughs, and eventually ending with renderings in color and scale models. These examples are from a proposal for an outdoor zoo habitat.

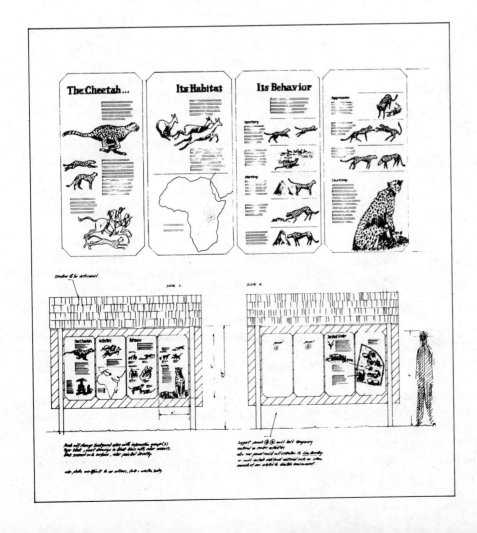

DESIGN RESOURCES

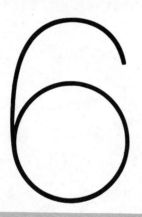

Acquiring Personal Resources

Artists and designers are often asked, "Where do you get your ideas?" or "How did you think that up?" Answering such questions might require psychoanalytic research into one's motives—or a look at the latest clipbook art directors annual. An important aspect of your design career is considering appropriate sources of information that can inspire you in your work.

Ideas or concepts for designs come from understanding the problem at hand and the background issues related to it. Extensive research is always not necessary to solve a particular design problem; rather, ongoing research should equip you with a pool of knowledge from which you can develop solutions of direct value to a specific problem. Any unapplied experience becomes part of your creative well, which fills remarkably fast during a lifetime and upon which you will constantly draw—consciously and unconsciously. As you study design and begin your design career, be open to any and all experiences. Even briefly pursuing tangential ideas that naturally crop up places them in your repertoire for later retrieval.

Many designers save their sketches, notes, and preliminary roughs in job or information files. Do this. After a period of time, as this file builds up, you will be surprised at how much browsing through it can help redirect you out of a rut and refresh your outlook. As you continue in your design career, looking back a bit might also help build some confidence—you will see how far you can progress in a surprisingly short time.

The more visual experience you acquire, the more you will build an individual commitment toward your work. Observe everything, view films—contemporary and classic—study television and its trends, analyze what is memorable and why and how things are done. Become aware of design trends in fashion, fabrics, automobiles, architecture, appliances, and consumer products.

Observe and understand the graphic systems that extend throughout our urban environment: traffic directions, apparel, symbols in public institutions and business, uniforms, personal gestures or body language, naive signage, graffiti, bumper stickers, decals, buttons, balloons, t-shirts, hats, and so on.

Become familiar with how products are promoted in supermarkets, pharmacies, special retail shops, hardware stores, and so on. Notice the visual differences between discount outlets and high-quality department stores. Note the competing variety of service stations, fast-food chains, and theaters. Observe the different attitudes they convey through their appearances, even if they offer similar services.

Be aware of the best in graphics nationally and internationally by keeping up with the major annuals of graphics, such as the *New York Art Directors Annual, CA Annual,* the *AIGA Annual, Creativity, Illustrators An-*

Figure 6.1
The spontaneity and impulsivity of graffiti are almost always expressed in its resulting forms.

nual, Print Casebooks, and *Graphis Annuals.* Several periodicals are also available that have fine articles and examples of current design activity (see the Bibliography). Subscribe to some of these for continual exposure to the ideas and creations of contemporary innovators.

Also seek out examples of the work of established leaders in design; (see box). Most of those listed have had their work reproduced or reviewed in publications such as *Print, Art Direction, Communications Arts,* or *Upper and Lower Case (U&LC).* In addition, many of them have written excellent books or articles describing their ideas and showing their work. Some also speak at national design conferences and workshops, which you should try to attend.

SOME LEADERS IN THE DESIGN WORLD

Herbert Bayer	Leo Lionni
Saul Bass	El Lissitsky
Max Bill	George Lois
Peter Bradford	Alvin Lustig
Josef Muller-Brockmann	Noel Martin
Alexy Brodovitch	John Massey
Will Burtin	Herbert Matter
Ivan Chermayef	James Miho
James Cross	L. Moholy Nagy
Rudolpf De Harak	George Nelson
Lou Dorfsman	Paul Rand
Charles Eames	Alexander Rodchenko
Adrian Frutiger	Herbert Spencer
Alan Fletcher	Bert Stern
Bob Gill	Ladislav Sutnar
Eric Gill	Bradbury Thompson
Karl Gerstner	Jan Tschichold
Milton Glazer	Theo van Doesburg
David Goines	Mussimo Vignelli
Morton Goldshall	Don Weller
Malcolm Grear	Henry Wolf
John Heartfeld	Herman Zapf
Gyorgy Kepes	Piet Zwart

Figure 6.2
Through casualness and clutter a discount outlet declares that if you dig in, there are bargains to uncover.

Figure 6.3a
Paul Rand's work shows a consistent desire for precise and simple, yet elegant, design. Notice his use of strong basic design elements in this early (1947) Disney hat ad for *Time* magazine. *Design: Paul Rand.*

154

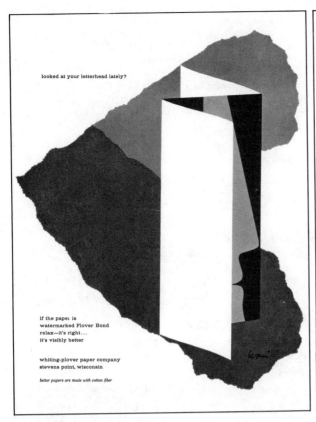

Figure 6.3b
Leo Lionni is an extremely versatile designer who has worked with every conceivable design form from architecture to children's books and sculpture. *Design: Leo Lionni.*

Figure 6.3c
Herbert Matter is well known as both a photographer and a designer. *Design: Herbert Matter.*

Figure 6.3d
Henry Wolf merges photography with typography in this lively informal layout for the American Institute of Graphic Arts. *Design: Henry Wolf.*

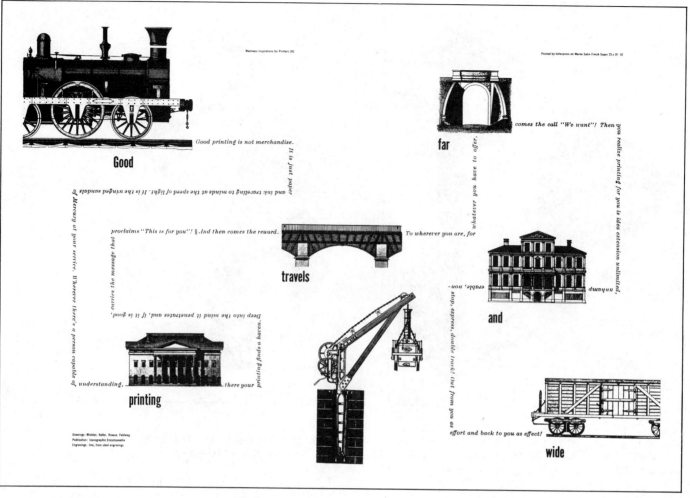

Figure 6.3e
Alexy Brodovitch greatly influenced many prominent designers. His work in magazine design is particularly notable. *From Westvaco Inspirations for Printers No. 161. Alexy Brodovitch Designer. Reprinted with permission by Westvaco Corporation.*

Utilizing Technical and Fine-Art Resources

The design profession and the graphics industry are noted for their openness. Most capable professionals in these fields are willing to discuss the business in general as well as their own individual activities with students or others curious about career opportunities or simply about what they do and how they do it.

A cornucopia of valuable, free, printed technical reference material is available from suppliers and manufacturers. Printers freely distribute examples of their work with descriptions of how their facilities achieve the technical qualities or conveniences clients may require. Typesetters and manufacturers of typesetting equipment have booklets, folders, and posters showing the range of styles available. Some of these must be purchased but they are well worth the price if they show extensive styles in many sizes. Paper manufacturers also produce abundant material of value to designers. Distributed widely through regional sales representatives and professional mailing lists, these materials demonstrate graphically how a variety of images, colors, and printing techniques will appear on their particular papers. Other booklets are offered that display the array of colors, textures, and weights of each type of paper available. Some of these publications have outstanding design quality and are collected eagerly by other designers. In addition, the sales representatives themselves can be helpful sources of practical information on their products or services.

The world of visual resources is as comprehensive as knowledge itself. Consider the micro and macro investigations of science, the new images brought back from space, and the amazing accumulation of visual material emerging from computers, lasers, and holography all as potential inspirations for your designer awareness. Such specialized imagery has to have an effect on how we perceive our environment and radically change our technical processes of communication accordingly.

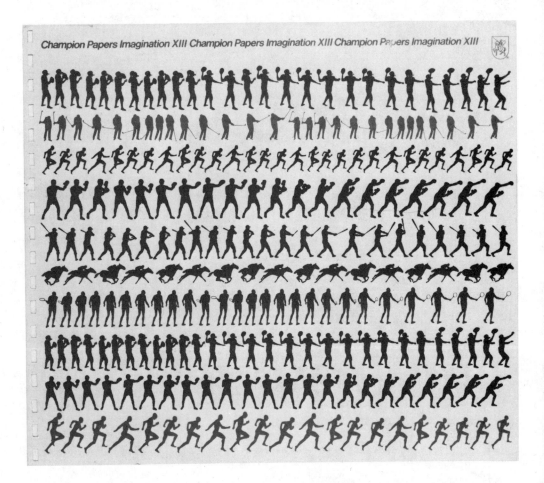

The underground parking lot beneath Ghirardelli Square has eight levels. But the management hasn't lost a vehicle yet. They designed a foolproof numbering system in keeping with the Square's overall graphic flair (which is anything but square). If the grown-ups forget the "4," the kids will remember the "blue fish." The vintage cable car routes are lined with unique signage that's functional as well as colorful. They make sure you get where you're going. San Francisco signmakers are metalworkers, stonemasons, ceramicists—or artists in colored glass or gold leaf. Often, the medium is the message. Sometimes it's as simple as a single brushstroke. Or, changing a few letters to convert a defunct bank into a baroque bar that pays better dividends.

Figure 6.4a
James Miho's designs for the *Imagination* brochures for the Champion Paper Company are widely collected. They demonstrate a rare merging of a designer's personality with a graphic concept. Not only are these handsomely organized but they also contain many innovative techniques.
Imagination XIII. Designer: James Miho.

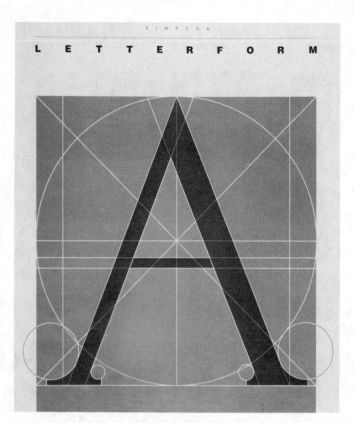

Figure 6.4b
The *Letterform* portfolio pages designed by James Cross for Simpson Lee are elegant "keepers." Promotions such as these express the finest development of graphic design and promotional motives; the results are not only effective in concept but they are also valid as artforms in themselves. *Design: Cross Associates, Los Angeles and Newport Beach, California. Reprinted by permission of Simpson Paper Company, San Francisco.*

Figure 6.5
Specialized scientific and documentary information are frequently fascinating and eye-opening sources of pattern and design structure (a) and (b). An abstraction is created by the digitalized, manipulated image from (c) an aerial photo of a city and (d) an X-ray of a monkey brain.

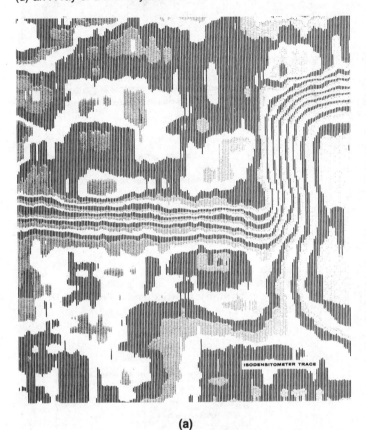

(a)

Cover of Science: 6 January 1967. Copyright 1967 by the AAAS.

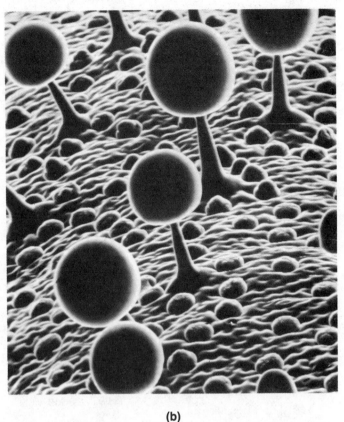

(b)

Cover of Science: 9 January 1970. Copyright 1970 by the AAAS.

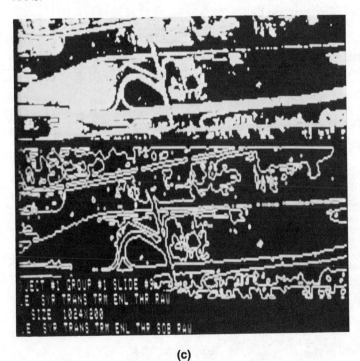

(c)

Photo Credit: Washington University Department of Computer Science.

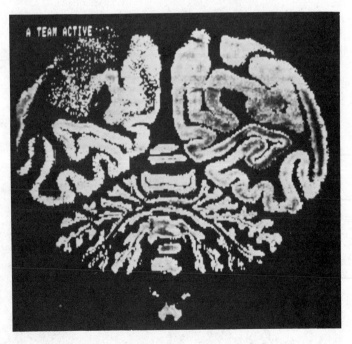

(d)

Photo Credit: Washington University Department of Computer Science.

Visits to art galleries are good stimuli, too. Remember: Inspiration is not a matter of looking for ideas to translate to commercial graphics, but rather of relating your visual experiences to other visual activities.

Some artists whose strong design techniques and creative use of graphic materials are worth studying are listed below.

Ideas and attitudes come from communicating with stimulating, creative people. Artists and designers communicate through their work. If you observe them and enjoy it, you will also be absorbing valuable input based on a substantial body of proven work. Do not avoid influence. Everything is connected; your talent will ultimately emerge as a development and extension of your unique personal observations of the work of others.

ARTISTS WHOSE WORK SHOWS STRONG
DESIGN QUALITY:

Josef Albers	James Rosenquist
Joseph Cornell	Kurt Schwitters
Ralston Crawford	Ben Shahn
Stuart Davis	Saul Steinberg
Red Grooms	Frank Stella
Wasily Kandinsky	Theo van Doesburg
Paul Klee	Andy Warhol
Rene Magritte	Tom Wesselman
Kasimir Malevich	
Henri Matisse	
Joan Miro	PHOTOGRAPHERS:
Piet Mondrian	
Ben Nicholson	Harry Calahan
Kenneth Noland	Walker Evans
Pablo Picasso	Charles Sheeler
Robert Rauchenberg	Aaron Siskind
	Minor White

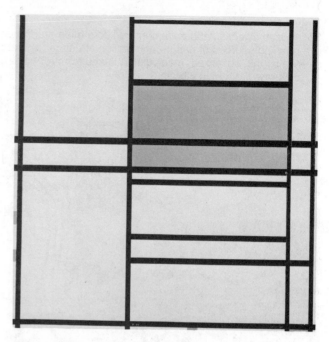

Figure 6.6a
Piet Mondrian is probably the single most widely acknowledged artist whose work directly influenced today's design forms. *The St. Louis Art Museum.*

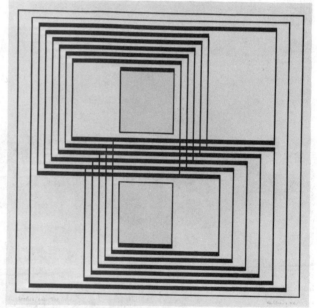

Figure 6.6b
Josef Albers' paintings and prints are readily recognized as a reference for the design of logos. In his early work at the Bauhaus Albers took great interest in letter forms and graphic-design basics. *The St. Louis Art Museum.*

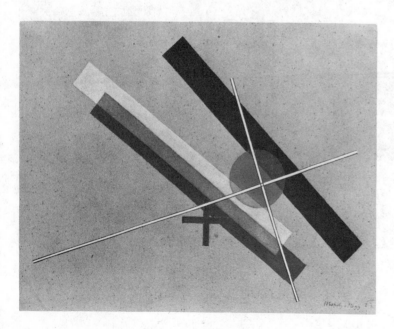

Figure 6.6c
Moholy-Nagy, a design educator in Germany at the Bauhaus and later in Chicago, has probably been the most important influence on the development of basic design principles in our century. *The St. Louis Art Museum.*

Figure 6.6d
Tom Wesselman frequently includes advertising graphics in his collage and assembled art. Through his visual translations these artforms take on new aesthetic meaning. *Washington University Gallery of Art, St. Louis.*

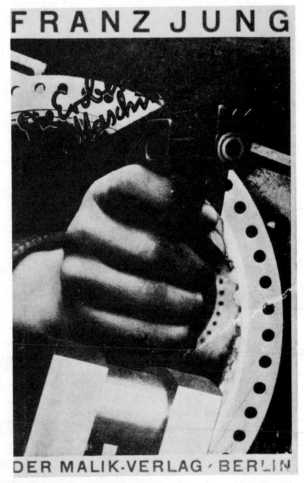

Figure 6.6e
Picasso, like many Cubists and Dadaists, frequently constructed his art almost entirely from graphic sources such as newspapers, tickets, labels, and the like. *Washington University Gallery of Art, St. Louis.*

Figure 6.6f
John Heartfield is one of the pioneers of collage for graphic purposes. His political-social commentary in this medium is powerful and rarely matched. *Design: John Heartfield.*

BIBLIOGRAPHY

The following Bibliography may seem formidable in such a basic book as this one. However, the publications listed here are intended to be a source for more extensive or specialized study. Because there are a few journals or reviews concerning graphic design, it is difficult for designers to be aware of what is available. I hope this list will be particularly helpful for instructors selecting references for their research and teaching programs.

Graphic Design

The American Institute of Graphic Arts, *Symbol Signs*. New York: Hastings House, 1981.

ANDERSON, CHARLES R., *Lettering*. New York: Van Nostrand, Reinhold, 1969.

BALLINGER, RAYMOND A., *Layout*. New York: Reinhold, 1956.

BERRYMAN, GREGG, *Notes on Graphic Design and Visual Communication*. Los Altos, Calif.: William Kaufmann, 1979.

CAPITMAN, BARBARA BAER, *American Trademark Designs*. New York: Dover Publications, 1976.

CRAIG, JAMES, *Graphic Design Career Guide*. New York: Watson-Guptill Publications, 1983.

CROSBY/FLETCHER/FORBES, *A Sign Systems Manual*. New York: Praeger, 1970.

DONAHUE, BUD, *The Language of Layout*. Englewood Cliffs, N.J.: Prentice-Hall, 1978.

DONDIS, DONIS A., *A Primer of Visual Literacy*. Cambridge, Mass.: MIT Press, 1973.

EKSELL, OLLIE, *Corporate Design Programs*. New York: Reinhold; London: Studio Vista, 1967.

FLETCHER, ALAN, *Graphic Design: Visual Comparisons*. New York: Reinhold, 1964.

GARLAND, KEN, *Graphics Handbook*. New York: Reinhold, 1966.

GERSTNER, KARL, *Designing Programmes*. New York: Visual Communications Books, Hastings House, 1964.

GERSTNER, KARL, *Compendium for Literates*. Cambridge, Mass.: MIT Press, 1974.

GILL, BOB, AND JOHN LEWIS, *Illustration: Aspects and Directions*. New York: Reinhold, 1964.

HURLBURT, ALLEN, *Layout, The Design of the Printed Page*. New York: Watson-Guptill Publications, 1977.

HURLBURT, ALLEN, *The Grid*. New York: Van Nostrand, Reinhold, 1978.

HURLBERT, ALLEN, *The Design Concept*. New York: Watson-Guptill Publications, 1981.

KAMEKURA, YUSAKU, *Trademarks of the World*. New York: George Wittenborn.

KEPES, GYORGY, *Sign, Image, Symbol*. New York: George Braziller, 1966.

KINCE, ELI, *Visual Puns in Design*. New York: Watson-Guptill Publications, 1982.

LOIS, GEORGE, *The Art of Advertising*. New York: Abrams, 1977.

MODLEY, RUDOLF, *Handbook of Pictorial Symbols*. New York: Dover Publications, 1976.

MULLER-BROCKMANN, JOSEF, *The Graphic Artist and His Design Problems*. New York: Hastings House, 1961.

MULLER-BROCKMAN, JOSEF, *Grid Systems in Graphic Design*. New York: Hastings House, 1981.

NELSON, GEORGE, *Displays*. New York: Whitney Publications, Inc., 1955.

NELSON, ROY PAUL, *Publication Design*. Dubuque, Iowa: William C. Brown, 1983.

RAND, PAUL, *Thoughts on Design*. New York: Wittenborn, Schultz, 1947.

THOMPSON AND DAVENPORT, *The Dictionary of Graphic Images*. New York: St. Martin's Press, 1980.

WILDBUR, PETER, *International Trademark Design*. New York: Van Nostrand, Reinhold, 1979.

WILSON, ADRIAN, *The Design of Books*. Salt Lake City: Peregrine Smith, 1974.

Typography

BIGGS, JOHN R., *Basic Typography*. New York: Watson-Guptill Publications, 1968.

CARTER, DAY, MEGGS, *Typographic Design: Form and Communication*. New York: Van Nostrand Reinhold.

DAIR, CARL, *Design With Type*. Toronto: University of Toronto Press, 1982.

LEWIS, JOHN, *Typography: Basic Principles*. New York: Reinhold, 1964.

LEWIS, JOHN, *Typography: Design and Practice*. New York: Taplinger, 1978.

McLEAN, RUARI, *Jan Tschichold: Typographer*. Boston: David R. Godine, 1975.

ROSEN, BEN, *Type and Typography*. New York: Reinhold, 1963.

RUDER, EMIL, *Typography*. New York: Visual Communications Books, Hastings House, 1981.

TSCHICHOLD, JAN, *Asymmetric Typography*. New York: Reinhold, 1953.

VAN UCHELEN, ROD, *Word Processing*. New York: Van Nostrand, Reinhold, 1980.

Basic Design

ALBERS, JOSEF, *Interaction of Color*. New Haven: Yale University Press, 1963 (paper, 1971).

ANDERSON, DONALD M., *Elements of Design*. New York: Holt, Reinhart & Winston, 1961.

BAZER, HERBERT, WALTER GROPIUS, AND ISE GROPIUS, *Bauhaus 1919, 1928*. Boston: Charles T. Branford, 1952.

BEHRENS, ROY R., *Design in the Visual Arts*. Englewood Cliffs, N.J.: Prentice-Hall, 1984.

CARRAHER, RONALD G., AND JACQUELINE B. THURSTON, *Optical Illusions and the Visual Arts*. New York: Reinhold Book Corporation, 1968.

CHEATHAM, FRANK, JANE CHEATHAM, AND SHERYL HALER, *Design Concepts and Applications*. Englewood Cliffs, N.J.: Prentice-Hall, 1983.

DE SAUSMAREZ, MAURICE, *Basic Design: The Dynamics of Visual Form*. New York: Reinhold, 1964.

FIRPO, PATRICK, *Copyart*. New York: Richard Marek Publishers, 1978.

GREGORY, RICHARD L., *Eye and Brain*. New York: McGraw-Hill, 1966.

GREGORY, RICHARD L., *The Intelligent Eye*. New York: McGraw-Hill, 1970.

HANKS, DURT, LARRY BELLISTON, AND DAVE EDWARDS, *Design Yourself*. Los Altos, Calif.: William Kaufmann, 1978.

HOFFMAN, ARMIN, *Graphic Design Manual*. New York: Van Nostrand, Reinhold, 1965.

ITTEN, JOHANNES, *The Art of Color*. New York: Reinhold, 1981.

KEPES, GYORGY, *Language of Vision*. Chicago: Paul Theobald, 1945.

KEPES, GYORGY, *Education of Vision*. New York: George Braziller, 1965.

KEPES, GYORGY, *Sign, Image, Symbol*. New York: George Braziller, 1966.

McKIM, ROBERT H., *Experiences in Visual Thinking*. Monterey, Calif.: Brooks, Cole, 1980.

MOHOLY-NAGY, LASZLO, *The New Vision*. New York: Wittenborn, Schultz, Inc., 1947.

MOHOLY-NAGY, LASZLO, *Vision in Motion*. Chicago: Paul Theobald, 1947.

MURARI, BRUNO, *Design as Art*. Middlesex, Eng.: Penguin Books, 1966.

RAND, PAUL, *Thoughts on Design*. New York: Van Nostrand, Reinhold, 1971.

RICHARDSON, JOHN A., FLOYD W. COLEMAN, AND MICHAEL J. SMITH, *Basic Design*. Englewood Cliffs, N.J.: Prentice-Hall, 1984.

SCOTT, ROBERT, *Design Fundamentals*. New York: McGraw-Hill, 1951.

TAYLOR, JOHN A., *Design and Expression in the Visual Arts*. New York: Dover Publications, 1964.

WINGLER, HANS M., *The Bauhaus*. Cambridge, Mass.: MIT Press, 1975.

Production

ADAMS, J. MICHAEL, AND DAVID D. FAUX, *Printing Technology*. North Scituate, Mass.: Duxbury Press, 1977.

BAHR, LEONARD F., *ATA Advertising Handbook*. New York: Advertising Typographers Association of America, 1969.

BOCKUS, H. WILLIAM, JR., *Advertising Graphics*. New York: Macmillan, 1979.

BORGMAN, HARRY, *Advertising Layout Techniques*. New York: Watson-Guptill Publications, 1983.

CAMPBELL, ALASTAIR, *The Graphic Designer's Handbook*. Philadelphia: Running Press, 1983.

CRAIG, JAMES, *Production for the Graphic Design*. New York: Watson-Guptill Publications, 1974.

CROSBY/FLETCHER/FORBES, *A Sign Systems Manual*. New York: Praeger, 1970.

FIELD, JANET N., *Graphic Arts Manual*. New York: Arno Press, Musarts Publishing, 1980.

GATES, DAVID, *Graphic Design Studio Procedures*. Monsey, N.Y.: Lloyd-Simore Publishing, 1982.

GOODSHILD, JON, AND BILL HENKIN, *By Design*. New York: Quick Fox, 1980.

GOTTSCHALL, EDWARD M., *Graphic Communication 80's*.) Englewood Cliffs, N.J.: Prentice-Hall, 1980.

Graphic Artists Guild Handbook, Pricing and Ethical Guidelines. New York: Graphic Artists Guild, 1984.

LETISSIER, DAVID, *Instant Graphic Techniques*. Kent, Eng.: Graphics World, 1981.

SANDERS, NORMAN, *Graphic Designer's Production Handbook*. New York: Hastings House, 1982.

STANSFIELD, RICHARD H., *Advertising Manager's Handbook*. Chicago: The Dartnell Corporation, 1970.

The Type Specimen Book. New York: Van Nostrand, Reinhold, 1974.

Historical Background

BARNICOAT, JOHN, *A Concise History of Posters*. New York: Oxford University Press, 1972.

BAYER, HERBERT, *Herbert Bayer*. New York: Reinhold, 1967.

BOJKO, SZYMON, *New Graphic Design in Revolutionary Russia*. New York: Praeger, 1972.

BOOTH-CLIBBORN, EDWARD, AND DANIELE BARONI, *The Language of Graphics*. New York: Harry N. Abrams, 1980.

CONSTANTINE, MILDRED, AND ALAN FERN, *Revolutionary Soviet Film Posters*. Baltimore: Johns Hopkins University Press, 1974.

FEREBEE, ANN, *A History of Design from the Victorian Era to the Present*. New York: Van Nostrand, Reinhold, 1970.

GERSTNER, KARL, *The New Graphic Art*. New York: Hastings House, 1959.

LEWIS, JOHN, *Printed Ephemera*. London: Faber and Faber, 1962.

MARGOLIN, VICTOR, *American Poster Renaissance*. New York: Watson-Guptill Publications, 1975.

MARGOLIN, VICTOR, *The Promise and the Product: 200 Years of American Advertising Posters*. New York: Macmillan; London; Collier Macmillan, 1979.

MENTEN, THEODORE, *Advertising in the Deco Style*. New York: Dover Publications, 1975.

MULLER-BROCKMANN, JOSEF, *A History of Visual Communication*. New York: Hastings House, 1971.

NEUMANN, ECKHARD, *Functional Graphic Design in the 20's*. New York: Reinhold, 1967.

SPENCER, HERBERT, *Pioneers of Modern Typography*. Cambridge, Mass.: MIT Press, 1983.

Visual References

American Institute of Graphic Arts, *AIGA Graphic Design, USA*. New York: Watson-Guptill Publications, 1980 to present.

Art Directors Club, *Annual of Advertising and Editorial Art*. New York: 1921 to present.

CAPITMAN, BARBARA BAER, *American Trademark Designs*. New York: Dover Publications, 1976.

COYNE, RICHARD, *CA Annual of Design and Advertising*. Palo Alto: Communications Arts Books, 1958 to present.

HERDIG, WALTER, *Graphis Annual*. Zurich: Graphis Press; New York: Hastings House, 1952 to present.

HERDIG, WALTER, *Graphis Diagrams*. Zurich: Graphis Press; New York: Hastings House.

HERDIG, WALTER, *Graphis Posters*. Zurich: Graphis Press; New York: Hastings House.

KAMEKURA, YUSAKU, *Trademarks of the World*. New York: George Wittenborn.

KOSTELANETZ, RICHARD, *Imaged Words and Worded Images*. New York: Outerbridge and Dienstfrey, 1970.

Print Case Books. Six volume editions of graphic design, 1975 to present.

SOLT, MARY ELLEN, *Concrete Poetry: A World View*. Bloomington, Ind.: Indiana University Press, 1970.

WILDBUR, PETER, *International Trademark Design*. New York: Van Nostrand, Reinhold, 1982.

WOODS, GERALD, *Art without Boundaries*. New York: Praeger, 1974.

Periodicals

ADS. New York.

Art Direction Magazine. New York.

Communications Arts Magazine. Palo Alto, Coyne and Blanchard.

Graphic Design. Japan, Orion Books.

Graphis. Zurich, Switzerland, Walter Herdig.

Ligature, New York, World Typeface Center, Inc.

Print Magazine. Washington D.C., R. C. Publications.

Push Pin Graphic. New York, Push Pin Graphic.

Typographica. London, Lund Humphries and Company (sixteen issues published between 1949 and 1967).

U&LC. New York, International Typeface Corporation.